ACCORDING TO G

Also by Geraint Thomas with Tom Fordyce

The World of Cycling According to G
The Tour According to G
Mountains According to G
Great Rides According to G

ACCORDING TO G

GERAINT THOMAS

THE AUTOBIOGRAPHY

Written with Tom Fordyce

QUERCUS

First published in Great Britain in 2025 by Quercus
Part of John Murray Group

1

Copyright © 2025 Geraint Thomas

PICTURE CREDITS (in order of appearance)
1–8 Author's private collection; 9, 12, 14, 15, 16, 28, 30 Alamy;
10 Getty/Bob Thomas; 11 Getty/Bryn Lennon; 13 Getty/Ryan Pierse;
17, 20–25, 27, 29, 31 Russ Ellis; 18, 19, 33–36 Alex Duffill;
26 Getty/Marco Bertorello; 32 Chris Auld Photography

A CIP catalogue record for this book is available
from the British Library

HB ISBN 978 1 78747 909 8
TPB ISBN 978 1 78747 908 1
EBOOK ISBN 978 1 78747 911 1

Typeset in AgfaSerif by CC Book Production

Printed and bound in Great Britain by Clays Ltd, Elcograf S.p.A.

MIX
Paper | Supporting
responsible forestry
FSC
www.fsc.org   FSC® C104740

Papers used by Quercus are from well-managed forests and other responsible sources.

Quercus
Carmelite House
50 Victoria Embankment
London EC4Y 0DZ
John Murray Group
Part of Hodder & Stoughton Limited
An Hachette UK company

The authorised representative in the EEA is Hachette Ireland,
8 Castlecourt Centre, Dublin 15, D15 XTP3, Ireland (email: info@hbgi.ie)

To Sa and Macs.
What a journey. Without you I'd never have achieved
anywhere near what I have. And I certainly wouldn't
have enjoyed it as much. It's been a hell of a ride,
so now for the next chapter. I can't wait!

And to you lot.
Thanks for all your support along the way.
On the roadside, online or from the sofa.
It means so much.

Diolch, grazie, merci.

Contents

1: Tour de France 2007, stage one   1

2: Junior Kuurne–Brussels–Kuurne 2003   31

3: Kampioenschap van Vlaanderen 2005   55

4: Olympics 2008, Beijing, team pursuit final   79

5: Tour de France 2010, stage three   109

6: World Road Race Championships 2011,
Copenhagen   129

7: Olympics 2012, London, team pursuit final   151

8: Commonwealth Games 2014, Glasgow,
road race   169

9: Tour de France 2015, stage twelve   191

10: Olympics 2016, Rio, road race   213

11: Giro d'Italia 2017, stage nine   231

12: Tour de France 2018, stage twelve   247

13: Tour de France 2019, stage nineteen   273

14: Giro d'Italia 2023, stage twenty   297

15: Tour de France 2025, stage twenty-one   323

Index   331

Acknowledgements   341

Chapter one

Tour de France 2007, stage one

'*Ciao*, Thomas. *Tuto bene?*'

    '*Ciao*, Claudio. *Si bene, grazie.* Erm, *poco stanco. Tu?*'

'*Molto bene! Noi stiamo andando Giro do Francia!*'

'The Tour? The Tour de France?'

'*Si!*'

'Barloworld have the wild card?'

'*Si!*'

'Wow, that's amazing!'

'*Si*, and you, Thomas, have a spot on the team. Keep doing what you're doing. Good training, good food, good rest. Speak soon.'

That was how it all began for me. A call from Claudio Corti, team manager of an unfancied second-tier team, to a young rider sheepishly coming off a three-day bender celebrating his twenty-first birthday. My initial thought, when I saw Claudio coming up on my 2007 flip-screen mobile phone, was that he'd somehow found out I'd been out on the lash.

Quarrata, the town in Tuscany where I was living, was not large. The nights out had been.

My second thought was that I'd better burn off those beers, fast. I rode for six and a half hours the next day, then six hours forty-five, then six hours forty-five again. I felt better after that. Better in the way you do as a professional road rider, when better means exhausted, skinnier and not allowed to eat most of the things you want to eat.

Punishing myself after a big night out was nothing new. I would go out, let rip and then add on the extra kilometres the next day. As a junior, my coach once said to me, 'Why did you go out last night? It's a Wednesday. You need some consistency.' Okay, I thought. I'll go out every Wednesday, then.

I was still known as a track rider, really, at that point; part of British Cycling's Olympic academy, based in Quarrata, out there with Mark Cavendish and Ben Swift and Ian Stannard, all of us young kids with our eyes on distant goals. I was built like a team pursuiter, an athlete designed to go 4000m round a velodrome as fast as possible, not up French mountains in a baking hot July. But I'd started the year okay for Barloworld, an Italian team registered in Britain with a South African sponsor and a South African sprinter as its best rider.

Robbie Hunter had a reputation as an angry man. When I met him for the first time, at the team hotel, he was in his pants and I was his room-mate, turning up late at night. But he accepted I hadn't booked the flight which led to my delayed arrival and took me under his wing. He began to teach me what it took to be a pro on the road. When we did lead-outs in training, I used my track speed to blow a few of the other guys off my wheel. That worked for Robbie, so I became part of his train.

I was sent off to the Tour Down Under to help with his lead-outs. My flat speed was great, my climbing less so. When I got back to Italy, I got a call from Claudio. Robbie and Fabrizio Guidi, another fast sprinter in his day, then in the final year of his career, were impressed enough to want me at Etruschi, a pan-flat, one-day race that opens the racing calendar in Italy. It was a good feeling, proving what I could do, being noticed for it. Robbie ended up fourth as Alessandro Petacchi won and Daniele Bennati came third. World champion Paolo Bettini was there, big teams like Liquigas. And me. It barely made sense, in the best possible way.

I went back to the track for the World Championships with the GB pursuit team – where we won gold – and then I rode the Giro del Trentino, four days in the Italian and Austrian Alps, where I took an absolute pasting. Every time the tarmac went up, I went swinging all over the road.

The Tour de France was a target for many riders, but not for me. As a Pro-Conti team, Barloworld had no guaranteed entry. The Tour might be starting in London, but I surely wouldn't be. Which is what made that phone call such a shock.

What made it worse was where I was sat when Claudio

rang. It was our favourite café in the square in Quarrata. Cav and the rest of us would meet for breakfast, have a cappuccino and a brioche, and start discussing the day's route. Often you'd stay and have another cappuccino and maybe a double brioche, filled with jam or creamy custard. This is what you can do as a track rider, when it's more about power than weight. It's exactly what you can't do when you're about to ride three weeks of the greatest and hardest bike race in the world, through the high Alps and the Pyrenees, against men who are still your sporting heroes.

There were no more brioches after that call. Espressos replaced cappuccinos. My daily mileage increased dramatically and my calorie intake plummeted. On 8 July 2007, in my first season as a professional, in my first race in the elite ProTour calendar, I was brought to the front of the field on Tower Bridge, before the first full stage from London to Canterbury, with the previous winners, national champions and the four other British riders starting on home soil: Bradley Wiggins, David Millar, Charly Wegelius, Mark Cavendish and me.

I glanced at Cav, pristine in his pink and white T-Mobile jersey. He glanced at me. Two friends who had been racing each other since the age of fourteen, who had shared a house in Manchester as young hopefuls, who had cared about the same tiny nuances of a sport that hardly anyone else seemed to know about in Britain.

'Cav . . .'

'Yes, G.'

'Flipping heck . . .'

'Yeah, I know.'

'Cav. Seriously. What the hell are we doing here?'

The first bike I was ever given was a little black speed machine made by Raleigh called a Street Wolf. It was Christmas and in that moment it was everything I'd ever wanted. I say speed machine. It had one gear and the wheels were only 16 inches in diameter. There's a reason why Cav's bikes have never had 16-inch wheels. But the Street Wolf did come with a little sound box that made different siren noises, a sleek paint job and excessively large mudguards. It was beautiful.

I learned how to ride it in the lane out the back of our house on Cromwell Road. A classic row of Cardiff terraced houses, red brick, cars parked out front. Up the road was Heath Park, which was where I adventured once I could turn, brake and get going again. The park had woods. It had gravel paths. It had sketchy corners where the keen young Street Wolf rider could go in too hot and come out on his backside. I learned early that skin always mended and blood never flowed for that long.

I shared a room with my little brother, Alun, in that terraced house. A set of bunk beds, me getting the top one as senior sibling. I was a Postman Pat man at the start, until Fireman Sam came along. If Sam's home village of Pontypandy didn't actually exist, it sounded believable enough to my young Welsh ears to win me over.

With all due respect to Pat and Sam, my cultural life was limited. I was bang-average at art, music and drama. I could copy a picture to acceptable levels, but that was about it. I could play 'Three Blind Mice' on the recorder. When the time came for the school play, I was given the part of a rat. I've always thought it was a nativity, but whoever heard of a rat in the story of Jesus's birth? I had socks on my hands for paws. I had no speaking lines. I was a rat, why would I? My grommets fell out mid-play as I tried to stay in character. If the arts were calling me, it was by a rude name.

So it was always all about sport. Being outside, running about, kicking a ball, catching a ball, sliding the Street Wolf into corners. Alun and I would never seriously fight, but we'd play-fight, and we'd play-fight seriously. Being four years older, I'd always win, although I'd keep him in the game for as long as possible on the basis that first-round knock-outs suit no-one when you've got a whole day to swerve colouring-in and recorder practice.

We took our inspiration where we could: after watching *Gladiators* on ITV on a Saturday teatime we'd fetch our pillows off the bunk beds and spend the rest of the evening standing on chairs, trying to whack each other off them. When we went on holiday to somewhere warmer than Birchgrove, once a year, it was races in the swimming pool. It was us watching my dad struggling with the underwater sections and thinking him being out of breath and slightly panicked was a lot more amusing than it actually was for him.

You do that much exercise, you get an early appreciation of fuelling strategies. My mum's Sunday roasts were good, but my auntie in Ebbw Vale, Christine, aka Chris, used a lot more salt, so hers took top step on the podium. My nan would bring the Welsh cakes and butterfly cakes. There were no old-school Italian team managers on my case at that point, so I could fill my boots. Once sated, my cousins would whack on Sky and we'd watch *The Simpsons*. My dad's actual job was in the boiler room at the local power plant; watching Homer Simpson at Mr Burns' place meant we imagined my dad's working environment to be exactly the same.

It was swimming that led to the great change, to the sliding doors moment. I was down at Maindy leisure centre, across the A48 and down the main road into the city centre, when I saw a poster on the wall advertising a kids' cycling club starting up on the oval tarmac track out front.

I'd seen some of this bike racing before. People racing flat-out on big tracks with banked turns. There was no gravel evident, but a huge amount of speed. This was my sort of game. The poster talked about bikes with one gear and no brakes – even better, I was halfway there already. There was a mention of five lessons, being shown how to ride this bike, how to race. I asked my mum and dad. They could see the same thing as me. What was on offer was all the things I naturally wanted to do anyway. It was close to home. It was cheap. There were no cars on the track and the parking was adequate. We were in.

I loved it. After a couple of sessions, Debbie Wharton, the woman who had set the whole thing up, shouted, 'Can you go faster?' This was an easy one to answer. 'Oh yeah ...' After our five-session graduation they got us to do a flying lap. Build up your speed, come in hotter than you ever could in Heath Park, smash it for one lap, throw yourself and your bike across the line. At the end of the evening, they totted up everyone's times. I'd won. Not only that, I'd taken the newcomers' record for my age. It didn't matter to me that there had been very few newcomers and that my age category was small. I was a record-breaker. I was guaranteed to come back again the next week.

I kept going down, that winter. Still playing football, still playing rugby, still smashing my brother off kitchen chairs with a pillow, but now with something else I was enjoying slightly more than all those things. In March they organised an omnium-style event for us: a handicap race, a scratch race, an elimination, a 200m time-trial. I won that too. With victory came my first ever prize – a red cycling jersey with white horizontal stripes. Something clicked inside. I loved doing this thing. I seemed to be good at it. Now I wanted to do it more.

Soon I was down the track twice a week with my new mates, Chris Gould, Mike Davis, Ross, Mikey P and the Rowe brothers. Twice turned into three times a week. On a Wednesday night we would have 'Maindy mini-league' – three or four races every week. Without any of it ever being structured like a lesson, all of us were learning all the time. We were racing our bikes for the thrill of it, for the chance to win, or come close, and in the process very naturally and easily soaking all of it up. The scratch race: easy, first across the line. Points race: multiple sprints over a longer period. Elimination – or the devil: last one across the finish line every couple of laps is out. The devil takes the hindmost.

I loved the riding and I loved the aftermath. Fresh from the track on a Wednesday or Thursday, we might pick up fish and chips on the way back, or pile home and have Marmite on toast and a pint of milk. Once the food was in and your feet were up, you'd get this lovely sense of satisfaction spreading through your belly and out into your body; the best sort of tiredness, where you feel you've achieved something good, and now you can kick back and enjoy it.

Cycling was starting to spread its way through the entire house. On my bedroom wall I now had posters of a few cyclists, as well as Ryan Giggs. I had an A3 calendar with track nights and a few races neatly entered in Biro. Downstairs in the kitchen was a monthly planner with all my dad's work shifts. An 'M' for a morning shift, 'A' for afternoons, 'D' for days, 'O' for off. I'd calibrate the two and see if he was free at the same time I was on my bike. If there was a clash, he'd always try to swap his shifts around.

Whatever happened, we'd always have the same conversation

in the car driving home. If I'd won, I'd offer him a leading question and he'd always respond in the same way.

'Did you expect me to win today, Dad?'

'Oh no, not at all. You did very well.'

If I'd been beaten, he had a lovely way of still finding a positive and making it feel like a victory.

'Jack is massive, I'm sure you'll have him soon. But Sammy was a good scalp to get today. First time you've beaten him. I didn't see that coming, you did very well . . .'

You start obsessing with something like bike racing and you want to absorb all of it. You want to do it all the time, but you want to watch it, too. To see how fast and how far the real riders can go. To see where they ride and how they do it. What these races look like, the ones round far smarter tracks than Maindy and the ones out in the real world, on perfect smooth tarmac, where the sun always seemed to be shining and everyone had an awesome jersey, not to mention legs that were three times bigger than mine.

This was where the Tour de France came in. After a year or so of constant badgering, my dad agreed to get us a Sky dish like our cousins. Not to watch Homer Simpson taking grievous health and safety risks at a more serious sort of power station, but for Eurosport. Eurosport came free with the basic Sky package, which was an attractive proposition for my dad. Eurosport had endless coverage of races I had never heard of in places I could never realistically go, which was outstanding news for me. I'd run home from school to catch the end of the race. If it had been a particularly fast day and the stage had already finished, it wasn't a problem. My mum would have recorded the last hour for me. Volume on mute, covering my eyes so as not to see the stage result on the screen, I'd rewind and watch the final.

Everything about the race made you fall in love with it. The racing, the sprints, the climbs and the scenery. The time-trial bikes looked like something from the distant future. The kits, I had to admit, were even better than my red and white striped one. Not all of it made sense; there were multiple complicated tactics I couldn't always understand and multiple ways to be a winner. You could finish minutes behind the rider who took that day's race and yet still be in the lead. You could come in last on a tough day and everyone thought you were a hero.

A lot more did make sense. A yellow jersey for the best overall rider, a green one for the best sprinter, a red polka-dot one for the quickest up the mountains – which were ridiculously big, by the way, and looked almost as insane to go down as they looked to go up. Then there were the riders. There weren't many British ones. Usually there was only one, a time-trial specialist called Chris Boardman. My eyes were drawn to a young German rider in a pink and white T-Mobile jersey. He won the first Tour I watched, as I was racing my own equivalent, the kids' Youth Tour in Manchester. Four stages over three days, racing in parks and on city centre pavements, a lovely yellow jersey for the leader. The German kid was called Jan Ullrich and he became my new hero. The Giggsy poster moved further down the bedroom wall. The Ullrich one, cut out of *Cycling Weekly* magazine, went up.

The idea of ever riding the same Tour as him? It was ludicrous. It wasn't even a daydream. How could it be? It wasn't just that so few Brits seemed to or that there were no British teams. It was that very few people in Birchgrove even realised the race was happening. Everyone knew the Tour de France and yellow jersey, but that was it. Kids at my school talked about Man United and Arsenal, and Ieuan Evans and Scott Gibbs. Quite a few had been to Cardiff Arms Park; everyone dreamed of going to Old Trafford or Anfield.

No-one I knew had ever been to watch the Tour de France. It was fine me getting in from school and parking myself in front of the telly and listening to David Duffield's commentary. I was never going to see it in the flesh. It looked impossible to get a ticket for *Gladiators*, let alone this race that went up the Alps.

There were no mountains near my house, unless you counted Caerphilly mountain, which you could if you were Welsh, but not if you had ever seen the Tour. I rode my bike round a bumpy concrete track built on the site of an old rubbish tip. Thinking about the Tour wasn't like wondering about going to the moon – you could see the moon most nights and everyone at school was aware of its existence. It wasn't even like the idea of playing at the Arms Park. There were two kids two years below me at school who everyone reckoned were going to do that, a lad who loved rugby called Sam Warburton and a football-obsessed kid called Gareth Bale.

The Tour was impossible, not just improbable. It wasn't even worth dreaming of. It was incredible and I loved everything about it, but it could never be for me. How could it be?

Nothing made sense, that weekend in July in 2007. The Tour de France was starting in London, which was mad enough. And so was I, on a time-trial bike, wearing a pair of Specialized sunglasses which, astonishingly, had been given to me for free. I was cruising past the Houses of Parliament, reconning the prologue, which was a short time-trial past the city's most eye-catching sights. I knew Mum and Dad were in the crowd, my brother Alun, and my auntie and uncle Chris and Ade, which made it hard to concentrate on the recon. Then I spotted Chris Gould, my old mate from Maindy, and a load of the other midweek warriors. I actually stopped. I got off my bike and we took photos. That's how bewildering it all was. I was acting like a tourist at a race I would shortly be competing in.

The Italian pros in our Barloworld team seemed to have an unjustified faith in my abilities. A few days before, on a training ride from our Surrey hotel, they had expected me to lead the way. 'Thomas, you show us a route, yes?' I tried to tell them I was from south Wales, not the south of England. I was as familiar with the lanes around Box Hill as someone from Milan. Neither did I have access to any mapping software on my phone, because my phone was a flip-open one which made calls and sent texts and that was about it. Come to think of it, I didn't even have my phone. I'd left it in a café on the previous ride. The free sunglasses barely made up for it.

Then there was my Cannondale TT bike. The team only had two of these. One had gone to Mauricio Soler, our young Colombian climber who they had big hopes for in the mountains and young rider classifications. They gave me the second one. Did they think I was the next best prospect in the team or was it because I was a British rider in London, and the youngest starter in the race, and so likely to be in more photos? I didn't care. This was a bike you couldn't buy. It was built for the pros and even then only a few of them.

Earlier in the year the team had asked me to trial a new riding position, where I was so low and so far back that the saddle was almost on the back wheel. The position didn't work, but these same guys were now coming to me for my thoughts on our TT set-up. I felt like Fabian Cancellara, at least until the actual Cancellara won the prologue, with Bradley Wiggins in fourth. Remarkably, I finished forty-fifth, the fastest man in our team. I was a single second behind Tom Boonen and Philippe Gilbert. I was ten seconds in front of Fränk Schleck. I was ahead of 144 elite Tour riders. The next day, before the first stage proper began, came the Tower Bridge moment. Of course I was going to ask Cav what the hell we were doing there. Who could compute all of this?

It was so fast, that first stage. So fast for so long. How were you supposed to ride at this pace for 200km and then sprint at the end? The crowds were vast. How could you stop for a roadside comfort break without peeing on a spectator's flip-flops? Everything was turned up exponentially from anything I'd experienced before: bigger, shinier, flashier. The noise was relentless, the colours brighter. Then we crossed into France, and it really became the Tour as I'd watched it and studied it.

Barloworld were not a fancied team. Respect in the peloton went to others before us. This made even holding your position in the bunch a constant fight. No-one would let you in, no-one would let you pass. Had the men around me just been what they were – vastly more experienced, more confident, much stronger – this would have been tough enough. Then there was the other thing they were: heroes I had only previously ever seen on television. Now I was rubbing shoulders with them.

One day I bumped into the legendary Andreas Klöden. Quite literally. He looked at me, pointed at my brakes and said, 'See these? Use them.' A couple of days later, in close to 40 degrees heat, I poured water over my head. Klöden was behind me and may have caught some of my overflow. I got another ear-bashing for that. Some of the old pros would have a go even without a reason. Murilo Fischer was a Brazilian rider at Liquigas who seemed at war with the world. I had enormous respect for these guys, but it looked like I'd have to earn theirs. Just you wait, boys . . .

I had no expectations of actually finishing the three weeks of the race. I hoped to make it through the first week. If I could, I wanted to do a mountain stage, just like the ones I'd been loving on TV for the past ten years. I wanted to see those roads winding up to impossible heights and the crowds parting in front of our wheels as we rode through. For now, though, it was about pure survival. I was never at the front and usually in the grupetto, the last bunch of riders on the road. I finished stage five, won by Filippo Pozzato, convinced that riding another day was impossible. Doing another kilometre seemed a stretch target.

During that stage, Robbie had wanted a bottle. 'Of course, mate . . .' Off to the back of the peloton I went and loaded up with six or seven bottles, enough for all the boys, not just Robbie. I was already carrying a bit of excess weight, but the extra 3.5 kilos of water almost killed me. The race was stretched out in one long line; making progress back up it was almost impossible.

I started ditching bottles. That seemed to help. I got to within about ten riders of Robbie, couldn't get any further and ditched some more. One final sprint got me alongside. I gave him the bottle and boom! – went out the back for the final 50km. I spent the rest of the stage grovelling round with a bunch of the big sprinters. When we eventually crossed the finish line I went back to the team hotel, had a massage and some food, lay on my bed not moving for a while and thought, I'm still here, so I may as well get dressed in the morning and go again.

Team manager Claudio had decided to room me with Robbie Hunter, which made sense even as it also intimidated me. Our most experienced rider with our most fresh-faced. Robbie would look at me lying there motionless on the single bed next to his and he would impart all the knowledge he'd built up over his long, combative career. He'd open up the race book, a huge thing. I was used to five-day races at the most, not twenty-one. That, in itself, was intimidating. The book contained a map of every stage, its profile, a breakdown of any categorised climbs, the percentage gradient every 500m – all enough to give you nightmares. In detail would be the final 5km run into every finish. Robbie would review the profile of the next day's stage and give me targets that felt more achievable than getting through the entire day.

'Right, it's going to be hard until … Well, it's going to be hard all day, but you need to bite the bullet and get to this point of the race. The gruppetto will form here. Sit tight with those boys, stay in the wheels and you'll stay inside the time-cut.'

After a few days I realised it didn't matter which point on the map he had pointed to. I was inevitably dropped before that anyway. I became quite used to riding on my own. Riding on your own is a lot less efficient than riding as part of a group. I knew that I just didn't have a choice. It's surprising how lonely you can feel in a field of 189 riders.

Everything about almost every kilometre was hard. I had steeled myself for the horrors of the mountains. What surprised me was how hard the flat days were. The intense French heat didn't help. Forty degrees, melting tarmac. This was as far from Cardiff as it could get. Everyone just went faster.

One moment I was towards the back, chatting with Brad as we came into a feed zone, unaware that crosswinds were looming. Maybe we should have been paying more attention, maybe our team DSs should have warned us. Astana attacked with Alexander Vinokourov and it all split apart. Suddenly I was out the back with five pure climbers. They hated the flat. I should have loved it. I was a track rider. This was my terrain. This was where I bossed it. Instead, I was getting my head kicked in. When the crosswinds like these blew and the peloton broke apart into echelons, you went backwards even faster than when the road jumped to 10%.

That was when, for just a split second, I got swamped by self-doubt. 'I can't do this anymore. I can't do this . . .' I stopped pedalling. Just for a couple of pedal strokes, but enough to put the fear into me. Enough to detach from everyone else by a bike length. That cleared my head. 'Fuck no. Hold the wheel!' I got out of the saddle and sprinted back. I closed the gap. I stayed with the last group and I got through another day.

Then there were the rolling days. The ones where it was

neither flat nor properly mountainous, but a horrible in-between. The days Duffield would refer to as transition days. These turned out to be the hardest of all. No-one sat up on the rolling days. No-one got dropped, so no grupetto formed. If you got spat out the back, you were on your own and staying within the time limit, and thus the race became incredibly hard. You saw a fourth cat climb coming up – basically, one so easy an old car could get up it in fourth gear – and a sense of dread settled over you.

Barloworld did not have a big budget. We were old-school in the ways you wished we could be new. For breakfast they'd give us sloppy pasta made in the kitchen of whichever Campanile we were staying in. Other days it was a ham and cheese baguette, as if we were spectators getting ready for a day in deckchairs rather than riding 200km flat-out. During the stage we had a choice of ham panini, crostata or whatever cakes were at the breakfast buffet that morning. It was nowhere close to the 120 grams of carbs we needed an hour, and it definitely wasn't the right mix of glucose and fructose. We did have a supply of energy bars from the team's sponsor, but they weren't great. I took to stashing my own supplies of SIS GO bars in my jersey pockets, even though they were like bricks back then, hard and chewy. Post-race recovery? The team offered us Italian biscuits. I went rogue again and made my own SIS REGO shakes from the supplies I had via British Cycling. Italians looked at protein shakes the same way they looked at sliced white bread and processed ham.

I might be making it sound like I wasn't enjoying being there. I was. It was just a different form of enjoyment to the one most people organised their lives around. I was in constant pain. I was exhausted. My legs hurt, my back hurt, my wrists ached. That was absolutely fine. If I thought it had been satisfying going home after a track night at Maindy and eating Marmite on toast with my feet up on the sofa, then surviving another Tour stage and getting back to a bang-average hotel room to a nod of approval from Robbie was the sweetest feeling I could imagine.

Slowly I began to take little bits of help everywhere I could. There was no Sa in my life at this point, but there was a new flip-top mobile phone. With barely a thought for my data allowance I'd call my mates back home in the evenings and talk about anything but cycling, just to take my mind off things. When I was ready to return my head to the race, I'd call Max Sciandri, who had seen it all as a pro and was now running the academy in Quarrata with Rod Ellingworth. I could be honest with him. He could keep it simple in return.

'Max, I'm so screwed here. I'm absolutely on the limit. I can't see how I'm going to be able to get through.'

'G, just take it day by day. Don't see it as a big thing – just start tomorrow, dig in, try and get to the point where Robbie says, "That's it."'

I'd talk to Brad when we'd go to sign on each morning. We'd hang out in the Tour village, all the remaining Brits plus an odd Aussie or American making a guest appearance.

Dave Millar and Charly Wegelius were more continental and cultural. Brad, Cav and I were fully British and track boys at heart. That bonded us, even as the race was changing us, too. I was alongside Brad on the last climb of one mountain stage and he looked absolutely nailed. I asked him where he would rather be – here, suffering on this bleak French mountain, or back on the track. He looked at me without any doubt on his face. 'Here. Definitely here.' That helped. This suffering had a purpose. It was taking us all somewhere.

The worst day in the mountains? Stage eight, the last one before the first rest day. Dropped on a cat two climb after 37km, so gone and so lost that the police motorbike in front started handing me water. I thought I was done until, flying down the final descent, desperation in my lungs and legs, I saw team cars ahead. The grupetto? No way ...

The grupetto was big in those days. You might find seventy riders, all of us locked together in the same misery and same desire to survive it. My Barloworld team-mates looked genuinely surprised to see me and gave me any food they had left in their jersey pockets. I got a pat on the back from Brad. It cemented a feeling I'd had growing inside me as the days of agony piled up: I might get dropped, but I was never stopping. Stopping was quitting. I was never going to give up. No chance. As long as I could pedal, I could get to the finish. End of.

My old Maindy Flyers mate Mike Davis had come out to France to watch. Each night before a mountain test he'd send me a similar text message: 'See you on the Glandon, mate, I'll bring water.' He was riding the stages himself, earlier in the day. That meant the water he handed me was warm enough to make a cup of Earl Grey tea, although I didn't have the heart to tell him, but the thought of seeing a mate from Cardiff out on the road was a boost enough on its own.

When we finally got to that first rest day, those older lads spent it with their families. I got a two-hour full-body massage and zonked out all day. When I came back to, I realised three riders had failed to make it inside the time-cut the day before. Five more had DNF'ed, each with their own war story. I'd made it. Somehow I'd made it. All that time in my own little world of hurt and pain and I hadn't thought that loads of others were going through the same horrors, too.

David Millar did an interview, about ten days in. He was asked how I was doing. I quite liked his answer: 'G has a soft face, but he's like one of the penguins in the film *Madagascar*. He looks cuddly, but every now and then you get a look from him which makes you realise he's anything but.' The stage after the rest day was a monster; we started up the Col de l'Iseran (15km at 6%), dropped down, and then went up the Télégraphe and the Galibier (12km at 6.7% and 17.5km at 7%). Mauricio Soler went on to win it, which made it a great day for our team.

I should have been in bits. Instead, I was up for it. I treated it almost like a monstrously extended team pursuit: plenty of caffeine in advance, a proper warm-up, Eminem and Tupac blaring down my headphones, game time. I'm ready for this. Bring it! Boonen was in the green jersey. He could also climb. When I saw him starting to be dropped, I made sure his wheel was the one I was on, because he could keep going and had plenty of team-mates with him to power us through the valleys that linked the big climbs. That was victory for me, as the youngest rider in the race: choosing when to be dropped, rather than having my sentence handed out to me.

But every day would still be a learning day. Coming into a bunch sprint finish one day, I was trying to look after Robbie. With about 600m there was a sharp right-hand corner. Robbie came past me and divebombed into the corner, so I followed him. We went underneath one of the other big sprinters and his lead-out man, and the sprint began.

I couldn't hold Robbie's wheel. It was too much. I flicked my elbow, telling the other lead-out guy to come past. Nothing. I flicked again. Half a bike between Robbie and me, then a bike, then two bikes. Frantically flicking my elbow, thinking, 'Ah shit, please come past, I can't hold this . . .'

He did come past me. I heard the swearwords first. Then – all of this at about 40mph – he punched me in the stomach. It was a proper one, balled fist, right into my guts. All the breath I had left whistled straight out of me. I freewheeled to the line. Then I started pedalling again, straight to Robbie's side. If he came for me again, I wanted to be with someone who'd take pleasure in getting in the way.

Something else, too. When I say us five British riders had

been lined up on Tower Bridge before the first stage – that's not quite true. There were stage winners and there were great champions, like Boonen and Cancellara. But there was no-one who had won the yellow jersey at the Tour, for one simple reason: none of them were in the sport anymore. Floyd Landis, winner the previous year, had been banned for doping. Lance Armstrong, winner of the seven before that, had retired amid a cloud of rumour and suspicion. My hero Jan Ullrich was thrown out of the Tour in 2006 for doping. Six weeks before this Tour set off from London, Bjarne Riis had confessed to taking EPO, growth hormone and cortisone from 1993 to 1998, including during his victory in the 1996 Tour de France. Marco Pantani? He was dead, gone at thirty-four from cocaine poisoning.

This was not something that was left in the past. First the Astana team were kicked out of the race on the second rest day after Vinokourov tested positive for an illegal blood transfusion. Then Spain's Iban Mayo tested positive for EPO and went the same way. Cofidis were next, which meant Brad was out of the race, despite having done nothing wrong personally. Then the biggie: GC leader Michael Rasmussen, fired by his Rabobank team after lying about his whereabouts to hide from anti-doping checks. It meant the race began its final week without a rider in yellow.

Maybe it was all obvious to the older riders. To us younger ones in our first Tour, in our first year on the road, it was not. There was no social media, there was no internet on your phone. You heard rumours on the bus that someone might be kicked out, but when the rumours are in Italian you're only half tuned into them. It was only on that rest day in Pau when I saw all the TV crews and reporters clustered round the Rabobank bus that I realised something serious was happening. You see something like that and it makes you ask yourself serious questions. What is this? Why am I getting into this whole world? Is this what this sport really looks like?

I was an innocent in a world of the cynical and habitual. When I'd been told by the team that I was riding the Tour, at a point when I was knackered from training and racing, our doctor had given me a prescription to take to the pharmacy. It was for vitamins and minerals – B12, magnesium, potassium. They came in small bottles. I tried taking the lids off, but I couldn't open them, so I lobbed the bag under the bed in my apartment and forgot all about them.

A couple of years later, then British Cycling coach Shane Sutton was staying at my apartment. One morning I got a call from him.

'G, what's all this under your bed, mate?'

I had no idea what he was talking about. 'What? What do you mean?'

'All these bottles! Have you been to the pharmacy?'

Suddenly I twigged. 'Oh yeah – the Barloworld doctor told me to get that a couple of years ago, but I couldn't get the bottles open to drink, so I just threw them under the bed and forgot about them.'

'Yeah, mate. They're for fucking syringes, you dickhead!'

So that's what they had wanted me to do. Cycling in Europe was a place that was fine with syringes, suppositories and injections. It wasn't illegal, taking vitamins, but I was never going to use needles, even if it was legal and safe. I was never going to do that to myself.

As the Tour wound its way back towards Paris, scandal in its wake, I got asked a question by a journalist. You've come from British Cycling, from the track. Road racing on the continent is a different sport. They've done things you wouldn't. Why the hell do you want to be involved in this?

It was a good question and one I'd given a great deal of thought to, but to me it was also pretty simple at the same time. The first thing was that I'd seen they were prepared to catch the big guys. You could be leading the Tour and they'd throw you out. You could be a great champion of the past, like Jan Ullrich, and they'd go back and re-test samples and not care about protecting your reputation. I didn't see a conspiracy to cover things up; I saw a sport trying to change and making obvious headway.

The second thing was more personal and straightforward. It was my dream to be a pro, and to ride and survive races like this. If I did a few years and then got spat out for refusing to compromise myself, or if it kept cleaning up and I could be more competitive or win a few races, that was all I wanted. I wanted to live my dream, not anyone else's. If it wasn't possible or I couldn't make it, that was fine. At least I'd tried.

So I kept going. The final big mountain day took us up the Col d'Aubisque in the Pyrenees. At the finish line, I knew for the first time that I could finish this race. I was still in pieces, but the greatest challenges had been surmounted. I turned to one of the reporters, smiled at him and pointed into the distance. 'Mate, you can see the Eiffel Tower from here.' He looked over his shoulder, confused. I was too tired to explain that I'd been making a broader philosophical point. Also my French was not yet capable of explaining any sort of philosophical point, broad or narrow. But I knew it, even if the last week was still a brute.

The breakaway days were the worst, because you had two hours of relentless fighting before the break finally established and escaped. Dave Millar even gave me a push over a fourth category climb, three days out of Paris, which I felt slightly uncharitable about – 'Where the hell have you been for the last three weeks, mate? While I've been grovelling around, spitting blood, chewing the stem, where were the pushes then?'

But then, suddenly, we were rolling towards Paris and Dave was alongside me again. 'Congratulations, G. We really can see the Eiffel Tower now.' And he pointed into the distance – and you actually could. A few kilometres or so later, we were riding laps of the Champs-Élysées, swinging under the arm of the big camera boom I'd seen so many times on TV.

To be on this side of the screen gave me goosebumps. No

longer was I watching the race from the sofa in my parents' front room. People all over the world were sitting on sofas in their front rooms watching me – or at least watching me flash through the shot, unrecognised. But still. I could hear the roar of the crowd in my ears. I felt strong and I felt fast. I felt like ten men. Barloworld even rode on the front for a few laps. Robbie would end up second in the green jersey standings, Soler won a stage and the polka dot jersey. We'd done a good job in the end.

Physically I had nothing more to give when we crossed the finish line for the final time. Mentally I was even emptier. It seemed strange to me that most of the team flew home that night. Only Robbie and Soler stayed, and that was to make some money in the usual post-Tour crits in Belgium and the Netherlands. No crit wanted me, not yet. So I went out for dinner with my family and, while I love my family and it was absolutely a treat, it also felt strangely anticlimactic. It summed up the Tour for me, in some ways: no party together for the team, off in my own little world, desperate to go to bed.

I finished 140th out of the 141 who made it through all three weeks. Chapeau to Belgium's Wim Vansevenant for beating me to the lanterne rouge, although he seemed to be making something of a deliberate habit of it: he had also finished dead last the year before and would finish dead last again the next year. He went back to running his parents' farm after that, albeit after dipping his toes in the post-Tour crits pot. The lanterne rouge is a bit of a celebrity in their own right. Race for two hours as the crowds expected and there was a healthy bonus in it for you.

I flew back to Wales with my family for a week of rest and recuperation, significantly skinnier than when I'd left. Familiar roads, and a familiar question and answer as we travelled along them.

'Did you expect me to finish the Tour, Dad?'

This time he even laughed.

'Oh, not a chance, Ger. You did well. You did very well . . .'

Chapter two

Junior Kuurne-Brussels-Kuurne 2003

We were a small gang at the start, down at Maindy Flyers. Four or five of us at best, one of them my brother Alun. A couple of my mates came along and it didn't stick for them. They were confused by the Lycra and fixated on why you might want to shave your legs. These were fair questions, but numbers still grew fast. Soon there were four or five in each age category, boys and girls, and we were racing on our bumpy old track, but at other places round south Wales, too.

Then came the game-changer. One of the older coaches took us aside at the end of a session. 'Now then, you're all doing really well, but wait until you start training on the road. Then you'll see how much stronger you'll get . . .'

He was right in more ways than he realised. Getting out in the lanes beyond the city suburbs did indeed build your legs and lungs. It also opened up whole new worlds. When the lanes went up, small Welsh hills became local versions of Alpe d'Huez. When you raced your mates down long, straight, empty roads, you were doing lead-outs in bunch sprint stages. When we played football in Heath Park we pretended we were at Wembley and it was always easy imagining you were at the Millennium Stadium when you could see its white roof supports gleaming from miles away. These road rides were a new connection and a greater leap. Now, when I watched these big races on the free Eurosport channels, I could go out and recreate a version of them myself.

You watched the races, you climbed the small hills and you threw yourself into all of it. Alun was no longer coming down to the club as frequently, but there was a little lad called Luke Rowe and his dad had some nice gear. For a crit race round a deserted industrial estate I was allowed to borrow his Mavic Ksyrium wheels with cool aero spokes. I felt incredible, at least until I crashed. The wheels survived. My skin would mend. I jumped back on, caught up a group containing newly crowned world champion Nicole Cooke, went straight past them and won.

That seemed to change something else. Watching was an old-school Aussie called Shane Sutton, who at the time was head coach at Welsh Cycling, and the junior coach Darren Tudor. From them came a grant for a new bike that would be mine to love and to race. I went for a sensational red Cannondale with a big fat down tube, and allowed myself to indulge in happy fantasies of how much faster I would go and how many places I could gain when I settled into its speed-machine charms.

I didn't crash it, because something far worse happened. Running into our garage one morning, carrying a great metal file with a wooden handle to my dad, I decided to make a karate-style chopping motion, complete with a shouted 'Hai-yah!' That was when the file detached from the wooden handle, and clattered straight into my beautiful red Cannondale and its fat downtube.

Oh, the devastation! Oh, the number of chips to the paintwork! I was petrified to even tell my dad. He realised this, moderated his reaction as a result and set about touching up the damaged paintwork. I prayed it was still okay. When the time came for its debut, at an under-fourteens circuit race in Hillingdon, west London, it was preceded by a sleepless night – and not only because we were overnighting in portacabins in the middle of the racing circuit, all of us Maindy riders lined up next to each other in sleeping bags.

In my sights was a lad I'd never beaten before, Ben Crawforth, from a club, Palmer Park, who were perhaps our biggest rivals of all. On my new touched-up Cannondale I was in focused mood on the start line, which may be why I failed to tune in to the commissaires' lecture before we began. Apparently, in the under-twelves race just before, the winner had crossed the finishing line with both his hands in the air, Tour de France sprint-stage style. The commissaires weren't happy. They gave him the win, but warned us not to do the same.

How was I supposed to react when shortly afterwards my Cannondale gave me my first ever victory over Ben Crawforth? Of course I crossed the line with my hands up in the air. I felt like Mario Cipollini. The commissaires made it clear I was not Mario Cipollini by immediately disqualifying me. There was outrage from most of the Maindy Flyers parents. There was talk of official complaints. There was talk of unofficially booting off with these jobsworth officials. By contrast my own dad was a model of calm. 'We'll be okay, Ger. We'll get our revenge next time . . .'

Was it the new bike that made the difference or me? We had the chance to find out a week later, when Ben Crawforth rocked up to that weekend's race on a bike even shiner, newer and less chipped than mine. I put him away again, and this time went across the line with both hands on the bars and a hard stare at the officials. So focused was I on keeping my hands where the commissaires dictated that I failed to notice the sharp 90-degree, left-hand corner 20m after the line, slammed the anchors on last minute, hit the kerb and flew into a bush.

On the way back along the M4 to south Wales, the conversation was tactfully steered to the usual places. Driving was always a good place to talk: no eye contact necessary, both of you looking into the distance, both of you happily weary and bonded by what you'd just been doing.

'Dad, did you reckon I'd beat Ben Crawforth today, when you saw his new bike?'

'No, no, I definitely didn't think you'd beat him today. You did well there.'

If I got beaten, there was always a positive. I'd always get them next time, according to my dad. There was always a scalp I'd never taken before. And there was never any pressure put on me – no shouting, no stern pep talks in the car on the way over. It was easy for me, in some ways, because all I wanted to do was race my bike and get better at it. I didn't need anyone to push me. And all I had known, since I could remember, was everyone around me working hard: Dad with his shifts at the power plant, Mum doing long care hours at the local Velindre Cancer Centre. No-one ever whinged, no-one ever complained about their day. If something difficult happened, you tried to find the silver lining.

A lot of what I was doing was strange. I may have been the only boy in south Wales who was shaving his legs before he was shaving his cheeks. My version of looking good prioritised smooth calves over hairy top lips, even if puberty had given me the option, which it wouldn't for a number of years. But I never questioned any of it, because it was all so obviously worth it. I was noticing something else at these races, although I didn't share it with anyone else: once I beat someone, that was it. I never lost to them again. I seemed to keep moving up as some of the other boys stayed where they were.

Through the English schools system I got an invite to a three-day stage race in Berlin. They obviously hadn't anticipated selecting many from the Welsh school system; the jersey they gave us to compete in was white with a St George's Cross on it. I wasn't happy. Don't get me wrong. I love being British, but I'm not English. Growing up in Wales, it's anyone but England, especially in sport. Don't hate me for it, it's just the way it is.

The other aspects were more pleasing: a prologue time-trial, then a road race around a similar circuit. These were adventures beyond anything I could have hoped for, but the circuit race baffled me. How come we were going faster with less effort than I'd had to make going flat-out solo in the prologue? The only aspect of aerodynamics that made sense was shaving my legs and even that went wrong. I hacked away at them with a blunt razor in a locked Portaloo, cut slices in most areas and left hairy patches in others. When questioned about it at school the following week, I denied all reports, wore trackie bottoms in PE and double-bluffed the most persistent by inviting them to pull up my trouser leg if they didn't believe me. No-one dared. Maybe I was better at acting than I'd thought.

Most weekends we were on the road. It was a sporting and cultural education, a convoy of cars or a minibus heading east from Cardiff and then to all points of the British com-pass: Herne Hill in south London, Palmer Park in Reading, Brighton, Scunthorpe and Kirkby. A drive of five or six hours, camping, eating out, playing some football or quick cricket, racing the next day, and then turning round and driving all the way home. We learned things we expected and things we did not. Mike Davis could reel off every service station on the M5 and M6 in geographical order, which was not the sort of thing you expected from a fourteen-year-old. I was more concerned with booing when we crossed the border from Wales to England or cheering when we crossed back the other way.

You took your pleasures where you could. It might be Mike and I making mix tapes for the boom box at the back of the minibus. It might be mooning a coachload of OAPs or the person manning the toll booth at the Severn Bridge. It might be letting a full toilet roll unspool from an open window, marvelling at the length of dangle you could achieve before it snapped, panicking when you were pulled over by the police, getting your trousers caught on the door latch as you trooped off and then standing there with your trousers flailing in the wind as an officer of the law gave you a stern telling off.

Like I say, a cultural education, but it was worth every mile on the clock. There was a national series called the Talent Spotter, where the winner of the omnium won a yellow jersey with the words 'Pocket Rocket' printed on the front. It's almost impossible to overstate how much I wanted to win this.

Here's how the omnium would go. A 200m time-trial, a 1.5 or 2km pursuit, a scratch race, a points race and then a handicap. The handicap was by far the most fun. Held over 500m, it would see the slowest rider from the time-trial given the biggest head-start, all the way down to the fastest. The idea was that we should all cross the finish line at the same time, although it seldom ended that way. The trick was to have the parent with the strongest arms holding your saddle at the start, so they could launch you down the track with maximum illegal speed. It became a competition within a competition: whose father could launch their rider the fastest? My dad would play it cool, which was fine, as my ideal choice was Mike Ball. He had a right arm like a trebuchet. Confidence would truly flow from your veins when you heard Mike Ball whispering in your ear: 'Don't worry, Geraint, I've got you for this one . . .'

Even with this reassurance I'd still get super-nervous at times. It wasn't unusual for me to throw up on the pavement outside the track at Maindy as I made my way in. Perhaps the southern fried chicken and pasta in ragu sauce that I usually demolished half an hour before didn't help. Other times I would go so hard in every race that I barely had enough left in the tank for the points race. If I was ahead going into that one I would often pray for rain to save me. I did, however, always love it.

Riding round the pavements of Platts Fields in southern Manchester shouldn't have been alluring, but when it was part of the Manchester Youth Tour, my first stage race and only a week or two after the Tour de France, I felt like Jan Ullrich. I finished second, one place ahead of a young Ben Swift, beaten only by Sean Arthur, who was not only from the Isle of Man, but was so much bigger than me the rumour was he had been served alcohol on the ferry over. We were fourteen. Different times.

It wasn't cool to be a cyclist at school. Not cool in the same way as it was to be a rugby player as good as Sam Warburton or a footballer so obviously gifted as Gareth Bale. I was okay at rugby, usually put on the wing for my speed and engine. We had a sevens tournament where the extra space played straight into my skillset. Was I running circles around the opposition defenders? It's not for me to say. But there were times when I rubbed a little more mud on myself, just so the opposition thought they had actually tackled me a couple of times. Either that or so I could pretend I had actually been making some tackles.

Other kids were approaching the hairy upper lip era of adolescence more rapidly than me. Being small made me elusive. It almost made me crumple when tackled by the bigger lads. Scoring a dramatic try in the corner, I was mangled by the last covering man, twisted my knee and was carried off. While in the moment I saw myself as Ieuan Evans being stretchered away a match-winning hero, a more sober assessment in the cold light of day was that my rugby days might be over. This hunch was confirmed a couple of weeks later when, about to dot down what I felt was a magnificent solo score, a lad from the opposition team grabbed me round the waist and threw me 10m back towards my own try line. On a bike I could win things and earn a bit of cash through the prize money.

In rugby, big lads were sitting on my head and lobbing me around like a toy doll. It was an easy decision to make.

I decided not to talk about cycling too much at school. I didn't want to draw too much attention to myself. The teachers were good at giving me time off to get to races, but there were few requests for me to go on stage during assemblies to wave my trophies triumphantly at some bored year eights. Instead I hung my medals on a board on my bedroom wall, watched obscure races on Eurosport and listened intently when the commentators explained which tactics were cunning, and which were madness.

Football was everywhere: on terrestrial telly, in newsagents, in most playground conversations. You didn't have to go looking for it; it came for you. Rugby was the same. Cycling was still a pretty obscure world. If you wanted to find out who'd won a race in Spain or the Netherlands, you had to hunt it out. *Cycling Weekly* was essential from the age of twelve onwards. If you spotted your name in the results section at the back, flicking through until you found Talent Spotter or Maindy Mini-League in bold, it was a heady thrill. If you rode a bigger race and did well enough to see the results posted in the *Western Mail* newspaper, something even ordinary people bought – well, that gave you extra swagger as you strolled the suburban pavements to school and back.

My new world remained opaque. Detailed information was hard to come by. No-one told you what to eat or when to eat it, so you stuck with your glasses of milk and Marmite on toast. There was nothing about periodising your training, so you just did everything: chain gangs on the track, chain gangs on the road, hill climbs and sprints, club rides and races at weekends. Sometimes I would be exhausted and not be able to work out why. The idea that I might be overdoing it never occurred to me. I was obsessed and, like a lot of obsessed teenagers, I never questioned the object of my affections. The more I rode, the more I watched. The more I watched, the more I raced and the more I fell in love with it.

None of it was ever hard work, even though I was still so raw I didn't really know anything at all. Aged fifteen, I decided to meet one of the guys from a local club, on the basis that he was a grown man and would thus push me harder. I have no idea how old he actually was; when you're fifteen, someone is either at school or they're a veteran with decades of experience.

We met at Treforest, outside Cardiff, just after 5pm. It was the depths of winter, already dark and cold. I didn't worry that it was snowing. I didn't worry that I didn't own a pair of cycling tights to wear over my usual bib-shorts. I didn't worry because I didn't know they existed. I wasn't even bothered that I was early and he was late, so I had to roll up and down the road waiting for him, trying to keep warm.

We still rode for three hours, because I wanted to. When I eventually got home, I didn't complain about the cold. I just couldn't get my key in the front door, because my hands no longer worked. I had to bang on the door with my elbow to get my mum to open it. She told me to run my hands under the hot tap to get some feeling back, which was maybe the worst point of all. It was so painful that I was almost crying in the kitchen – and no-one cried in our kitchen. I got into bed for half an hour with all my clothes on to get warm enough to even attempt a bath.

You learned by making mistakes. The next morning I was straight to Cyclopaedia, the bike shop on Crwys Road, to buy my first set of tights. Shortly afterwards I was on a long solo ride into the valleys north of the city when my tyre blew. It wasn't the inner tubes – I was prepped enough to have two of those in my jersey pocket. It was the tyre itself. When I spun the wheel, I could see there was a big tear in it. I had no phone. There were no train stations nearby. So I took the banana out of my other pocket, ate it, carefully inserted the skin inside the tyre over the hole, stuck in one of the spare inners and started pedalling back south. It worked. It got me home.

The same bike shop gave me some advice. Don't ruin your nice red Cannondale on these long cold rides. Get yourself a cheap winter bike with components you won't need to wash and oil after every ride. So we got one for £100 and I took their words at face value. I rode the bike all winter and I didn't wash it once. It was a disgrace – covered in dried mud and animal muck, the chain brown with rust and squeaking with every pedal stroke, road salt all over the bottom bracket and derailleur.

Reflecting on the banana skin hack, I bought the most puncture-resistant tyres I could find – thick rubber, heavy, super-slow to ride. I went into full tank mode, trying to make the bike indestructible, not caring how heavy and cumbersome it became to ride. Keeping up with others was a nightmare – it felt like I had to ride twice as hard – but as a result it was also an absolute dream. I had to ride twice as hard as anyone else, so I was getting fitter and stronger without going any further. When it came to races and the red Cannondale, I felt like I was climbing on to a slightly chipped rocket. I barely needed to pedal. I was flying.

Years later, this was to be the way of the British track team. You did your training on standard bikes and standard kit. Only when we got to major championships did they let us have the lightweight stuff and the aero gear. It became a significant physiological and psychological advantage. What we never did, in the GB team pursuit squad, was add weights to our bikes, which is what I started doing as a teenager.

It seemed obvious to me: make your bike heavier, work harder, get quicker. My bike already weighed more than anyone else's. Add in the big cylindrical battery packs for front and rear lights and you already had a decent amount on top. Add on a few of those bean-bag weights you might attach to your ankles or wrists with Velcro for an aerobics class and you had a bike that was best friends with gravity.

Gradually, the local boys weren't quite as comparatively strong as they had used to be. On my first long ride I'd been convinced throughout I was going to be dropped. I was convinced I was going to be dropped with no idea of where I was. I thought these old boys would leave me out in the wilderness. As a result I'd carbo-loaded to the point of collapse: a massive curry the night before, doubling up on rice and naan bread; sticking loads of jam sandwiches in my jersey pockets. If I got another tear in my tyres the sandwiches were going to be less effective than the banana, but my tyres were so thick a direct hit from a Stanley knife would have struggled to pierce them.

But I didn't get dropped. I survived and I realised that, if everything else went wrong, you could follow road signs back to Cardiff. I began to understand that the sketchiness of some of these rides was one of the reasons I loved them. This wasn't just riding your bike. It was an adventure. On one ride I realised we were at the Storey Arms outside Brecon, an adventure centre where you could go rock climbing, pot-holing, gorge walking and canoeing. I'd been there for a couple of nights with school and it had taken us at least an hour in a minibus to get there.

How could we have ridden our bikes so far? That was the whole point. It was freedom and discovery and thrills all rolled into one. Fresh climbs, unfamiliar descents. Going further than you ever thought you could, all under your own steam. All because of your own legs.

Even more of an impossible buzz was being taken out to the Netherlands to watch Amstel Gold, aged fifteen. I'd loved watching the one-day classics on telly, but this was something else. I wasn't one of the lads taking photos of the team cars and bikes. I liked bikes, but for me they were for riding rather than putting on your mantelpiece. It was the racing paraphernalia that got me: standing near a feed zone, watching the riders grab musettes without breaking cadence; picking up a Rabobank bottle, and knowing I could keep it and take it home.

We rode to the T-Mobile team (then Team Telekom) hotel the morning before the race to get some autographs and then for a short while, in a slightly stalky way, followed the riders, the actual T-Mobile team, the same team as Ullrich – Erik Zabel, Vinokourov, all of them. It was genuinely astonishing. I didn't want to get within 10m of them. I was terrified I'd get in their way or cause a crash or something. To take all those fine details and colours back to south Wales turned my imagination and obsession up another load of levels. This fantasy world was real. I had been there. I could see it in my mind on every valley road or climb.

I still enjoyed the track, but the road was even better. Every time you went out you could push your boundaries. You could go longer, ride a loop quicker, do a steeper climb or beat your previous time up it. Gradually you could do it all without doubling up on rice and naans the night before. Each weekend could be better than the one before. The hard stuff became easier, so you found harder stuff and rode it until that became easier, too.

I went out one day with my friends Mike Davis and Chris Gould. The idea was to get far enough out to watch the Five Valleys race, but we kept egging each other on – another climb, another loop, another half-hour. We must have done 80 miles, sunburned, starving, thirsty as hell. But none of us wanted to stop. None of us wanted to be the one to say no.

It was a world where once you were gone, you were gone. Your parents couldn't do hands-on supervision when you were 40 miles away. You might be where you said you were going, but you might not be, because you were never sure where that was. If you were, you had no phone for them to check anyway. If you arranged to meet someone somewhere for a ride – say, a particular crossroads or outside a certain shop – you had to be there or else they might leave. The one time I did take my mum's phone I went way too long and got home to find I'd got loads of missed calls from her, thinking something catastrophic had happened. I didn't take her phone again after that. I quite liked the hanging around waiting for people. I liked going where no-one else knew. Ignorance could be blissful.

I was racing now against kids two years older than me, when two years older meant quite a lot. My birthday is in May, so after my sixteenth birthday I'd be able to ride up an age category and race against juniors, who might be coming up to their eighteenth. There was a national junior road race series named after Peter Buckley, a brilliant rider who'd won Commonwealth gold for the Isle of Man back in the 1960s, before his untimely young death. The series was a big deal. It had been won by Matt Stephens, Charly Wegelius and Bradley Wiggins, years before, and would later be won by Simon Yates. Some kid called Luke Rowe would finish second in consecutive years. I'd win the whole series when I was the right age, but I also managed to win the first round I competed in after turning sixteen.

I was quiet in the changing-rooms before the start, listening to the bigger lads talking about races, cars and girls. Out of those three topics, no-one asked me about the one I knew anything about. As the race developed, however, I felt at home. I got away with a couple of others. One of the older lads, a second-year junior with plenty of wins to his name, bigged me up to the other lads. I decided to back up his chat by attacking on the tougher part of the circuit, got away and won solo.

The name of the race might not have been as catchy as Amstel Gold. The Bath Road Road Race barely made sense, but winning it still changed things for me. My success meant that in early 2003 I got picked to ride the junior version of Kuurne–Brussels–Kuurne. I didn't know then how big a deal this was. I knew it was in Belgium, on the opening day of the season, so late February and often freezing cold, and I knew there were cobbles at some point. That was about it. I was racing so often that I would literally just roll into the next adventure. I didn't worry about failing. There was no failing when there was so much to learn at every race.

It was John Barclay who took us over. He'd done the same for the best young British riders over the years – Jeremy Hunt, Dave Millar, Charly Wegelius – and just to be a part of that heritage felt inspiring to a boy from Birchgrove. Most of the GB team seemed to be from London, maybe because John lived in Croydon, maybe because Belgium was a lot harder to get to if you lived in Yorkshire or Glasgow. I went down the night before and stayed in a bunk bed in his spare room. Then it was a ferry over and suddenly being in a country where it wasn't just about football – and definitely wasn't about rugby – but a place where cycling was on the front page of all the newspapers and being shown on the TV screens in every pub.

I found it all rather mesmerising. Old boys in bars drinking Duval and talking about cycling. News reports on TV talking about cycling. Every other rider except me talking about tactics and how to position yourself to get a win, because my approach was straightforward: get on your bike, race the race.

I didn't feel like an intruder. Cycling was my world, even if my world had much less cycling in it than this one. I did feel like an outsider. When I walked into the changing-rooms before the start, the other riders were having heat balm rubbed into their legs or Olbas oil shoved up their noses by a parent or coach who'd been there and done it himself. My dad grew up on a dairy farm, played rugby and ran a bit of cross-country. He was also hundreds of miles away in Cardiff.

This was a different world. The aromas were powerful,

almost overwhelming. Even a sniff of Olbas oil now takes me straight back there to those shiny Belgian boys with their properly shaved legs and cyclists' tans from training miles in warmer climes. Everyone was chatting away in Flemish. I had to assume it was Flemish. I didn't know enough Flemish to be sure.

I had a decent bike now. My development meant the lads down at Cyclopaedia had managed to sort me out with a nice new Giant, but when we lined up on the start line I realised it just wasn't in the same league as the ones being checked and finessed all around me. You couldn't move for deep-rim wheels. Their jerseys were bright with the names of multiple sponsors. Negative thoughts started jumping into my mind.

'Look how big these boys are. Those bikes and wheels must be worth thousands. How the hell can I compete with this?'

Then my dad's voice would fight its way back.

'Ger, it's just a bike and some flashy kit. We'll see once we get racing. What's the worst that can happen?'

Another thought popped into my head. 'Someone here on this start line is going to win today. Could it be me? Why not?'

It was cold. Thick gloves weather. I also felt small. Most of the riders were bigger than me. One of my GB team-mates, Ian Stannard, fitted in a treat. He looked custom-designed for the cobbles and frozen, muddy lanes. He looked even more Belgian than some of the Belgians.

We were supposedly each man for themselves in our team,

but I reasoned that Stannard would make an excellent bench-mark. I could also use him as a make-shift team-mate. If he went away, I wouldn't chase, because one of these Belgian lads would. If he stayed away, I could try jumping across once the others had done all the work. If I was up the road I could always say I was waiting for Stannard, my leader, or just revert back to the simplest of cycling rules when you're in a break: only do as much as the rider doing the least.

Lots changed that Sunday morning. Initially, it was the thrill of the terrain. Kuurne is not a hilly, cobbled race. It's why the senior version is often won by a sprinter. That's how Cav won it twice, later in his career. But bouncing over those cobbles, flying down those lanes – if doing a two-minute climb in south Wales had made me imagine I was at the Tour, then racing here was another level again. I felt like Peter van Petegem or Andrea Tafi or any other of those big-boned boys I'd watched winning the Spring Classics on Eurosport. I was so raw to it, so ignorant of any consequences, that I threw myself into every element. I dived into slippery corners too hot because I didn't really know how wet cobbles reacted under warm rubber. I went with attacks I probably didn't deserve to be in, because I'd never really blown up in a race before. I just tried to stay at the front with Stannard.

Maybe that was why I found myself in a group of seven or eight who seemed to have got away. Maybe that's how I stayed there as others were gradually whittled away. When I looked around and Stannard had gone too, the buzz was intense. 'Phwoah, I must be going well, because he's not here anymore, and it's just me and these three Belgians. I could win this . . .'

It was one of those days when you're almost confused. Where had everyone gone? Had it been that hard? I was feeling alright. I was feeling good. With a couple of kilometres to go, I chipped off the front. No-one could follow. I came down the run-in, a typically narrow Belgian street lined with terraced houses either side, and I was out on my own. I was free. I was going to win.

There had been no overthinking. No telling myself I couldn't do it or that I'd probably fail. It was take the pin out and go. It was do what feels right at the time. Just go balls to the wall and see what happens.

I saw a quote, many years later, on Instagram. It talked about keeping two people happy as an adult: the eight-year-old you, when you have no barriers or set beliefs and go out and do things for fun, and the eighty-year-old you, who looks back and thinks, yep, I gave it everything and I enjoyed it. That was something I always tapped into as an established rider in the pro ranks, because that's how it had naturally been for me. In those last thousand metres or so in Kuurne, I never stopped to think about what it might mean. I didn't worry about being caught. There were no consequences. There was only instinct. There was only this moment.

So the feeling when I crossed the line was not astonishment or ecstasy, it was more, 'Wow, how has that happened?'

Hearing all that chat afterwards, getting a different kind of look from the big local lads with their shiny bikes and kits, the ones whose world this was, really, piling back into John's car and then on the ferry, I just had a big grin on my face. 'Cheers, boys, thanks for having us . . .'

In any professional sport, the margins are so close, physically. What makes the difference is the top two inches. If you can somehow relax under the most intense pressure – if you can avoid overthinking things and not stress about the outcome – that's a huge advantage to have. I was lucky because that was me, and that was the way I'd been brought up by my mum and dad. Doing my best, doing everything I could to succeed, but not worrying about the outcome. Of course I still felt the nerves. I always did, all the way through my career. There were always doubts and negative thoughts. Your mind needs the same attention and work as your body. You will always feel these big emotions, but you just have to learn how to cope with them.

I was naturally intensely competitive. That was the other thing. I hated losing board games with my family or on the Xbox with my brother. In the guts of a bike race I loved how those flat-out moments made me feel, when some people found it a pressure or weren't arsed enough about it to keep pushing deeper and deeper. Training and racing were taking my competitive instincts and refining and driving them further. I was never content with each fresh level I reached. I wanted my long rides to get longer. I wanted my sprints to get quicker. I wanted to be faster than I was the week before and finish higher in the field in my next race, but I never assumed I would keep progressing through the age grades and ranks. To get to each new level I knew I would have to push harder each time.

I wanted to perform in every race I did, but I also knew I couldn't win them all. There were still areas in each one I did that could feel like success. You didn't need to necessarily cross the line first. If you took a scalp, or did your job and delivered someone else, or you did your quickest time or best placing – all those things were small wins. You just had to look for them. Even mistakes could be good as long as you learned from them and didn't repeat them.

From my academy days until the end of my first year as a professional, I'd write down the good things and the bad things I'd done in every race. Except they were both the same, the way I looked at it. They were lessons. That's what they were. Every one of them took you forward. They didn't go neatly into a journal. I'd scribble them down on the back of the race programme or a random bit of paper, but they all ended up together in a plastic wallet. The process of writing them down was the key bit. It allowed me to assess the race, to be self-critical, but also positive.

It was the same with the sacrifices I had to make to do what I wanted to do. They never felt like sacrifices, for exactly that reason. Now I was getting older, most of the lads from school were going out on Friday and Saturday nights. There was hanging out in the park after dark. There was chatting to girls. There was going to gigs or down the Arms Park, or just chilling after school. But my bike wasn't going to ride itself.

I did enjoy a night out. This was an era of blue WKD, of vodka shots and Jägerbombs. Sometimes I just couldn't say no. My best mate Ian would call the house phone. 'Ger, we're heading out to town in half an hour. Fancy it?'

I was still young. If I'd restricted myself too much and never gone out, maybe I would have jacked the riding in. My mum and dad saw that. What I had to learn was that there was a time and a place, and work it out for myself. As we all know, the spontaneous nights out are always the best. They were the hardest ones to sack off. But I never missed training, however big we went.

One Saturday morning I was due to ride with Chris Gould. When he turned up at my house, he threw up outside the back gate. We still went out and did four hours. Even one Christmas Eve, out with the boys in town at lunchtime, I didn't drink because I had to go home for a turbo session in the afternoon. No-one had told me to do an afternoon turbo session on Christmas Eve. I thought I should. And the 'should' came from me, not from anyone else.

Chapter three

Kampioenschap van Vlaanderen 2005

The more I raced, the more reasons I could find for thinking it might be possible to turn this happy obsession of mine into an adult occupation. In spring 2004, I went to the junior version of Paris–Roubaix with the GB squad. You got to race on the same morning that the pros raced in the afternoon and on the last 100km of the same historic route. Those two things meant you also rode with the same crowds lined deep along the roadside.

I had watched Roubaix so often I thought I knew what I needed to do. In the absence of proper specialised kit I borrowed a pair of strong steel-rimmed wheels from a friend, put foam pipe-lagging under the bar tape on my handlebars and did my best to get away in a break with Stannard. Coming into the famous velodrome, the two of us were clear. That's when Stannard decided to follow the diversion meant for cars. I'd fancied my chances of beating him in the sprint anyway, but it simplified things. Winning a race over such a hallowed parcours, and in an arena where so many heroes of mine had won, all seemed rather unreal.

The prize? My own weight in chocolate. There was only one issue: I had no idea what I weighed. I came up with a figure based more around my enjoyment of chocolate. They looked at my skinny arms and legs and raised their eyebrows, but delivered all the same. Actually, there were two issues. As a rider, I wouldn't be allowed to eat my own bounty. The hundreds of individually wrapped mini cobblestone chocolates would end up being divided between the non-riding staff at the Manchester and Newport velodromes, while I went out to the European Junior Track Cycling Championships in Valencia and won a silver medal. The university application I'd made to keep my mum happy started looking more like an emergency back-up plan than a genuine bid for academic betterment.

I was getting advice from all corners now. I had an old mate from school, Mark Sweeney, who'd left young to go to work in a suit shop in Cardiff city centre. Part of his job entailed wearing his employer's merchandise at all times, which had triggered a simple yet effective new nickname: Suit Man. Suit Man always talked a good game, which may be one of the reasons why he'd got the gig in the first place. On my eighteenth birthday, just before those Euros, he'd already done the maths for me. 'Ger, that race in France was good, hey? That means you could maybe get a medal at the Europeans, which puts you maybe fifth or six in the world. Next year you could get a medal at the Worlds. And if you keep improving at that rate, why couldn't you be world champion a few years after that?'

Suit Man was not an expert in cycling. Shane Sutton, who by contrast mainly favoured polyester tracksuits, was. A new GB academy programme was being established, looking to develop the best under-twenty-three riders in the country. I asked Shane about it. Tracksuit Man was as unequivocal as Suit Man. 'Ah mate, you don't want to do that. It's a mess at the moment. You want to get yourself on a good continental under-twenty-three team, like Rabobank. Learn the ropes on the road there, go win some medals on the track as you're developing.'

Suit Man turned out to have the power to look into the future as well as a full-length changing-room mirror. I went to the World Junior Track Championships in Los Angeles in July 2004 and won gold in the scratch race. The race was so chaotic I didn't want to believe I'd won. I barely celebrated. When we lined up for the medal ceremony the guy I thought was second even tried to stand on the top step of the podium. It was only when I had the rainbow jersey on my back that it became real. I went back to the Holiday Inn where we were staying with my parents and my brother, and raised an illegal beer in Suit Man's direction. Uni could wait. There wasn't much more I could do to prove to myself that I was taking the correct turn.

I went down to the velodrome in Newport when I got back

from the US. The GB track team were there doing their final prep for that summer's Olympic Games in Athens. I was in awe of every one of them: Chris Hoy, Brad Wiggins, Victoria Pendleton, Steve Cummings. They were so far above my level that the gap between where I was and where I wanted to be seemed wider than the track. The notion that this velodrome might one day bear my name was so laughably impossible that even Suit Man didn't flag it. Shane, meanwhile, had seen enough in the background to change his tune. The system, which had Chris and Vicky at its pinnacle, was starting to function in a way it hadn't before. There was Lottery funding and there were outstanding coaches like Rod Ellingworth getting involved. Shane made it clear: get on the under-twenty-three programme, race on the road, aim for the Olympics on the track.

I went home and watched them all race in Athens' velodrome. Brad won pursuit gold, Chris won the kilo despite the riders before him all breaking the world record. How did you get that mentally strong? How did you get that fast? I wasn't sure, but I hoped it would involve packing your bags straight after your A-Level results and moving into a shared house in Fallowfields, Manchester, with two young riders called Ed Clancy and Mark Cavendish.

These were houses looked after by British Cycling and rented out to us at £280 a month a man. If that seems cheap, the houses were cheaper. Ours was terrible, an end-of-terrace with a shed for bike storage that was soon broken into and emptied of bikes at speed. We had a room each, a shared kitchen and lounge, and neighbours who had no idea what these lean young lads were supposed to be doing. We could have been students, but we spent too much time each day exercising and not enough time out at night, because that was Rod's plan: work us hard, teach us to look after ourselves, see who could cut it as things got harder and home seemed further away.

Cav was the one who seemed to settle first. He struck up an early relationship with a man called Barry who lived over the road. Cav liked Barry, because he sold knock-off sports gear like Lacoste polo shirts with the crocodile on upside down or four-stripe Adidas tracksuit tops. Barry liked Cav because he bought them in volumes that suggested he thought they were genuine. I'd been there less than a week when Barry came flying down the road in an unfamiliar car considerably outside his price bracket and with his hand pressed down on the horn. As we walked out to say hello he dramatically accelerated away again, failed to see another car pulling out of a side-road, smashed into it and then careered off again once more. But no-one else came round and the illicit sports-wear deals kept taking place, so everyone seemed happy.

I barely unpacked, partly because there was nowhere to unpack to. There was no wardrobe in my room, just a bed, so I left my two bags of clothing and kit tucked away under that. At times I did miss the comforts of being at home: my mum's roasts, my mum's washing, my mum's adequately stocked fridge. But I was doing what I wanted to do, living with two very contrasting characters who were both equally enjoyable to spend time with. We were living our dream, even if that dream was not a familiar one to every teenager our age: dark and wet early mornings, riding through some dodgy old areas to the velodrome on the east side of the city, hoping the batteries in our bike lights were still holding; doing a whole day of hard track training, double sessions and sometimes triple ones, emptying the tank every time; pedalling back through the same streets of broken glass and staring kids to begin French lessons and Italian lessons, because who could make it as a road rider on the continent if you couldn't speak the language of the Tour and the Giro?

Cav was already the Cav that Cav would grow up to be. He was loud and brash and prone to temper tantrums and great generosity in equal measure. Ed was an introvert and often happier on his own than in a group. That one of them would go on to be knighted after winning more stages of the Tour de France than anyone else in history and that the other would become a triple Olympic gold medallist – it was as likely as Suit Man ending up in charge of Emporio Armani. If you'd looked at that run-down house in Fallowfield, you wouldn't have spotted cyclists of the future. You would have seen three young men who were permanently tired and not particularly skilled in the kitchen. Ed's signature dish? A bowl of cornflakes. He could serve it for breakfast, lunch and dinner.

Rod wasn't trying to make it as easy as possible to succeed. He didn't want it to all be about the training. He almost wanted us to fail, in the best possible way. To forget to make our food and thus learn how riding hungry was riding slow. To forget to tidy up, fail to find your cleats and then miss the first part of a session, so you never did it again. To not clean the kitchen or bathroom so we ended up getting sick and learned how important hygiene is to an elite athlete. It wasn't about the watts we could produce. We didn't have power meters to measure them, even if we had wanted to. It wasn't about winning races. It was everything else around it, because that was the stuff that really got you there and allowed you to stay. I may have missed out on the conventional uni experience, but this was something far better. It was much more serious and it was entirely specific. It worked.

We succeeded by failing. That first November we were sent over to Belgium to ride the under-twenty-three version of the Six Days of Ghent track event on the crazily short and steep Kuipke velodrome. The banking was so tight it turned out to be remarkably easy to crash, so high that when you did you had a long way to fall. After one guy put me into the barriers at the top, I fell left from such a height that I barely touched the wooden boards on my way to the flat concrete at the bottom of the turn. Rod stood over me, asked me if I was okay, picked my bike up, gave me a push and sent me off again. That was how it was. You didn't complain and you never stopped, unless you genuinely couldn't get yourself back into the saddle. You didn't worry, because you were loving every second of it. Where we wanted to be, when we wanted to be there.

We barely got massaged, that first year. It wasn't about the soft touch. And all of it was so much better than that alternative route of going off to an under-twenty-three team in Europe. I heard stories later from Richie Porte about his own adventures as a callow young Australian in Italy. The advice he got didn't stretch much further than to eat pasta and have a good sweat the day before a race. In rainy Manchester the weather may have been worse, but we were being given enough freedom to work it out for ourselves. There was a track series in Manchester four times each winter called Revolution. The competition was good and the prize money was enough to keep young sprinters in (misspelt) Sergio Tachini. Ed and I won some decent money the night before we were due to fly to Australia for the Sydney leg of the World Cup and some other smaller races and blew most of it on fish and chips, beers and sweets from the corner shop on the way home. It made our twenty-four hours of travelling about twenty-four times less comfortable. We didn't do it again, although worse was coming my way.

In this time I never looked too far ahead. I'd seen those Olympic riders up close, but I couldn't think about the Beijing Games in 2008. They were too distant to have any effect. I would be the same when I came to starting Grand Tours, years later. I would never roll off the ramp for a prologue at the Tour and think, Jesus, there are going to be twenty-one horrific stages between here and Paris. I would just deal with each stage in front of me and often just the next hour.

Turning pro was my dream. So was riding the Tour one day. But there was always something ahead of that. To get to the Olympics, to win a World title on a track, to be good enough to be picked for the GB squad to go to a Worlds, to win some European track races so I could be in the frame for selection, to win races at the academy so I could go to Europe. So many goals along the way to hit. Make them and I would do all the things I wanted to do. Don't worry about what's down the road. Just worry about what's in front of you this minute.

Including the piece of metal on the tarmac which caused the crash on that trip to Sydney which led to me rupturing my spleen and ending up in intensive care. The key part of the whole experience, looking back two decades later, is that the pain and the danger and the worry for all those around me never deterred me. It was never a question of if I would be racing again and putting myself in the exact same position. It was only ever when.

In the ambulance on the way to the hospital I'd turned down the paramedics' suggestion of morphine. I thought I was racing in two days' time. Then, after I'd had some scans, the consultant came to see me.

'Mr Thomas, you've ruptured your spleen. You're not going to be racing this weekend.'

'Are you sure? Can you patch me up?'

'No. I think we'll be taking it out.'

'Ah, okay, yeah. Give me all your morphine or whatever you've got, let's crack on.'

Two hours later: 'Mr Thomas, it's stopped bleeding, so we'd prefer to just leave it in. But if it does start bleeding again, then we'll take it out.'

'Well, why don't you take it out anyway? Just get it over with. And then we can crack on and I can get back on my bike.'

Maybe it was all a bit delusional. Dave Brailsford had been worried enough to fly my parents and brother out from Cardiff to Sydney. I was seriously unwell. I was also seriously into getting back as rapidly as possible. Just as I had loved all the challenges that had come my way when I had been learning the ropes at Maindy and in the lanes and hills beyond – going longer on my weekend rides, going faster up the Bwlch and Rhigos, getting lost and cold and wet and hungrier than I'd ever been before – so I was relishing all these fresh things being thrown at me now. Everything I was doing was new. Every step up I made the goals and challenges got bigger.

Cav was born to be a sprinter. He had the speed, but he had the attitude, too. He'd spell out what he wanted: 'Right, I'm going to win this race, then that one, then I'm going to beat that guy.' He was like a boxer talking hype before his next title fight. I was quieter and much shyer. With people I didn't know I often wouldn't say much, but I had the same belief, deep down, and I had the same confidence. I wasn't going to go around telling everyone about it, but I had the same real drive, the same ambition. I took the same pleasure in making all the necessary sacrifices. Every race, every week, I wanted to step up.

We moved out of the Fallowfield house when we got back from Australia. The suburban charms of Heaton Mersey were calling. The house was bigger, the neighbourhood was better, training roads were closer. It was still the tried and tested combo of me, Cav and Ed in one house, before Stannard and Ben Swift joined later, and Andy Tennant and Ross Sander got another similar place at the bottom of our road.

We didn't do everything right. Who does at that age? My nineteenth birthday coincided with the Champions League final between Liverpool and Milan. At the start of the evening we had no notion that it would shortly become known as the Miracle of Istanbul. When Liverpool went 3-0 down we didn't think it would be a big night. By the time Steven Gerrard had orchestrated an impossible comeback and Jerzy Dudek had become the hero of the subsequent penalty shoot-out, it was a significantly longer night and bigger bar bill than we had anticipated, which was maybe why we thought it was a good idea to stop off at Subway on the way home to buy up all their cookies and muffins, and then to wake up Cav when we got back.

I could still turn up for work the next day. I had to. We had a photographer and journalist from a cycling magazine coming over to chat to us before training, and then follow us with Rod in the car. The issue was the state of the house. There were cookies and muffins everywhere. I tried vacuuming, at least until the damage broke our hoover. Ever resourceful, I popped next door to borrow theirs. While I was out, Cav opened the microwave to make his porridge and a plant pot fell out and smashed on the floor. My name was taken in vain. When I returned, I couldn't find my cycling shoes anywhere. I had to call Matt. 'Erm, maybe try the freezer?'

Sure, I was hanging, but I still dropped Cav in one of our lead-outs. The issue was that Cav had already done some dropping of his own – us, in with Rod. We got called into the track the next day to see Rod, Shane and Dave Brailsford. We were asked what time we got in. I honestly couldn't remember. Kick-off was around 8pm, so I guessed at 10.30pm, which failed to build in the extra time and pens. We were asked how many drinks we'd had. I was tempted to say it was hard to remember after the seventh one.

Perhaps unsurprisingly, our first authentic bollocking fol-lowed shortly afterwards. I was banned from doing the Five Valleys race in Wales a few weeks later, which was exactly where to hit me to make sure it hurt. Instead, we were sent out on a long road ride with Brad and Steve Cummings, who had just got back from the Giro. With a certain amount of snitch karma, it turned out to be more of a punishment for Cav than the rest of us. Cav had to go faster up bigger hills than he wanted to. We got to ride with two of our heroes and quiz them endlessly on all the things they'd learned in the Grand Tours. Cav got to be spat out of the back on every climb and have to empty the tank on the flats to get back on. We even got to do some lead-outs at the end for Brad, who was maybe the one I looked up to more than any of the others, because he was always a few years ahead, doing what I wanted to be doing a few years later – winning Junior Worlds, winning on the endurance programme as a senior, turning pro, riding Grand Tours, winning Olympic golds.

So most of the time we only drank occasionally. We focused on our cycling, except when we felt the need to focus on something else. And we didn't live a true student lifestyle, apart from those incidents when we absolutely did.

It was a day when we were supposed to be going to Italian lessons. It would have helped me a great deal, a few years later, on Barloworld, if I had paid more attention in the classroom, but we were slightly late, this afternoon, and not that keen on walking in halfway through. At the exact moment of the umming and ahhing, we passed a shop selling fancy-dress outfits. In the window was a full *Scream* mask and costume, which led to the seed of an idea: what if we still turned up late for the Italian lesson, but did so in a *Scream* costume?

Like all great plans, the broader concept was soon finessed into something more refined. The Italian lesson was too big. It contained people we didn't know. Why didn't we target one of the lads? By this stage it was me, Ben Swift and Ian

Stannard in one house, Andy Tennant and Ross Sander in another just down the road. Andy was in Italian. He was easily spooked. It was all starting to make a lot of sense.

That evening it began. All of us were at our house. Swifty did some theatrical yawning, announced he was too tired for a movie night, went up to bed and then climbed out of his window and on to the wheelie bin he'd left against the wall for this exact purpose. Down the street to the other house, through the back door that Ross had left unlocked, into Andy's room and into the *Scream* outfit.

Meanwhile, we had begun to work on Andy. 'Ah, Tennant, get that DVD from your house, will you?' He was reluctant. He suggested Ross went instead. Conveniently, Ross was already in the toilet, so Andy was forced to walk down the street to his house, calling his dad on his phone as he went. He unlocked the front door, went up the stairs, pushed open his bedroom door – which was the moment he saw Swifty at the end of his bed in the full *Scream* outfit.

You could hear the screaming from our house. You could pretty much hear the sound of Andy taking the entire staircase in two leaps. You could certainly hear the panic in his voice when he phoned me from the street a second or two later.

'G! G! There's someone in the house! Someone's in the house!'

'Ah, mate, just get the DVD. What are you on about?'

Swifty, meanwhile, was experiencing his own adrenaline

explosion. He came down the stairs expecting to see Andy sprinting up the street. Instead, Andy came sprinting towards him, hell-bent on revenge.

The mask came off just before the first punches landed.

'Tennant! It's me! It's Swifty!'

There was some hugging after that. Hearts pounding, fight or flight all over the place. When it settled, which took a while, and the story had been told from all angles, which was most enjoyable and far more dramatic than the proposed DVD, a new resolve was apparent in all of us. The *Scream* costume had already more than paid for itself. But we were just getting started. What could we do with it next?

It was Andy who came up with the plan, perhaps through an understandable desire to be in the audience for this one, rather than on the stage. This time it would be Ed Clancy as the victim and Tennant as the main perpetrator. A scheme was set: Andy would get into the costume and hide in the boot of my hatchback, I would offer to give Ed and his girlfriend a lift to the local Tesco, and Andy would jump out at some point en route.

Weirdly, my car refused to start when we tried to set off. Possibly this added to the confusion in Ed's mind. Everything else went to plan. We drove to Tesco. I left the boot unlocked. Andy, in full *Scream* costume, climbed into the boot. When we got back in, with Ed's girlfriend fully briefed and on board, I slipped into the driver's seat again and Ed rode shotgun next to me.

The detail in the planning was extraordinary. I was to drive to a certain layby. Swifty would have his own car parked round the corner, ready to flee with Andy. When I turned up the car stereo and used the phrase, 'Now this is a tune ...' Andy was to jump out of the boot.

The execution was dreamy. We approached the layby. Swifty was parked up. I turned up the stereo, hit the central locking and uttered the fateful words.

To be fair to Tennant, he did a magnificent job. So did Ed's girlfriend, whose interpretation of Neve Campbell was worthy of an Academy award. Ed lost his mind. You've never seen anyone trying to exit a moving vehicle so quickly. You've never seen a man take so long to figure out how central locking works. By the time Tennant had legged it round the corner and escaped in the Swiftmobile, Ed was a messy wreck.

The genius of a great plan is the room it allows for riffs and improv. Seeing Ed's distress, I found new depths of creativity within myself.

'Mate, you know what? I reckon that was those lads who followed me home from the track earlier ...'

Ed had his hands on his head. 'What do you mean?'

'Yeah, I cut up some lads on the way home and they followed me all the way back.'

'Why did you go home? Why did you go home if they were following you?'

'I don't know, I was just ... I just thought it would be okay ...'

Escalations, everywhere you looked. We got home. Now Ross Sander wanted in on the fun. He had taken the *Scream* costume from Tennant, who had probably had enough of it for now, and was sitting on the sofa in the house.

I tried to give him a whispered heads-up. 'Mate, you need to start running now, because Ed's going to get you and he's going to kill you . . .'

Shouting back over my shoulder to Ed at the same time: 'Shit, Ed, someone's in the house!'

Ed ran in. Ross darted out the back door. Ed went after him like a police dog. Ross launched himself over the garden fence. Ed tried to grab his ankles and just missed.

I'd never seen the version of Ed we all experienced in the following few hours. He wasn't just wired. He was ready to go to war.

'G, these lads are lunatics. How did they get in the house? How did they get in your car?'

Now everybody wanted in on it. Swifty was next, putting it on and then tapping at our living-room window with a kitchen knife. It took a long time to bring Ed back down after that, and I think we realised we had pushed him as far as we could. I put the costume on, walked into the lounge, de-masked myself and told him all. Which took a lot of explaining and reassurance, and a fair few man-hugs.

'Ed, it was us. We were the boys. Nobody's following us. Nobody's trying to kill us.'

I'm not sure what development and junior teams are like

these days, but I'm pretty sure this sort of thing no longer flies. There's too much money in it, for starters. Young riders are more impatient to reach the top. We were focused, too, and we could definitely be serious, but letting our hair down and failing at things was part of it. And I always knew, even as a junior, that to get 100% out of myself I had to operate at 60% some of the time, not tick along the entire time at 90%. If we had tried to turn ourselves into robots at that age, we would have blown at some point. We would have got to twenty-five or twenty-eight years old and cracked.

Instead, most of us kept going deep into our late thirties. There's a reason why Cav won his last Tour stage aged thirty-nine, why I rode my last Tour at the same age, why Swifty looks like going the same way. Of course, some guys can be intense their entire careers. Maybe that's their personalities. I needed to enjoy myself. This looked like it could be my job, but it was also my passion.

I was maybe having a few more crashes than was ideal. Some of them were my fault. I was overly keen sometimes. I was always putting myself in the eye of the storm, trying to avoid the wind and save the legs as much as possible. That would often create wrong-place-wrong-time scenarios. When you're constantly fighting and battling in every race for each position, it becomes something of an occupational hazard. What irritated me was that I seemed to be getting a reputation for crashing. There were plenty of riders who didn't crash, because they backed out in sketchy situations. They couldn't and wouldn't get involved. I was fully committed for my own result and for the team's. If that meant I lost skin on the road – fine.

Rod and the other coaches could see we were getting strong. They could measure our efforts on the track. What they wanted to add was some elite racing smarts, which is why they decided to send us off for a spell in a couple of second-tier German teams in the later part of 2005.

It was arranged through the late Heiko Salzwedel, who was coaching as part of the British set-up at the time. I would ride for the Pro-Conti team Wiesenhof. Cav and Ed were sent to Dortmund to ride with Sparkasse. How much did we have to learn? Well, we thought it was good idea after one small race to wash our bikes in the hotel showers. We used degreaser to get the bikes really clean. It was an effective strategy; all the dirt came off the bikes – and attached itself to the shower tray, walls and curtain. It was a hard call to say who was more furious, the manager of the hotel or the manager of Sparkasse, who had to pay the manager of the hotel back to happiness.

A few days later we all rode the Sparkassen Giro Bochum, a one-day race that attracted most of the German pros. Only on the start line did I realise Jan Ullrich, my hero ever since he'd won that Tour back in 1997, was also in the field. So, too, was Ivan Basso. I pedalled along behind them like a shy super-fan, marvelling at the size of Ullrich's legs and the way all his muscle fibres seemed to be poking out of his skin. 'Holy shit, Cav, this guy is insane. Look at those veins!'

We went out for food afterwards, me, Cav and Ed. Dizzy with our surroundings, we celebrated with a massive surf 'n' turf, in my case a fat steak with two giant shrimps. A couple of hours later, lying on a camp bed on the floor of Ed's room, I noticed my chest was feeling tight. Next was the itching – first under my arms, then on my scalp, then around the sort of areas where you really don't want an itchy rash. It was like someone had given me a bath in stinging nettles.

It was only six months or so after my splenectomy. Could this be something to do with that? Since it was gone midnight, I decided to ride it out. Ed, being Ed, was much less sure. Ed had concerns I was going to die.

He slept even less than I did that night. It was like he was a new dad and I was his newborn son. He checked at least once an hour that I was still breathing. Without wanting to spoil the story, I lived. When we returned home a month or so later, an allergy specialist did some tests and warned me off shellfish for good. It sort of summed up where we were: doing scary shit a lot of the time, but going with it and always assuming it was all going to work out for the best.

Recovered, off my own back I went off to Leipzig with one of the older German riders, André Schulze. Now the adventure really began. If I'd thought parts of Manchester were a little rough round the edges, I wasn't prepared for the more affordable parts of an old East German city. Neither was the team based on the same founding principles as our academy back home. I went out on a training ride with a young André

Greipel and a young T-Mobile pro called Eric Baumann, who had also won junior Paris–Roubaix four years before me. We did a long training ride. I felt good. When we got home, they announced they were going out for an extra session, paced behind a motorbike. They asked if I wanted to come.

'Yes, for sure, let's go.'

We stopped at Eric Baumann's house to refill our water bottles. As we walked out of his kitchen, he picked up a beer, flipped the cap off and downed it in one.

'Do you want one, Thomas?'

'Erm, I think I'm alright actually, thanks . . .'

A few days later we drove to a race in Belgium. It turned out Leipzig is a long way from Belgium. Even the parts of Belgium that are closest to Leipzig aren't very close to Leipzig. We stopped at a bakery for lunch. The two Germans bought three different sorts of cakes each. I found myself asking questions about professional road racing that hadn't occurred to me before. What was normal – what Rod was making us do back in Manchester, or what these tough German dudes were doing on the long roads from Leipzig to Belgium?

We raced Kampioenschap van Vlaanderen, or the Championship of Flanders, a one-day race that had been going for almost a hundred years. It was a 1.1 event under UCI rules, so one level below the absolute top, but it was packed with the sort of pro riders who were used to cobbles and elbow-to-elbow bike combat. I did okay. I came eighteenth. And while that didn't count as an astonishing result, being there with a Pro-Conti team, as a stagiaire, a raw youngster, and surviving multiple laps and the cobbles, and a whole lot of super-experienced road racers – all that felt like a massive achievement.

I paid for it. We did another tough race the following day, undulating over classic northern European roads, always up or down, the speed so much punchier than a smaller race in the tail end of a season should be. This time I was completely spent. I could barely get round. When I did, there was another nine-hour car drive back to Leipzig. Upon arrival, I found out that André's female flat-mate had just finished shooting a topless calendar, along with eleven other girls. While this was a slightly different post-race scenario to those I was used to with Cav and the boys or my parents, the vibe was a good one, and they insisted on taking me out to see the best that Leipzig had to offer.

I didn't need much persuading. We ended up in some quite lively underground discotheques and I had a marvellous time. No-one wanted to talk about what it took to get a top-20 finish at Kampioenschap van Vlaanderen, but that was just fine. I was seeing things that even Fallowfield and Barry over the road couldn't supply. I couldn't wait to get back to Manchester and tell Cav and Ed all about it.

There was so much new stuff happening every day that you just had to roll with it. We could talk about it up in Manchester, I would phone my mates back home who were also bike riders to share war stories, and Rod was always there when you wanted to chew over all the stuff you'd learned about racing.

Cav and Ed, Stannard and Swifty – we were all different characters, but the academy was shaping us in the same way. We were working off the same blueprint, and then adding on our own individual bits and pieces. Everything is an adventure, when you're at this stage in your life, whether it's at a normal uni or the much more abnormal College of Rod. Everything points forward. Even the bumps in the road throw you onwards.

Chapter four

Olympics 2008, Beijing, team pursuit final

As 2005 became 2006 and I got ready to leave my teens behind me there was something people kept asking me: what sort of rider was I going to be? I rode track, I loved the cobbles. I liked climbing and I was good at time-trials too. Which route would I choose, now I was coming out of the age categories and into the big-boy leagues?

It wasn't that I couldn't give them an answer. It was that my answer didn't seem to compute for some of them. I loved it all. I enjoyed testing myself out in the varying disciplines and couldn't see why there was any hurry to ditch one for the other. I knew it all in my head. First I'd target the track, turn pro, then hit the Olympics on the track. Then commit to the road – first the Classics, and shorter stage races after that. Well, that was enough planning for someone still in his teens.

But I wasn't one to shout about it. I went to the Commonwealth Games in Melbourne a few months before my

20th birthday and won a bronze medal in the points race on the track. Thirteen months after Sydney had taken my spleen it felt like Australia was paying back its debt. Those Commonwealths were a great learning curve, a fine first taste of a big multi-sport event, even if it was strange turning up together as what felt like a familiar GB team and then getting separated almost immediately, even though we were all off to the same place. 'Are you guys from Wales? Sorry, this isn't your bus, it's England's. Yours will be here soon.'

A couple of weeks later I was back in GB colours at the World Championships in Bordeaux. We lost the team pursuit to the Aussies by a mere 0.004 seconds and I was the one to miss the back of the line on the final lap. There were only three of us left rather than the usual four. I didn't nail the change and was fractionally off the back as we crossed the line. Others tried to make me feel better about it, including my mum and dad on the phone, and then within the GB team. The consensus was that they'd got the starting positions wrong. I should have been the one at the front bringing it home, not last change. I still blamed myself. I was young. I thought I had to get everything right, whatever was thrown at me.

In any case, there wasn't much time to sit back and feel sorry for myself. There seldom is in cycling. Rod had set up a base for the GB academy in Quarrata in Tuscany. My road education was about to be taken to an entirely new level.

It wasn't just that Italian roads didn't behave like British roads – faster, smoother, slippery when wet – but that when they went up they went up for far longer and then when they went down you could go far faster. Of course I loved descending. It was the most thrilling thing of all when you rode your bike. In Wales you could go quite fast, but not for long. Sprinting to try to set off the 30mph speed limit camera as you dropped down from the top of Newport Road was a pleasure which lasted about thirty seconds. The Bwlch and Rhigos were fairly long by Welsh standards, but they were nothing compared to Tuscany. In Italy you could go into corners hot and pop out the other side hotter. You could dive-bomb down the inside of a team-mate or take them on a blind outside, if you were willing to believe you were invincible, which as young men of our age we did. Max Sciandri, long years in the pro peloton behind him, now responsible as a coach, would try to warn us on some days: 'Ah, boys, it's quite narrow, this one – maybe take it steady down the other side.' We'd get into an eyeballs-out battle, forget his words, meet a van coming up the other way and bail out into the gutter, sliding around on our back wheels and sometimes our backsides. Max would catch us up, bikes scattered across the road, riders picking gravel out of their palms, and shake his head wearily: 'Boys, what did I tell you?'

We always wanted to race – Stannard, Swifty, Ross Sander, anyone out on the ride. We'd have free-wheeling competitions, where you weren't allowed to pedal on the descent, and so had to conserve and amplify all the speed you could find. We learned how to hold a wheel and its aero pull; how to brake as late as possible, but never too late; you wanted the speed out of the corner, not into it. We were learning the skills, but not necessarily the control – too keen, too eager, too much blood rushing to the head. Within a few months most descents within a 40km radius of Quarrata had a corner named after the rider who'd decked it there.

It wasn't just going down where we were learning by getting it wrong. One of the key sessions we did was the infamous Monte Serra test, beloved and feared by all the pros in the area. It's a hard road, that one – just over 12km, an average gradient of around 7%, and it's harder still if you've gone out to a €15 pizza buffet the night before. It turned out that young British lads viewed a buffet slightly differently to the more cosmopolitan Quarrata locals. They saw the chance to sample small amounts of several dishes. We saw quantity over quality. We saw all you can eat.

Rod was alongside us on the scooter as we rode out to Monte Serra, asking how we were feeling. I did well in that I just about managed to tell him I was still feeling a touch bloated, rather than burping in his face. All you could eat transpired to be less than you could ride. Of course I still wanted to clock the fastest time, yet I was learning something specific about myself: I could go fast in training, when I didn't have thirteen slices of pizza slowly working their way through my lower intestine, but pin a race number to my back and I could always go faster.

I wasn't just a rider. I was a racer. The hill might still be the hill, but when places and a podium were on the line, there was a strength in your legs and desire in your heart that were just a little greater than when it was pure training.

I knew Cav was the same. He fooled the more scientific coaches at British Cycling for a while, because his numbers were not as impressive as some of the others. They missed the point. Put the finish line of a race 20km on from a tough climb that Cav believed he could get over and he'd bury himself, manage to stay within reach and then find the power to win the sprint at the end of it. You couldn't see that sort of real-world racing in tests on a stationary bike. You couldn't recreate that sort of ruthless desire in a lab.

Throughout my career I would be the same. Right at the other end of the arc, training with the Ineos gang for the Vuelta TTT in 2023, time-trial specialist Dan Bigham came out to help our prep. He put on all the best kit and prepped with bicarb drinks, as you would in a race. He kicked my head in, I got spat out the back and threw my dummy a little. His approach worked for him: 'You have to hit the numbers in training, because it's not like you can magically gain 20 watts in a race.' Mine was different. Yes, you have to be in the ball park, but training is about consistency and constantly going deep, not about PBs. To be fair, he was right that I didn't gain 20 watts. I gained 40.

From the outside, in 2006 this mix of old superstitions and learned habits was beginning to be supplanted by the new world of stats and sports science. Max was old-school, from the days of a wired cycling computer and heart-rate strap. The Monte Serra test to assess your form, 'a little sweat' the day before a race so you were ready to go – it was an art, but there was a historic logic behind it, and the science and data would often underline those traditions rather than contradicting them. A decade later, we'd be told to prep for a race by holding a certain number of watts for a certain period of time. You'd be a little bit sweaty after it. Hmm.

Races were professional. What exactly professional looked like depended where you were. Riding the Baby Giro I was climbing well on the penultimate stage and was positioned nicely around 20th on the road at the start of the final climb of the day. By the top I had dropped to fiftieth. I didn't blow up. Instead, four team cars came past me with five or six Italian riders holding on to each one.

That's pretty illegal, whichever country you're racing in, yet the commissaires seemed more concerned about the front of the race than the back. Sometimes the riders getting a tow would shout at me to hold on as they went past. There was more chance of me stopping by a roadside bistro for thirteen slices of pizza. I hated what they were doing and I hated they were allowed to do it. It went against everything I believed. Cycling is about suffering. If you can't finish the race yourself, you don't deserve to finish.

A few years later, at my first Giro proper, I'd see my old friend – the one who'd punched me in the stomach at the

2007 Tour – smacking a rival rider who had the temerity to glide past attached to a team car. It was quite reassuring to see him smacking other people for proper reasons, as well as young innocents whose legs no longer had the strength to pedal to his satisfaction. Here at the Baby Giro there were no policemen and no vigilantes either. On the following day's final stage I finished fourth in a sprint where I was leading Ben Swift out, but ended up going for it myself. Were the guys in front of me some of the boys who had freewheeled up the final climb the day before?

Maybe I was getting more professional in better ways. I went to the British Road Race Championships in Yorkshire in 2006 wearing a pair of red Specialized glasses that someone at the company had given me for free. No-one had given me free shades before. You had to be a proper rider to get free stuff. I didn't think I was a proper rider, but maybe this was more evidence I was on my way.

There were big names on the start line. Four former champions, including Jeremy Hunt, Matt Stephens, Roger Hammond and Russ Downing. Roger, as a serious Classics rider, was something of a hero to me. I'd been in the velodrome celebrating my junior win when he came in third at Paris–Roubaix two years before. There was also my good mate Dale Appleby, who I'd grown up with in south Wales, and who had already been responsible for something defining in my life. My nickname for Dale was D. It was hearing me talking to him on the phone from our rubbish Manchester house that led Cav to utter his fateful words – 'Right, well, if he's D, then that makes you . . . G.'

Maybe it was being with Dale that gave me the confidence to launch an attack. Maybe it was Tuscany and the track, and my legs. Either way, we were in the mix with Roger Hammond and a couple of others going into the final lap of the 5km circuit, and when I launched my sprint, with 200m to go, only Hamish Haynes and Roger Hammond came past me.

Third in the Nationals couldn't be fluked. Two years after watching him in wide-eyed awe, I was both racing against Roger and holding my own. I had beaten Jez Hunt, I had beaten Steve Cummings. A couple of weeks later, at the European Track Championships, the GB quartet of which I was part won gold in the team pursuit. I would occasionally see myself referred to in articles as 'Gee'. That could wait. Everything else was marching forwards.

Because this was 2006, the forwards wasn't always straight. Word of mouth still mattered. The elite could still be informal. In the middle of that summer, David Millar, returning from his doping ban, was training with the Saunier Duval team and staying with Max at his house in Tuscany. Saunier Duval were going to a one-day race in Bilbao, northern Spain, called Circuito de Getxo. They had space for a young rider. Would I fancy it?

I was too heavy for the road after the track Euros. My body was 4km of pursuit big, not one-day race slim. Saunier Duval had been a rider short, but the way I rode they may as well have started with one less, because I was absolutely useless. I had turned up feeling self-conscious about my track weight and tried to use my Italian phrasebook to communicate this to the team manager Mauro Gianetti, who in his previous life as a rider had won both Liège–Bastogne–Liège and Amstel Gold, and in his future life as a team principal would run the UAE team of Tadej Pogačar. My phrasebook failed its task, but the first steep climb, which arrived after only 20km of flat warm-up, soon did the job.

They didn't ask me back. Getxo wasn't even a truly elite race; it was another UCI 1.1, one level below the top, like Sparkasse the previous year. And yet all I had done was watch a load of skinny Spanish dudes disappearing away from me into the green Basque mountains. Beating a few pros in the British Nationals was one thing. When it came to racing in Europe, I clearly still had a long way to go. This was a world where everyone had free sunglasses, except for the ones who were actually being paid to wear them. I took my rejection as best I could. Okay, Saunier Duval would rather turn up a rider short than take me. I'd have to show them what I could do.

A year later, struggling round the Tour de France with Barloworld, the sight of the Saunier Duval jersey was often a very useful motivation for me. Every time I saw one I tried to overtake it. Every time I rode past their team car, I'd make sure I gave them a little wave, just to let them know I was still there; just to let them know that I was slightly less overweight for the road than a year ago and slightly less useless for my team-mates than I had been for them.

There was something else, too. I really wanted to be a professional cyclist, but at the same time I wasn't stupid. I was beginning to understand what the world of professional cycling smelled like in this era. In the summer of 2006 the Operación Puerto scandal broke. So many pro riders were implicated in blood-doping that it was hard to keep track of all the names, but two of the suspended riders could not be ignored: Ivan Basso and Jan Ullrich.

Hearing about Ullrich's suspension, and later his confession of doping, was devastating. I had my suspicions by this point, obviously, but the confirmation was still deeply upsetting. I'd looked up to him so much – as a kid watching him accelerating up Alpine mountains; as a junior dreaming of doing the same; as a young rider in Germany the summer before. I didn't want to believe he was doping, but slowly it became clear that he had been and, with that, the next realisation: good riders, clean riders, were being defrauded because of people like him.

Going to Circuito de Gexto was another part of a picture I'd hoped never to see coming into sharper focus. I had roomed that weekend with Riccardo Riccò, the young Italian whose results were already making people sit up and take notice. Riccò would later be found guilty of blood-doping on so many occasions that he would eventually be banned for twelve years. When I got to our hotel room, he was just opening his suitcase. It sounded very much like there were multiple needles or syringes in there. Injections weren't illegal, at this point. Riders could inject vitamins and legal recovery substances, but I wasn't naive. I had read about Puerto, and I knew what had happened to Dave Millar, and I never wanted to go anywhere near that world. British Cycling and the track scene was a very comforting place to be. It felt safe and totally clean. This other world – I wanted to be part of the good aspects of it, the big races and epic climbs, the Grand Tours and the one-day Classics. I was ready to push myself to my limits. But I didn't want any part of this dirtiness. When my suitcase opened, I wanted bib-shorts and racing jerseys to fall out.

So part of me was glad when the Saunier Duval thing never amounted to much. Both Riccò and Leonardo Piepoli would be fired from the team at the 2008 Tour for doping. The sponsors would withdraw in disgust. It was the same when a move to another pro team fell through. Phonak were a big deal in 2006. They'd won the yellow jersey at the Tour through Floyd Landis, which seemed completely different to the relentless domination of Lance Armstrong. I was told they were after a young British rider for the following year and that I was in the frame. I was in the box room at my mum and dad's house when I got the phone call. A company called iShares was going to replace Phonak as the main sponsor, with a budget big enough to compete at the very top. It seemed a fantastic opportunity, and not just because the contrast between a box room in a terraced house in Cardiff and a spot on a Tour-winning team was as hard to miss as a yellow jersey on the Champs-Élysées.

Then Landis tested positive for testosterone a month after the Tour and was stripped of his win. iShares cancelled their deal, the Phonak team folded and I wasn't turning pro. Looking back now, I'm glad it worked out as it did. Had I joined Saunier Duval or Phonak/iShares, I might have seen a whole other world. How would I have reacted, as a young man surrounded by the powerful and habitual? I'm fortunate I never had to find out.

I could still see a path forward. The track was so much cleaner than the road, that much was obvious to me. British Cycling were committed to doing it the proper way. That was my immediate goal and focus. The road in my eyes was slowly getting better, too; every race winner who tested positive was a blow, but it was also a way for the sport to show it cared. There were athletes from other sports also caught up in Puerto, but only cycling seemed to be taking action. Cheats were getting caught – by new tests, by police operations – and sponsors were forcing changes through simply by refusing to give their name and resources to dirty teams.

Us Brits still felt massively underrated. It was going to be harder breaking into the elite when you came from Cardiff or Manchester or Yorkshire than if you were a promising young rider in Spain or France. We were a laughing stock, sometimes, as we raced each other along Italian roads. We were outsiders everywhere. Road racing was a European thing. We were meant to stay on the track or specialise in time-trialling. We could win a prologue at the Tour, like Chris Boardman and Dave Millar, but anything else? Deep inside, Cav and I believed we could do it. Stannard and Swifty too. Cav believed it on the surface as well. Obviously.

So much of our world was in transition. Personal relationships still made things happen as much as agents and formal deals. Barloworld happened for me a few months later because someone spoke to Shane Sutton and Shane knew me. You could show team managers a few race results, but no-one had the depth of data and race coverage routinely available later in my career. Recommendations and connections mattered, and my world would change with a chat over coffee with Max Sciandri in Bar G, our local in Quarrata.

'G, Barloworld want to sign you – €25,000 per year, two years. You can carry on living here and drive directly to races or via Milan. Sound good?'

The excitement must have been all over my face. The cycling statto inside me knew that team manager Claudio Corti had been general manager at Saeco when a young Damiano Cunego won the Giro from his team-mate and reigning champ Gilberto Simoni in third. I would be joining a team with history. I was also heading into a whole new level of racing. What was that going to be like? There's a lot of climbing in Italy and the pros there go uphill fast. As soon as I got back to our flat I looked up the team's website to find the other riders in the team. I needed to know their names and their results. What were they good at? Who might I learn from because they were similar to me? Who might push me on? I wanted to continue getting faster. Having a target on my back or a scalp to hunt down was naturally my way of doing that. I could see there were a couple of South Africans on the team, a few Colombians and a lot of Italians. I'd better start working harder on my Italian.

A couple of weeks later I went with Max to the Barloworld service course in Bergamo. We met Claudio and Alberto Volpi, who was the team's head DS. I wasn't nervous. I was excited. Barloworld was a Pro-Conti team, the equivalent of road cycling's second division, but they were good enough to get invites to a lot of the biggest races in the world. I was amazed at the scale of the service course. The first thing that caught my eye as we entered was a huge picture, hanging across the entire wall, of Cunego in his pink Giro jersey, riding alongside his team-mates and Simoni. Underneath that were hundreds of wheels – light climbing wheels, deep rimmed carbon, big steel ones with fat tyres for the cobbles of Roubaix in their own specific section. I was mesmerised by it all. I could almost feel the Roubaix cobbles through my hands and shoulders. A race I had always dreamed about was closer than ever before.

There were an extraordinary number of Cannondale road and time-trial bikes. There was a pair of gold shoes commemorating the victory of the team's Spanish rider Igor Astarloa at the 2003 World Road Race Championships. When I made admiring noises, being incapable at this point of expressing myself more fully in their native Italian, Claudio and Alberto insisted on giving me my own pair of gold Diadoras. I tried to insist back that I could no more wear gold shoes than I could a replica yellow jersey.

All that felt incredibly new and exciting. We went for lunch and a plate of salad came to start, and then a pasta course, and then a meat dish. Then dessert arrived. Should I politely decline? There wasn't just more food than I was used to at home. I was also accustomed to it all coming at the same time on the same plate. Claudio had a post-lunch espresso. I was happy to do the same. Claudio then lit a post-lunch cigarette. That was an easier no.

We rolled back to the service course. Volpi already had his own name for me, part nickname, part basic misunderstanding of Welsh nomenclature.

'Tom, before we sign, do you have any questions?'

'Yeah. What's expected of me? How much racing can I do? I still have my track goals – am I going to be allowed time away for this? What are the team's goals for next year? Can I continue to work with my coach?'

It was a lot of questions. I blame the espresso.

'Tom, just fit in the team well, on and off the bike. We have a busy year of racing. Be ready. With the track – yes, you can prepare and race. I can write you a programme when you are on the road, building up to a big race, but yes, you can continue with your track coach. The Tour is starting in London. We want to ride.'

'Where do I sign?'

The time came to try on some kit. I found myself standing in front of the two men in my underwear. It didn't seem weird. It didn't seem weird even when I sensed them checking my body out. It was a technical appraisal. Max whispered to me afterwards, 'Ah yeah, you know, they were looking at your legs, you know, because at the moment you're a bit . . . heavy.'

It turned out to be the same at races. The bosses and the doctor would come over and squeeze you on your side every now and then – grab a bit of fat or loose skin and give it an evaluating pinch. The DS would give you lifestyle advice that felt similarly old-school. 'At home now, nice long training, Thomas. No pizza. Pasta, small bit of pasta. No Coca. *Si?*'

One thing that remained the same was how I experienced it all. It wasn't as much fun as it had been when I was younger. It was much more. The races were slowly getting bigger and the climbs longer and the descents faster. Everything I did was closer to the professional standards I aspired to. When we rode the Tour of Britain as academy riders at the end of 2006, Rod arranged for the experienced heads of Rob Hayles and Roger Hammond to join us. The lead-outs were our thing. We were up against legends like Tom Boonen and Filippo Pozzato, riding for Quickstep, but we backed ourselves and we raced them, shoulder to shoulder, and we came out on top. We led Roger out to a stage win in Liverpool.

With each other we were relentlessly competitive. I wanted to beat Stannard, Swifty wanted to out-sprint Cav. All of us pushed each other. People met me, and found me quiet and undemonstrative. It took them quite a while to work out how determined I was to be performing at my best.

So I adventured on the road and I kept learning, and all this good momentum kept driving us forward on the track, too. We all knew what was happening within the British Cycling camp. You saw it most days in the velodrome – the sprinters, like Chris Hoy and Vicky Pendleton, burying themselves in every maximal session; the endurance squad, wintering on the road, coming in to the boards to prep for the big comps – Brad Wiggins, Rob Hayles, the young ones like me and Ed and Andy Tennant.

It was just the outside world that was a little slow in catching up. We went to the World Track Championships in Mallorca in spring 2007 and won seven of the seventeen gold medals on offer. Our team pursuit quartet broke the world record set at the Athens Olympics by an Aussie team containing legends like Stuart O'Grady. A year later at the Worlds in Manchester we made it even clearer, had you not been paying attention the first time around: this time we won nine of the eighteen golds. Brad got two, Chris got two, Vicky got three. We won the team pursuit by three seconds, which was a margin that could have made you complacent if you were that way inclined, which we weren't. Brad won the individual pursuit by five seconds, which was even more unprecedented.

All of it was working: the coaching, the cool kit, the mix of different personalities and skillsets on the track. Brad was the superstar of the pursuit. We would joke that we were towing him round to his medal, and that he was taking all the glory and accolades. He was also the one who absorbed a lot of the pressure and carried it with him, so the rest of us could just get on with it in comparative obscurity.

You never quite knew what Brad was thinking, even back then. He'd flip-flop between being on a high and entertaining us all, to disappearing without warning and no-one knowing where he'd gone. Ed was the opposite – reserved, with a tendency to worry. If we qualified five seconds faster than anyone else, he'd theorise that the other teams were saving themselves and had a masterplan for the final. I wasn't cocky or over-confident, but I believed in our abilities and I had faith in the support structure all around us. I didn't worry about the other teams.

Then there was our fourth member, Paul Manning, who was even more reserved than Ed. We nicknamed him Bern, even though he was nothing like his namesake Bernard Manning. Neither was he a punchy rider. Ed would go first man, Paul second, me third, Brad last. These days man two is almost a kilo rider – much more power. But it worked for us in those critical years, and if the times and margins of victory made it look easy, it never was. The training camps took you apart physically and rebuilt you in a different shape. They pushed you mentally, because the characters could be combustible. The older ones like Brad, Rob and Steve Cummings knew what they wanted. Us younger ones weren't going to let anyone walk over us. And they were long days, double sessions, Steve and I doing zone-two-style training all morning, chopping off and then drills on the track all afternoon; drills under intense fatigue to ensure you still made the right calls.

These were hard yards that nobody saw. They just watched the end product in the big championships or up Alpe d'Huez. It's that strange paradox of elite sport: the best athletes make it look easy, but when they do it's less exciting for those fans who want to see a close race. Within the sport, everyone understood and it was never easy. It's like when you watch darts and see them nailing 180s, and then find a dart board and stand on the oche and it's really hard to even hit a 20. And don't get me started on snooker ...

Sometimes at meets you'd take a bit of a kicking, because you were knackered from training and peaking for something else. Manchester on winter mornings was no-one's idea of glamour. It was freezing riding in to the track before breakfast and not much warmer inside the velodrome when you got there. I was lucky that I had the road in the summer. I could ride out and see more of the world than the same wooden banking and straights every 250m. For Chris Hoy and Vicky Pendleton, for Jason Kenny, I had so much admiration. They had no variety. They were going to the track all year round.

Some sessions they might be in the gym, but it was the same building and the same shiny grey paint.

In lots of ways, I felt lucky. I knew from the older gang how hard it had been less than a decade ago, before Lottery funding kicked in. It was the era of borrowing a GB tracksuit for World Championships and then having to give it back when you got home. It was old bikes and heavy wheels and turning up just to take part, although during our annual summer holidays it had seemed amazing to the fourteen-year-old me to watch Yvonne McGregor win a bronze in the pursuit at the 2000 Olympics in Sydney, astonishing when Jason Queally won gold in the kilo.

Inadvertently, I had timed it brilliantly and arrived in the sport just as the British Cycling revolution was funded, finessed and blessed with great role models like Chris. It was the antithesis of when I had ridden with Wiesenhof or that one day with Saunier Duval, when no-one noticed I had turned up and very few had noticed by the time I'd left. On the track we had a collective confidence, founded on our training and buttressed by our results. There was a camaraderie in the British team that came from our successes and self-belief. I felt like we had an aura when we walked into a velodrome. At times we almost felt invincible.

That confidence mattered when you got to the biggest events. If Barloworld's service course had impressed me, the Olympic village in Beijing in August 2008 was astonishing. The food hall on its own was enough to destroy the best laid plans of the less wary. All the food was free. There was a McDonald's that never closed. Of course I wanted to sample everything. I also had Rod in my head. He'd warned us all that you could still wreck all those months of training by going off the rails in the last few days. Eating for enjoyment would have to wait. For now it had to be only about fuel.

It nearly caught me out, walking into the Laoshan velodrome for the first time. Velodromes had always done it for me – the swoop of the bends, the rolling thunder of bikes hammering round the boards. Even though we had ridden here in a World Cup event the previous winter, this was different. It was supersized. There were Olympic rings everywhere. For a moment I felt like a 22-year-old fan, not a contender for gold.

In the small room I shared with Ed we were normal. We talked about the same usual nonsense, we had fights with hand gel. Even our illicit kicks were hygienic. As soon as we walked out, we switched into focus mode. We would leave only to ride, eat or head to the track. At the velodrome we had tunnel vision. We thought about the team around us and we grew taller as a result. We tried one spin on local Beijing roads, saw overflowing drains and terrifying drivers, and came home with our white kit filthy with mud and pollution from the air. That a simple bike could take you from suburban Cardiff to here was an astonishing and beautiful thought.

One regret in this period, looking back, was that I was so focused on the team pursuit, so conscious of how hard all of us had worked over the past eighteen months, that when the opportunity arose to ride the individual pursuit as well I didn't take it. It was scheduled before the team pursuit and I didn't want to let anyone down. I didn't want to jeopardise an Olympic gold medal.

We had done a dress rehearsal in the velodrome in Newport before leaving for Beijing. Brad and I did an individual effort, the other boys a collective effort to see who the fifth man would be for the team pursuit. Brad had worn our full Olympic kit – skinsuit, the lot. I wore my basic kit plus some over-socks. He beat me by a tenth of a second. Shane Sutton thought he had seen enough. 'Ah, G, you're flying, mate. Do you want to do the IP as well?'

It was my first Olympics. I'd just turned 22. I looked at Ed and Bern and how much, like myself, they had committed to the team pursuit. I couldn't risk anything that could affect our chances, could I? I think I probably could have. I felt great. Brad was a little sick. Maybe I could have left with two golds, but maybe that was being greedy at my first Olympics. Because there are always things you don't expect. We qualified really well. We progressed to the final in untroubled fashion. The night before, the size of the occasion began to bite at me again. You lie there in your small bed and one thought keeps rolling round your head: tomorrow we're riding an Olympic final.

The morning of the race it came at me again. I went to the toilet and saw myself in the mirror. 'Jeez, it's today ...' It was these moments on my own when I felt most vulnerable. When I felt the chimp that psychiatrist Steve Peters had talked about rattling my cage. This was the time when sabotage was going to happen. With the boys I was okay. I could draw strength from them. I could take comfort from the fact I was almost always the least anxious one of the four. I had to be the calming one for them, in the same way that if you hit turbulence on a flight, and the person next to you starts panicking, you have to smile and turn it into an adventure.

Routine is your great saviour in those moments – a familiar pattern in a moment bigger than anything you've experienced before. We had done our warm-up so many times we barely spoke, each of us ticking off tasks, hitting numbers, focusing on our own clearly defined jobs. Only when we were sitting on the folding plastic chairs, seconds before, did I feel something needed to be said. I looked Ed in the eye, then Brad, then Bern. 'We've fucking got this, boys. Come on!'

We absolutely smashed it. We went so well we almost caught our Danish opponents. I was on the front with two and a half laps to go when I caught a glimpse of their last rider ahead. That was the moment I knew we'd won gold and that was the moment I let it all go. No more focus, no more process. Just unleash and open up, faster and faster with each turn, going through the line and knowing we must have broken the world record for the second time in two days. Could I have ridden the individual pursuit and experienced this wonderful sensation not once but twice?

Yes, but I missed it for the right reasons. That's what I tell myself today.

At those Olympics the GB cycling team won eight gold medals, four silvers, two bronzes. The next best was France with two golds. It was an extraordinary thing to be part of, even when you were on the inside and sort of expected it. Our kit was good, but so was everyone else's. We'd won the Worlds with normal kit and helmets with cracks in; we'd just won by less. We had the riders. And we had Dave Brailsford, who had a talent for bringing it all together: heading it up, getting the right people in the right places and keeping those people motivated. Rod Ellingworth was brilliant, as were Shane, Steve Peters. Dave led it, but everyone played their own critical part.

When you're involved in something like that, good things seem to keep happening. Chris Hoy won BBC Sports Personality of the Year. The cycling team won Team of the Year. We all rode down a big ramp on to the stage and tried not to run over Gary Lineker's toes. I got nominated for the BBC Wales version of SPotY and got to hang out with the deserving winner Shane Williams.

But something else would top all that. I got invited to watch the Wales Rally GB. That wasn't the thing. One of my best mates, Rob Partridge, had invited me on a double date afterwards. My role was classic domestique: do all the hard work so he could walk off with the girl he fancied. The girl's friend was from Cardiff. She was called Sara. She referred to herself as Sa. She referred to me as Gez. It was like we'd known each other before Rob had ever hatched his plan. An adventure began which is still carrying us both along. It would work out okay for Rob too, just not that night. Years later, I would set him up with another of Sa's friends, Soph. Those two have just had their second child.

Maybe, after 2008, Team Sky was always going to happen. James Murdoch had already been to visit the velodrome in Manchester before the Olympics. The team's success in Beijing, on terrestrial television, must have helped strengthen the appeal. We all knew that Dave and the rest of the management team wanted to do it, because they were feeling as confident in their processes and ideas after all these gold medals as us riders were. They also wanted a new challenge and that meant going to the road. It had been more than 20 years since a properly British team had ridden at the Tour de France, and that had ended badly when ANC-Halfords folded.

I liked all the rumours and the plans I was hearing. I was contracted to Barloworld for another year, but heard that Sky were putting a squad together to start in 2010. Perfect timing. I already knew the people heading it up and was confident I'd get the best out of myself with them. Of course, I could think about trying to get a deal at another team, but when you were comfortable and successful in an environment, and you trusted the coaches and the bosses, it all pointed your front wheel in a certain direction.

I was done with the track for now, at least until the next Olympics in London. No more Worlds on the track. I wanted to focus on the road and I wanted to get it right. I could see what Brad was doing with Team High Road and Garmin-Slipstream, and Steve Cummings, too. I just kept getting a few things wrong. Racing at Tirreno–Adriatico in the early part of 2009 I took too much of a risk on a tight corner in the time-trial, overshot it and crashed.

So much can go through your head in those tiny fractions of seconds between staying up and going down; questions that can seem theoretical before they're suddenly practical. Do I yank on the front brake now, just to hit the deck and slide, and maybe hit the barrier and stop? Or do I try to hold it up, but hit the barrier anyway and end up wherever I end up?

I went for the second option, which may have been an error. I hit the barrier, went over the top, hit a tree and landed on the gravel road below, only bouncing once. I'm not certain exactly how high the tree was, but our mechanic, who was six foot, struggled to reach the suspended bike with his long arms outstretched. I was probably lucky to get away with a fractured pelvis.

I went back to Manchester to rehab and recover, the thought of this potential British pro team the best possible motivation as I tried to get strong and fit again. From all of it I tried to take on other lessons: you don't always need to go into things hammer and tongs, and as you get older it's going to be up to you, because no-one's going to stop you. It was like when I went out drinking. I wasn't a quiet pint in the beer garden man. I committed fully, which was good for a short period and then less good quite quickly for a longer time afterwards. There was a time and place to take risks. A TT in Tirreno at the very start of the season where a top 20 would have been a realistic result was not one of them. If you wanted to take a corner faster than everyone else, it was worth reconning it properly in advance, so you knew that what you were trying to do was actually possible to pull off.

All the time I could see this new team taking shape. Sky were confirmed as sponsors. The budget looked good, really good, and everything looked super-professional, but because this was 2009 the moment still came in an informal, word-of-mouth way.

It was Shane who took me aside first. It was always going to Shane.

'Right. Yeah, yeah. You're going to be on the team obviously, G. A hundred grand a season. Are you happy with that?'

My negotiation skills were poor, partly because I was just too excited about the team, partly because I was on €25,000 for my first two years with Barloworld and €50,000 in my third. After somehow finishing the Tour in 2007 and then later the Giro in 2008, I was doubling my money. Clearly I'd done some pretty elite-level telepathic negotiating already.

'Yeah, sweet. Thanks, Shane . . .'

Looking back, I could have done with an agent. Other riders at my level were getting more, but it was never about the money. I did want what I was worth, but it was still an easy decision. I wanted to race my bike against the best, in an environment that would get the best out of me.

I'd seen Dave at Tirreno, scouting other riders. I heard the rumours of who else was going to sign and it became even more exciting. When they announced the first six of us, we were all British: me, Steve Cummings, Russ Downing, Stannard, Pete Kennaugh and some skinny dude who'd grown up in Kenya and raced with me at Barloworld called Chris Froome. You would watch Sky Sports News and they would be talking about who else was signing, as if we were a Premier League football team. Norwegian Edvald Boasson Hagen, who was one of the top young GC pretenders around, joined. Dave also told the media that we were aiming to win the Tour de France with a British rider within five years.

I liked the idea of aiming high, although that felt a little punchy. Easier to picture was the team bus they were talking about. We would have seats like airline business class. I had never travelled business class, but I guessed it was good. There was talk of mood lighting to help us relax after a stage or gee us up before, Bose speakers to pump out the tunes, WiFi and in-built chargers for our team-issue Apple laptops.

There was this attention to kit and training we'd had on the track, the search for small advantages that might all add up, the commitment to recovery and diet, making sure everything around you worked so that the work itself became your only focus. All these years of cycling being a niche sport that most people in Britain didn't understand and didn't care about, the Italian phrasebooks and the strange German apartments, the fat-pinching and the cakes for breakfast – all of it was changing. The challenge ahead would be huge. We were underdogs. Lots of people clearly thought we were going to fail. Even more wanted us to. But that was motivating too. We wanted to prove them wrong. I wanted to show I belonged.

Chapter five

Tour de France 2010, stage three

You know that feeling of being in comfortable surroundings, but never comfy? That was me as 2010 rolled around. I was no longer a track rider for now, but I was fully recovered from breaking my pelvis at Tirreno the previous spring and ready to push on from the Tour of Britain the previous autumn. Team Sky was many thing to many people: an adventure, a gamble, a threat, a mirage. To me it was people I trusted and a way of working that had brought out the best from me.

But never comfy. We started the season at the Tour of Qatar, wearing time-trial skinsuits and road helmets made aero by filling in all the air vents. Other teams stared and some sniggered behind their hands. We weren't given a race strategy before we rolled out, but a battle plan instead. Riders were no longer designated as domestiques or breakaway men. Instead we had assassins, but we were the ones out there to be shot at. Dave hadn't held anything back when talking about the team's ambitions, and you could feel the resentment and a little jealousy. Our big new bus got christened the Death Star. Our big new budget got called unfair.

In Qatar we wanted to show the doubters they were wrong. Before the team time-trial we did warm-ups on turbos as our rivals just rolled up and down the road. They also rolled their eyes, at least until we beat some of the big hitters, like Garmin, HTC and Quickstep.

'Who do they think they are?' became 'Yeah, but they won't do much the next few days.' Our sporting director at the race was Scott Sunderland, who was also going to be in charge of our first Classics campaign. Qatar isn't the most difficult race to navigate. You basically go straight in one direction for an hour, turn 90 degrees and repeat until the finish line. When the wind blows, it splits. On the first stage after the TTT I got caught in one of the back groups and was distanced. Scott never told me directly afterwards, but I got a clear sense from him. First of all, I had work to do to cut it at the top and, second, he rated lots of others in our team much more highly than me.

I've always liked proving people wrong. When I won the Tour de France in 2018 and some people said it was a fluke, that drove me on the next year to go back and nearly win it again. When they told me I was past it after a troubled 2020 and 2021, I went back to France with fire in my belly and took third. Same again when I was written off as too old after that. I came second in the Giro in 2023 at the age of thirty-seven, in part because I wanted to show the doubters how ill-informed they were.

So when I went into our first Classics campaign in the spring of 2010, I wanted to show Scott Sunderland what I could do. I finished in the front group at Flanders, sprinting in for fifth. I rode alongside Lance Armstrong, who was in his unexpected second coming with RadioShack. I felt good. I felt the benefits of a winter as a road rider, rather than a temporary track convert. I could hold my position in the peloton and I felt I'd given Scott a little evidence to change his mind.

Sa and I, meanwhile, decided to follow the Classics campaign with our first holiday together, to the cobbles-free zone of coastal Egypt. Two days into our week-long trip, Sa was struck down by a local illness and didn't leave the room for a couple of days. When she appeared to be on the mend I decided to bring some magic to the holiday and organised a day of watersports. It was a well-meaning catastrophe. She failed to leave our room for the rest of the week.

Okay, so the watersports idea had gone wrong. I had others. I called our new team's doctor and asked what the best medication for Sa might be. Armed with my precious knowledge, I walked into the local pharmacy and gave them my list. They had everything on it. They also had a suggestion of their own, as I went to pay. 'How about this? We have a special deal at the moment?'

It was a box of blue pills. Yes, it was Viagra. Had I spoken

Arabic, I would have said something along the lines of, mate, can you not see what else I've just bought? Do you really think with all that going on that I'll be needing your blue pills? Instead I returned to our room and played Brick Breaker on Sa's BlackBerry while she failed to hold down solid food and I ate only fruit, reasoning that if she was losing weight for unfortunate reasons I could lose weight for racing reasons at the same time.

It was around this point news reached us of a volcanic ash cloud that had grounded half the world's planes. We weren't going to spend a week's holiday in one small room. We were going to spend ten days. It would probably have been enough to end other young relationships, but it seemed to strengthen ours. If you can love someone who spends eight days in their bed when it's 30 degrees and sunshine outside, and that person can in return love someone who takes them snorkelling when they haven't eaten for three days and inadvertently lets a deadly lionfish swim up close to them – well, you get the feeling you could make it through anything. Swifty even drove from Quarrata to Milan Malpensa to pick us up, even if this was partly because he had no idea quite how far it was from Tuscany to Milan's equivalent of London Luton.

Dave B, however, didn't think the holiday had been a great idea in the first place. He phoned Steve Cummings and sounded somewhere between bewildered and angry. 'Would you go to Egypt mid-season? What is he doing? What's G thinking?' When word got through, I was robust in my defence. 'Dave, do you want me to go back to Cardiff with all my mates and go on the piss for ten days, or go to Sharm El-Sheikh with my girlfriend and eat three apples for my evening meal?'

We were all finding out what worked and what didn't in this brave new world. The battle plans didn't last long. Neither did the assassin roles. At one point we were going to races with a tent that doubled up as a sauna. Some of these little things felt they might be taking our attention away from the big things, which were train hard, eat well, rest, recover and repeat. The foreign riders or the older ones on the team were the ones who struggled with this scattergun innovation the most. Those of us who had grown up with it on the GB track programme were more open. Thinking differently had worked for us. You could respect the traditions of road racing while also looking at the background stuff like travel and nutrition, and seeing what you could improve with planning and some strategic thinking.

Some people continued to look at us like we were idiots, just as they had before the team time-trial in Qatar. Why did you need to warm up when riders had won races in the past without turbo trainers? Then we started warming down after stages. We would finish a mountain stage and get back on the turbo to cool off, when all the other teams would climb straight off their bikes and on to their team buses after breathing out of their backsides for the last forty-five minutes.

It's strange looking back now, when all these things are a

matter of routine for every single elite team. At the time, it was part of us proving ourselves, of showing that we weren't all big dreamy ideas and hard-edged big budgets. The newer teams were interested, the ones from outside road cycling's traditional heartlands. The older ones acted as if they were custodians of some timeless cycling orthodoxy. The road was not the track. This was their sport, not ours. You didn't have porridge for breakfast, you had a bowl of white pasta with some baguette with butter and jam on the side. You wore a jersey and bib-shorts. You spoke English only when you had absolutely no other option.

While the season matured, so did we. As a rider you could feel yourself having a decent number of good days. You could look around at your team-mates and see them having a decent number of good days, too, which overall was a good thing, but could sometimes cause problems. At Paris–Nice I'd done an average time-trial in the prologue. I hadn't troubled the top ten on the stage, when the team expected me to. Afterwards, sporting director Sean Yates – a tough cookie as a rider and a man who had worn yellow when the Tour came to Britain all the way back in 1994 – chose to push my obvious buttons again.

'Ah yeah, G, I don't know what it is. Maybe you need to do more than you are, but you've already done a couple of Grand Tours now, you should be stronger. I don't know why you're not sort of progressing like you should. I think we should take you out of the Milan–San Remo team, bring in Greg Henderson.'

Obviously this put grit in my gears. Okay, it had been an average TT. I was still moving forward. Hendy had won a stage at Paris–Nice, but only after I'd guided him all the way to 200m to go. Leading him out for one of the biggest wins of his career seemed to have deselected me for one of the most important races in mine. On the notoriously difficult final weekend of Paris–Nice I'd then looked after our leader Simon Gerrans and outperformed what had been asked of me. While this also failed to get me in, I did seem to have proved myself to Yatesy and he apologised that I hadn't been picked for Milan–San Remo.

He kept up with the tough love from that point on, I think because he'd worked out it was the easiest way to get the best out of me. He always had my back after that spring, and so did Steve Cummings. He and his wife Nicky continued to look after me in Quarrata like a little brother. Steve would bring the deep knowledge around training, racing and diet. Nicky cooked countless meals. And all the time Max Sciandri was the father figure – the fixer and the sorter-out.

Recovered fully now from the double whammy of gastro-enteritis and a lionfish swim-past, Sa not only came to visit me out in Italy, but started coming along to a few of my races. When I was home she was also spending more and more time at my house in Altrincham, and not only because her experience of student life along the M62 at Liverpool University was falling below expectations. I wanted to impress her. I wanted her to see why I ate half the amount of most

Welsh men my age and had the biceps of a teenage girl. I wanted her to see that it was all worth it, this eccentric life she was stepping further and further into.

The British Road Race Championships in June were held around the steep climbs of Pendle in Lancashire. Sa was there, and in the first few laps I was able to look out and wave to her in the crowd. If I needed any extra motivation, it was right there for me.

There were a few of us in the Adidas three-stripe Sky kit. I attacked early and a group of ten of us ended up going away. Slowly it was whittled down until I looked around and could only see two other riders, both also in Team Sky skinsuits: Ian Stannard and Pete Kennaugh. David Millar was in the race. So too were Jez Hunt and Simon Richardson. It was hard not to sense, as you looked at our kit and our bikes and the team's support and our form, that this might be something of a changing of the guard.

I felt like I was floating along. I was looking round and feeling surprised that so many riders were getting dropped so quickly, because it didn't seem that hard a pace to me. It can be strange racing team-mates; you know each other's strengths and weaknesses intimately, and their form, and their preferred tactics. I knew Pete was strong and fast and lived for the Nationals. Stannard was even stronger, but a bit big for these constant climbs. I was confident. I knew I was going well. I'd done all the work and I'd felt its benefits.

I knew Pete was keen and wanted to get rid of Stannard,

so I let him do the majority of the work. Sure enough, we dropped him on the penultimate lap. Pete wanted to make sure it stayed that way. 'Come on, G, let's keep going, share the work and race it out at the end . . .'

I'm not the fastest, but after a hard race I can hold my own. I backed myself for the sprint. So I sat behind Pete coming into the 1km-to-go banner and I stayed there – and then faked my sprint for the finish early. That got Pete moving. He inadvertently took me up to speed in his slipstream, I came around him in the final 100m and crossed the line hands in the air.

Before the race I hadn't given it too much thought. It was another part of our prep for the Tour a week later. Now, standing on the podium, I realised I'd be going to France in the jersey of the British champion. Rocking up to the biggest bike race in the world wearing that was going to be quite the buzz. That night I checked the results of the other national championships held all over Europe. There were some big names at the top of the standings and I was among them.

The Tour de France was now just around the corner. Sa and I discussed most nights whether I'd get picked. We felt the excitement and trepidation in equal measure. We had become a team of our own, without really trying to or noticing, and she was making as many sacrifices as me. While most uni students her age were hanging out with their partners whenever they wanted, I was always away. Summer was supposed to be a time to chill out and enjoy being free of adult responsibilities. Instead, she was finding hotel rooms to book on the Tour route, but not committing in case it didn't happen or she jinxed it. When Dave called me to say I was in, Sa was the first person I rang. These were the moments that made all the time apart worthwhile.

There were big expectations for all of us. I wasn't entirely sure what to expect from myself, but I did understand I was a different rider to the one that had rocked up so naively in 2007. There was so much I was looking forward to: helping Brad in his quest for the overall win, helping my good mate Eddie go for stages. There was a cobbled stage on the roads of Roubaix and there would be super-hard days in the mountains. I'd be doing it all in the colours of the British champion. For the kid who had dreamed of all of this, it was a heady mix.

Rain fell during the prologue in Rotterdam. As others stressed, I saw familiar conditions and committed everything. I finished fifth, one second off Lance Armstrong, ahead of Alberto Contador. I was only three seconds behind David Millar, who was third. Fabian Cancellara had smashed it to take yellow. Tony Martin had come in behind him. That I was on the same page of the results as these names felt like unarguable progress.

While I stayed fifth on GC after the first stage proper and held it after the second stage, won by Sylvain Chavanel, I went into the third stage with only one mission: look after Brad. He was our team leader. He had been fourth in GC the year before while at Garmin, a result that was later upgraded to third when Armstrong was retrospectively disqualified. Chaos was predicted that morning. The stage was long-ish, at 213km. That mattered less than the six sections of cobbles they were borrowing from Paris–Roubaix and putting in our way.

I loved it. Of course I did. We had riders who were skilled on this sort of terrain: Brad, Steve Cummings, Juan Antonio Flecha. Flecha had taken Sky's biggest win so far on the cobbles at Omloop Het Nieuwsblad. He'd go on to finish on the podium for Sky at Paris–Roubaix. Without question he was the man for me to follow.

The plan for the day was to get Steve Cummings into the break, so we had someone up the road ready to help Brad. My job was to just race my race, to get into the final stretch. To always be around Brad and Flecha, but never stressing about who might be on my wheel. When the cobbles kicked, I should help Brad, but also do my own thing. Pretty loose and pretty un-Sky for the time.

You couldn't help but feel the tension in the peloton – Classics guys wanting to win, GC riders wanting to stay upright, the ones deputed to help them not wanting to let them down. Then there were the little climbers who had never seen a fat French cobble in their lives. They looked as pale as Sa seven days into Sharm-el-Sheikh. Me? There's something so special about this stage of your career, when you think all the good big stuff is ahead of you, whatever that may be, so you're riding with freedom. You don't overthink things. You make a move without even realising you're doing it – accelerating at the right times, battling with everyone, squeezing and pushing to hold your position.

I looked around, deep into the stage, and it hit me: I'd been in a pretty good position pretty much all the time. I can remember the key secteur of cobbles vividly, even fifteen years later – the noises, the sensations. Coming off a narrow, straight road, maybe four abreast, me second wheel, hiding from the wind, Flecha about somewhere. A few sections where it narrowed as the pavement came into the road. A big farmhouse on the right, all of us racing hard into a left-hander. Everything suddenly changing – from smooth and silent to the mad rattling of frames and bouncing of wheels, from tarmac to dust and the screaming of supporters. Everything in your head suddenly turned up to twice the intensity.

I was still close to the front. I could see Fabian Cancellara up ahead, powering over the uneven cobbles and the gaps like he was still on the main road. A sudden cloud of smoke and dust to my right as someone went down. Was that Fränk Schleck colliding with another rider and keeling over? Don't look around. Don't look back. Eyes in front, focused on the wheel ahead. There's still a slight gap, just close it. Drilling it to get across, head down, thinking I could see Cancellara, maybe Thor Hushovd.

Another corner and a sharp right turn, and suddenly no more cobbles. Silence, the crowds gone, the rattling and chaos

Christmas, 1987. Bow ties are not something the young Welsh boy chooses to wear, but I think I carry it off.

First day at nursery, 1988. The sartorial experiments continue, at least this time with a practical edge.

It's not the size of the trophy that counts, but the pride with which it's held.

You can't teach casual sporting style like this. You've either got it or you dream of it.

Actually no need for the photo finish at my school sports day in May 1994. I was probably just disappointed the race didn't go on for longer. Or go uphill.

You can't beat that podium feeling. Bikes lobbed on the grass is a nice touch too.

I have no idea why the Speedo went out of fashion. When worn well – for example, with medal on chest and trophy held aloft – it's a magnificent garment.

Yes, that's who you think it is in the middle. The early stages of a long and beautiful cycling relationship.

The prologue of my first ever Tour de France, in 2007. I was the youngest rider in the race, and wow how I suffered.

The GB gold rush in Beijing, 2008. Bern, Ed, me and Brad. A fast team, and a happy team.

Above: Celebrating Cav's victory at the World Road Race Championships, 2011. He didn't need my lead-out, but he needed my manly hug shortly afterwards.

Left: Winning Olympic team pursuit gold once again, London 2012. A giddy few weeks for the entire nation, and specifically for me when we went out celebrating afterwards.

Left: Oh, I loved this day. Winning the Commonwealth Games road race in a very wet Glasgow, 2014. Doing it for Wales felt magical.

Below: I'd always loved the cobbled Classics. I'd always thought I might win one. So when E3 Harelbeke came along in 2015, I wasn't going to let the chance slip away.

Above: Being hunted down by Alberto Contador at Paris–Nice in 2016. The early days of the stage-race chasing days. Strong sunglasses game.

Left: This pretty much sums up what it's like to crash on the last corner of the last descent of the Olympics road race when you think you have gold in your sights. I launched into the caipirinhas after this one. They only helped for a short period.

Above: My soigneur and friend Marko helping me with my yellow jersey at the Tour in 2017. Note for jersey aficionados: this is the podium-issue one, hence the zip at the back.

Right: Seven years later, Marko and me in another happy touchy-feely moment. He's a good man, the best soigneur a rider could hope to have.

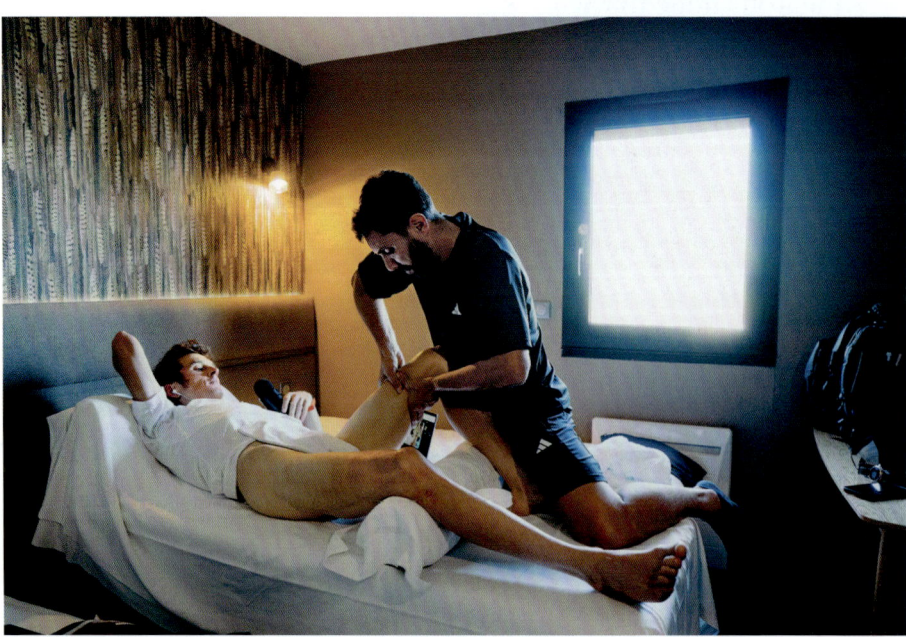

It's all glamour, at the Tour. The only unusual thing about this massage from Marko is that I'm not recording my podcast at the same time.

gone. Just a small group of us left. I had almost been caught up in a crash, but I'd avoided it. That had caused a split and the guys behind hadn't been able to close the gap. I'd been the last one to get across. Now I looked around. Now I looked behind. 'Jesus, there's only five or six of us here and one's Cancellara, and there's Cadel Evans and Thor Hushovd, and Andy Schleck, and then there's me . . .'

We'd caught the final two guys from the break, Ryder Hesjedal and Steve Cummings. Steve had the call on the radio to sit up and help Brad in the group behind. I needed clarity. Was I doing my job?

'Guys, what about me?'

'G, you stay there . . .'

Fabian was drilling it at the front for Schleck, his team's big Tour hope that year. I stayed in the wheels. I was here so Brad could win the Tour. I wasn't going to help one of his rivals gain time. The most convenient of excuses to sit on.

As we entered the next cobbled secteur, you could see the TV helicopter low in the sky ahead of us, maybe 10 o'clock in my vision. Your eyes went to the flashing rotors and then the big flags of the different nationalities on the roadside up ahead, so many of them Norwegian for Hushovd.

Fabian on the front, me third or fourth wheel. For the first time all day I briefly switched out of the race. 'Holy shit, I'm in the Tour here, in the British champion's jersey, in a group of six over cobbles. This is insane. Last time I rode this race, I finished 140th. Fuck, I've made it. I'm here!'

I held on. Got my head back in the game, and buried myself. Kilometres passed in a blur and I was now alone, too far away from the team car to hear the radio. With 3km to go, coming towards the finish in Arenberg, just before the entry into the forest, I started to do the maths. Okay, could I win this? How could I win this?

There was Hushovd, winner of the green points jersey the previous year, king of the bunch sprints, and we were going into a headwind. So I stayed on his wheel for as long as I could, until Hesjedal tried going for a long one, jumping down the right-hand side.

I didn't hesitate. I went straightaway, brain in autopilot, not thinking but reacting after all those hundreds of tiny lessons from the years down on Maindy velodrome and pavements and parks all over Britain. I tried to use Ryder as a launch pad. Maybe the others wouldn't react immediately and we'd get a small gap. Maybe I could gain some free speed from Ryder's slipstream. Maybe Hushovd would be tired. Maybe he wouldn't be expecting anything from me.

He was. He came past me with 50m to go. I was second. I was also in a daze. I had no idea where Flecha was or that Brad was coming through about a minute down. I had no idea I was also almost a minute up on reigning champion Alberto Contador or two up on Armstrong.

I rolled back to the team bus, took a recovery drink and climbed on to the turbo for a warm-down, head still spinning.

I was about to get stripped off for an on-board shower, when Fran Millar came running on.

'G, you've got to go to the podium for the white jersey!'

'Shit, are you sure?'

'Yeah, yeah, yeah, you've got to get down there ...'

I rode back to the presentation area and suddenly I was in a whole different world. I stood on a podium and had the jersey for leading young rider zipped on to me. I was being given flowers and then taken through levels of media interviews – TV, then radio, then written press. I had gone into this Tour purely for Brad. Everything had been about doing all I could to help him. Individual glory had never even entered my mind. Now I was on the podium. I was second on GC. Second? It didn't make sense, even when the reporters kept repeating it to me in different languages.

Looking back, I could have been a touch greedier. I was in such a daze in those final kilometres. I was in the land of pink unicorns and flying fairies. Had I been more experienced, had I had a DS whose attention wasn't naturally drawn to getting Brad across the line with minimum possible time losses, maybe I could have tried something else.

I could have tried hitting them with 1.5km to go – attack from the back of the group, hope they would hesitate because I was just a kid, if they knew me at all, and most of them probably didn't. Fabian might have been cooked, because he'd ridden 20km flat-out, and there was that headwind, and if I had got a little gap, who was going to really bury themselves to close it? The others would be watching Hushovd, and Schleck was about GC rather than the stage, so . . .

I'm sure Thor would have been straight on to me. Without doubt I would still have been totally up against it. What options do you really have, as a young rider, when you see Fabian Cancellara drilling it on the front? Who rides away from a raging Fabian? I'd actually got on the right wheel and I'd tried to sprint. A decent idea, I just didn't have the legs. Not yet.

I was buzzing that evening, back at the hotel. I was rooming with Flecha and he seemed genuinely happy for me. There was no social media to read messages and massage my ego, the internet connection at our Campanile too slow even for Facebook. I stayed, instead, in my own little world of contentedness. I spoke to Sa, away on holiday with her family. I was chuffed that she was happy and proud. The thought of them all watching from the poolside in Spain was weirdly inspiring.

The team? They didn't seem to care too much. The investment was all in Brad. 'Right, guys, decent day. On to the next. What does Brad need tomorrow? Oh yeah – and good job, G.' That's just how it always was in Sky. Process, process, process. Always on to the next thing. Maybe that was one reason why we were so successful. We were never content. We were always looking ahead.

I held second on GC behind Cancellara for another three days. Cav won a bunch sprint on stage six and the ghosts of our younger selves in our rubbish house in Fallowfield laughed their heads off. The next day was a mountainous one, from Tournus to Station des Rousses. Halfway through it, Lance pedalled up alongside me and gave me a sideways look.

'Hey man, good job the other day. You can get the jersey today.'

I was still in too much awe. 'What do you mean?'

'Yellow jersey, man. You can get it today.'

I just laughed. 'Ah yeah, mate. Yeah, whatever.'

Lance is nothing if not persistent. His way is the way.

'Nah, the last climb's not that hard and for sure Fabian's going to get dropped. Hey man, good luck. You can do it. You can kill it.'

Off he rode, leaving me to my dazed thoughts. I was already in a state of shock after realising I was climbing with Andreas Klöden, who had twice finished second in the Tour, someone I'd watched racing on telly for years. Now Lance Armstrong was giving me tactical advice.

'Fucking hell, if Lance Armstrong's just told me I can get the yellow jersey today, maybe it's possible, then ...'

As we hit the last climb, Fabian had already been dropped. For a brief moment I was the yellow jersey on the road. Chavanel was in the break, hunting the same prize. I was clinging on to the peloton for dear life – jersey nearly fully unzipped, the French summer and relentless pace on the climb getting to me. With 5km to go I started to lose contact. I tried desperately to keep going, to hold the wheel. I couldn't. My legs were gone, all out of energy. Chavanel stayed away and took yellow.

If I could have hung on for another kilometre or so, the road flattened off a little before kicking up again. Could I have dug deeper? Would that flat part have made the difference? You can torture yourself with these retrospective reassessments. The next day, Lance came up to me again and apologised.

'Yeah, that climb is a lot harder than I remember.'

I wasn't about to kick off. 'Yeah, no worries, mate.'

It was all too surreal. It was all too mad and impossible. It was also pretty much downhill from there. Brad wasn't as strong as he had been the year before. He floated around the top 20 on GC and with each stage slipped further back. You could see the staff gradually losing morale. We continued to try for stages, but it never quite came off. I made it into the break on one of the mountain days and got on the radio to ramp us all up. 'Come on, guys, let's push harder, gain more time!'

Then we hit the climb. The heat caught up with me in the same moment and I was out the back of the break in no time. Lesson learned. A few stages later, descending into Gap on the same road where, in 2003, Joseba Beloki had crashed so badly it ended his career, Lance came up to me again. The memories were fresher for him: when Beloki went down, Lance had famously ridden through a field and over a ditch to avoid him and get back to the race. Now he seemed to want to be friends. He seemed to want to offer me better advice.

'Hey man. Be careful on this descent. It's a widow-maker . . .'

I wasn't married. Not yet. But I was thinking about it now, just as I was seeing other elements of the future more clearly. We hadn't succeeded as a team as we had hoped, but it was coming. Armstrong was almost the past. We were looking forward.

Chapter six

World Road Race Championships 2011, Copenhagen

When I look back at the end of 2011 there are a couple of things that strike me as significant now to the young man I was back then. The first was at BBC Cymru Wales Sports Personality of the Year. I wasn't on the shortlist for the award and that was fine, but I was still invited and I was in Cardiff, so I went along. When they played a montage summing up the best of Welsh sport from the year I did hope, having worn the white jersey for best young rider at the Tour de France, that I might feature. It was a good montage, too – highlights from the nominees, clips of other athletes from lawn bowls to kite-surfing. When the four or five minutes of slow-motion clips and inspirational music had finished, I realised I hadn't featured. I'd like to say I wasn't upset, just disappointed, but I was definitely irritated, just as I had been around the time of the Commonwealth Games the year before.

I had been advised by our team doctors not to travel to Delhi. Losing my spleen in Sydney five years before meant I was too susceptible to bugs and infections. BBC Wales had asked me to go on their 6pm news programme to explain. I didn't really want to, but I did. The way the questions went I then felt like I was on trial, in a strange court where Jason Mohammad was the judge. Both these incidents went straight into the increasingly large file entitled 'Screw you – I'll show you.'

Then there was the Flanders recon we went on after Team Sky's December training camp in Mallorca. We stayed in a B&B with a bar featuring many of Belgium's tastiest and most potent beers. It was a few days before Christmas and we'd been worked hard, so I got stuck in. I got on a roll. I got carried away.

The weather the next day was terrible. Instead of riding the recon through puddles of freezing rain and animal effluent running off the fields, our DS decided we would drive it instead. I could have handled it. I'd rugged up and got my bike ready, but I was still delighted, at least until I got out to the car to discover that the only seat left was up front next to Carsten Jeppesen, one of the senior management team.

While I did everything I could to convince him that I was well rested, fresh-faced and keen to crack on, I'm pretty sure he saw straight through me. It didn't matter. I was my own harshest critic. Once back in Cardiff I thrashed myself into the wet tarmac in training over the next few days. This was the strange balance I used to strike at the time: I felt the need to let my hair down, so I could then endure and flourish in the tight regime the rest of the time. But when I did get loose, I had to punish myself afterwards. A sensible compromise wasn't for me. It was all or nothing, whichever direction that fell in.

That hasn't surprised me, looking back fifteen years. I'm still like that now. What I had forgotten, because it makes less sense in the logical narrative that follows, is that I was featuring at the business end of quite a few sprints. Pro sport likes to fit you into neat categories. I'm supposed to be the pursuit rider who turned to the Classics and then converted into a GC rider who peaked only for one Grand Tour a year. Some of the stereotyping about me was accurate. In the early days I did struggle in the heat of a high European summer, because I'd grown up in a country where 22 degrees Celsius is considered a heatwave. Some of it was not. I could get results all year round, not just in the build-up to my main target. I could also sprint better than my later career might indicate. At the Dauphiné in 2010 I had worn the green points jersey for a while; I'd won the Nationals in a sprint; I'd stayed deep in bunch sprints at stage races. My winters in the velodrome were over, but I was still carrying a lot of track speed. Come the end of the year, that would make quite the difference to both me and one of my closest friends.

For now, it was about learning the ropes, earning my stripes and continually trying to improve. I started the Classics season free of any temptation around the local ales and, at a race in the build-up to the Tour of Flanders, I went away with a proper Classics specialist, a real strong man. I was buzzing – toe to toe with a legend, up and down steep narrow roads that until recently had existed for me only as something on the TV in my parents' front room. We mopped up the remnants of the early break, but the peloton was still close behind. With 10km or so to go, the race was still in the balance. Could we stay clear?

That was the moment he offered me €25,000 to give him the win. This was the first time this had happened to me. I had to check what he was saying. When he repeated it and I understood, I said no. I wanted the win. It was easy.

He beat me in the end, so none of it mattered. Maybe if I'd been a bit more tactically cynical, I could have agreed the deal and then competed for the win anyway. If it was close, I could have claimed I had to make it look real. If I'd won, it wasn't like he could have kicked off afterwards – 'Hey, he agreed to sell me the win!' For now, I just accepted that these things happened in more races than I might have imagined. Wins mattered. They made careers. Deals got offered and deals got made.

Second was still okay, for now. It confirmed to me that I liked racing in this part of the world – the flat countryside, the cold winds, the cobbles and the short, steep climbs. For now, this was the landscape that suited me, more than the endless long climbs of the Alps or Pyrenees.

I went to Flanders full of confidence. My job was to be in the final to help our leader Juan Antonio Flecha. I was on a good day, good enough to lead us into a lot of the key secteurs, and the pleasures of it all were flowing through me. I wasn't thinking about myself or worrying about conserving anything. I was just racing in a race I loved, one of the greatest in my new world.

We were on the old route, the traditional one, so the Muur and then Bosberg were the final two climbs. We were in a pretty select group of around ten, albeit rammed with big names. I dropped back from the first six riders on the Muur, but then I looked around and George Hincapie was with me, and the thrill of riding and talking with someone I'd been watching contest cobbled Classics since my teenage years gave me fresh energy. We chopped off and made it back to the front group, where Fabian Cancellara had been brought back after attacking from way out, and I got up to Flecha and asked what we should do. 'Let's just try to get up the road. Alone or following the attacks. If neither of us is in front, we need to bring it back.'

It was only later, watching it back on TV, that I realised Fabian had just sat at the back of the group once he'd been caught, doing nothing. Nick Nuyens noticed. That's why he went and sat on Fabian. So did Sylvain Chavanel. Meanwhile, the rest of the group were attacking each other, chasing stuff down, burning their legs with every passing kilometre. Had Flecha and I been a little more level-headed, had assessed the situation properly, one of us could have gone to sit behind Fabian as well. We should have gambled – one sit on, the other wait for a draggy technical section or lull in the group to launch an all-or-nothing attack. Because neither of us was going to win in a sprint against these boys.

Looking back, it seems obvious, but after 250km of full-gas racing your mind doesn't function as clearly as when you're sat on your sofa analysing the race with a cup of tea. I was also a young kid, and I was focused entirely on doing my best for Flecha. I was focused on the stellar quality of those around me. 'Jeez, man, I'm in the final of Flanders here in a group of ten or eleven, going for the win, and there's Cancellara and Boonen and Hincapie and Philippe Gilbert, and Flecha's got a chance here if I bury myself for him . . .'

Sure enough, Fabian did go again, with 2 or 3km to go, and he dragged Nuyens and Chavanel with him, and I was too empty to follow. They got a small gap, no-one could close it and that was the podium. Nuyens came round them both in the sprint, and Flecha and I ended up coming in at the back of the group, both 100% committed, but with almost nothing to show for it.

I don't want to blame anyone. It's my career and it's my result and it rests on my shoulders how I race. Could the DS have given us more direction? Seen what was playing out with experienced eyes, not those of an emotional and adrenaline-filled youngster? Maybe. I did what I thought was right in that moment. These guys were my heroes. I admired them and looked up to them. I wasn't ready to give anyone wins, free or otherwise, but I just lacked the experience.

A couple of days later, riding the Scheldeprijs one-day race, the well-known cycling photographer Tim De Waele came up to me on the back of his motorbike. Tim has been around the pro peloton for almost thirty years. He's seen even more than I have. And he told me what a strong ride I'd done in Flanders and how I'd always been in the wind, and maybe because of his expertise, and his nationality, those compliments felt more authentic than they might have done from someone else. At least I had learned some fresh lessons on that cold windy day. Keep your head up and assess what's happening. Do your homework, understand the riders around you – their strengths, their weaknesses, how they usually race. When the moment arrives, take your opportunity and back yourself. More than anything else, if you see a way to win, go for it. There'll be too many other days when you have no possibility whatsoever of a podium. Chances are rare and they're there to be taken.

The rest of our season as a team? It was all about Brad and it was all about the Tour. The 2010 race had not turned out as the team had hoped. Brad, having struggled in the Giro, had failed to finish within the top 20 on GC. This year was looking better. I roomed with Brad on our first training camp up on Mount Teide in Tenerife, Simon Gerrans and Xabi Zandio in the other room. Brad had climbed well. Actually, he was flying – efforts behind the scooter, smashing power

PBs all over the shop – and off the back of that he had won the Dauphiné, one of the two key build-up races to the Tour.

But when does the Tour ever go the way people are expecting the Tour to go? On the first stage, which took us across the Passage du Gois on the French Atlantic coast, a road that's underwater at high tide and treacherous at low tide, a major crash towards the end caught up quite a few of the big GC contenders. I was in a good position up front, got away unaffected and came in sixth on the day. Cancellara tried a late Cancellara-style attack, but this time it didn't come off. Philippe Gilbert went over the top of him for the win with Cadel Evans second. I was there right in the mix of it all. Once again I was in the white jersey and once again there was a genuine chance of going into yellow the next day.

It was a team time-trial. Not a long one, at 23km, but with Brad and Edvald Boasson Hagen on form and me feeling good, Sky were among the favourites. If I'd enjoyed wearing the white jersey a year ago, this skinsuit version was even better. I was thinking about the team first, which meant thinking about Brad, but I also allowed myself the occasional thought about how it might feel to wear yellow. It was good and bad at the same time: motivation and also distraction.

It turned out to a classic Sky TTT from that period: close, but not quite good enough. Garmin and BMC beat us by four seconds, which put Thor Hushovd into yellow and Cadel Evans third behind David Millar. I was fourth on GC. The difference this year was that it almost felt normal. I didn't feel giddy at my progression, and I kept riding well and getting myself in the right positions. The next day I was fifteenth in a bunch sprint. On stage five, another bunch sprint, I came in fifth as Cav won from Gilbert. I was ahead of André Greipel.

Looking back, this all seems something of a mad dream. What was I doing fifth in a bunch sprint? It almost seems like a typo. Eddie was up there so maybe I was positioning him and then Cav came late. In the second week, on stage ten, when Greipel won from Cav, I was ninth.

There are times in a bike race when it feels like you can go wherever you want. You have a clear mind and you have the legs to take you through the gaps you've spotted. It's a beautiful feeling to have, since even when you're young and every month seems to bring improvement, you know it's not going to be there every day or at every race. That's how it was on stage six from Dinan in Brittany eastwards to Lisieux in Normandy, when we were hunting a stage win for Eddie. It all felt so gradual, moving through the bunch in the final kilometres, Eddie glued to my wheel. Hitting out at the right time and delivering him with speed at 150m to go. There's a nice photo of Eddie celebrating his win with me in the background, one arm raised in the air, the other off the bars by my side, as if I'd never had that run-in with the commissaires at Hillingdon and never learned the lesson they were intending to dish out.

Sometimes when a team-mate wins you feel you haven't really done anything. It's great for the team and you all buzz off it, but it's their win and not yours. This time I felt like I was an important part of it. And it was Sky's first stage win at the Tour, which felt like both a partial justification of everything we had been trying to do and an augury of what might soon follow. It was one of those days to enjoy in the moment and savour in harder days to come.

This being cycling, it all came crashing down the next day. Specifically Brad, who went down in a big pile-up about 40km from the finish in Châteauroux and broke his collar-bone. I was gutted for Brad and I was also annoyed at the way it all played out. It had been one of those super-tense days when the wind blew enough to cause a lot of stress, but never enough to cause any splits. Simon Gerrans and I were in the front group; the rest of the team were in the group with Brad or further back. When Brad hit the deck it was all chaos on the radio. You couldn't work out what was going on.

Gerro and I had a hurried conversation. Did we keep riding, have a go at the finish and fight for a second successive stage or did we wait? If Brad was coming back he would need all his team-mates. Brad was the priority. That couldn't be any clearer now. And it was now or never. If he needed us, it wasn't in 2 or 3km, it was now.

So we stopped pedalling and we rolled along, and there is no worse feeling than seeing the back of the front group just riding away from you when you should be there. You're suddenly drifting in no-man's land and it's abruptly so quiet.

The peloton is always noisy – the sound of all those bikes, the crowds, the braking, the shouting for team-mates or just at each other. Sometimes it's just the breathing. Your concentration is at 100% just to hold your position. Gerro and I had gone from those intense sensations to feeling like we were on a training ride. There were the same number of fans on the roadside as there had been for the main bunch, but they didn't care so much about two guys who were clearly just rolling along having a conversation.

Me in the white jersey, watching the peloton getting smaller and smaller in the distance. Thinking and hoping: 'Phwoah, I hope Brad comes back quick now so we can get back to that group. Get him home safe and I can keep this jersey too . . .'

A couple of minutes later the radio cleared. Brad wasn't coming back. We were told to just keep going. And it felt like it had all gone, then: all the sacrifices made by Brad and the people around Brad; the chance of the stage; the hopes of staying in the white jersey. What was our purpose now? Where would we throw our efforts for the remaining two weeks?

We thought about stages. We thought about pushing Rigoberto Urán for the white jersey, at least until he injured his knee and started to struggle. So we turned our attention to breakaways. I got in the escape five days later on the stage to Luz Ardiden, a big climbing day that would take us over the Tourmalet, and at one point we had a lead of nine minutes. What I didn't realise was that there was a €5,000 prize for being the first man to summit the Tourmalet.

Riders kept dropping from the break. What had been nine of us became six and then four. Suddenly it was just me and Frenchman Jérémy Roy. Teide was in my legs. I was climbing well. Without really trying, I dropped him, too.

Which is where my naivety kicked in. Beautiful though it was to be leading the way up the Tourmalet in the Tour, if I had slowed slightly and let Roy get back on, we could have ridden together, and I could have used him on the descent and the valley road, and maybe started thinking about the stage. It was a long shot. We were being chased by the big GC guys: Alberto Contador, Cadel Evans, Damiano Cunego, Fränk Schleck and Andy Schleck, Ivan Basso, Samuel Sánchez. But it was my only shot.

Roy knew more than I did – 300m from the summit he jumped me. I was angry in the moment. 'What you doing, you idiot! I just waited for you!' I would be angrier still at the finish when a reporter told me about the €5,000 prize.

Things continued to go wrong as soon as we crested the summit. My back wheel slipped out on a right-hander, which meant I had to correct my line, but now couldn't make the corner. I saw a car in front of me and then the side of the road, no barrier between me and a very long drop. I realised I had a choice: hit the deck here or hit the deck much further down.

It's never a great feeling, having to crash on purpose. At least it was grass. But it got worse as I remounted and entered the next hairpin too hot. With mud already all over my tyres I feared I'd crash again if I banked it out too much and instead went straight on to the grass verge again. The TV commentators blamed a fan with a Welsh flag for distracting me. This time they were wrong.

The GC guys, this select group of superstars, caught us on the last climb to the finish. And as they went past, about ten or twelve of them, I glanced at their faces and tried to take it all in: a sense of what they were going through, of what it was like to be in that elite company. I had never before been on the last climb of a Tour stage at the front of the race. I was only there now because I had been in the break, allowed to get away because I was no threat to anyone more important. But I wanted to stay with them, if only for a kilometre, to experience what they were experiencing, to live the exact thing I'd been watching on TV ever since I fell for this crazy and cruel sport; to hold on to some element of it and carry it with me into the long winter of training ahead; to tell myself, 'Yeah, I'd love to be here one day. Fighting for a mountain stage in the Tour. And I'm going to fit in. I'm going to belong.'

The 2007 Tour had been, 'Holy shit, this hurts.' 2010 was, 'Wtf, here I am at the Tour and I'm in the white jersey.' This time around, for the first time, I felt like I deserved to be here. I knew I was improving all the time. Maybe not next year, but in years to come, I wanted to be climbing with these boys.

We weren't quite finished. On stage seventeen, from Gap

over to Pinerolo in Italy via five categorised climbs, Eddie and I made it into the initial break again. This time maybe we would have stayed away, but we had the German rider Linus Gerdemann with us. His team, Leopold Trek, were in the mix for the team classement, so Garmin began to chase us full gas.

These are the sort of scenarios where riders fall out with each other fast. Linus wasn't even taking turns on the front. He was asked in relatively spicy language to start riding.

'Nah, nah, nah, my DS is telling me I don't have to ride.'

'Well, don't even stay with us, then – they're chasing because of you.'

'Nah nah, I can't.'

I don't need to spell out which part of the body rhymes with Linus and how the combination became his nickname from this point on. Linus stayed at the back of our group. The rest of us buried ourselves for 30km. Garmin kept riding full gas. Garmin caught us.

Pretty much as soon as it came back together, Eddie went again. I'd switched off for a moment, annoyed the move should have been the move but wasn't. Another lesson learned: don't switch off once a break is brought back, because another can go immediately. I was gutted to have missed Eddie's move, disappointed I hadn't spotted the possibility. I wanted to be there racing in the final for the stage, alongside my mate. I had the legs to be there, that's what made it worse. Yet I was chuffed for Eddie when he stayed away on the descent to the finish.

We celebrated hard when we reached Paris four days later. There's always a party when you reach Paris, although some are better than others. This time, even with Brad back home a fortnight previously, we had enjoyed some success to go with the adversity. Something the team was doing was coming right. Four years on from finishing 140th in the Tour I'd ended up thirty-first on GC, when GC had never been my aim. I'd gone from every day just trying to survive, to being up there in bunch sprints, and wearing the white jersey and thinking, even briefly, about taking yellow.

Of course, I was completely spent by the end. You're always on your knees come Paris, however the preceding three weeks have gone. But I had options now. If I was in the grupetto, it was because I chose to be. I could get in breaks, I could hold my own with all but the very best on climbs.

We had a good few drinks, that Sunday night. A year before it had all been a little too formal, riders sitting at tables, insufficient beverages. Even when I made the executive decision to switch the music up to Eminem and Jay-Z it failed to go off. This time, the party started. Rigo Urán brought the Latin American vibes. Riders' families piled in, the staff. Abstinence went out of the window.

What sort of rider was I, then, after all this? I had watched Brad develop from pursuit rider on the track to time-trialler and now GC hopeful. I saw in Eddie someone who had been signed to compete at the top and was now winning multiple stages at the biggest bike race in the world. Me? I thought of myself as a Classics rider who could feature in week-long stage races. I could see how I could fight for Flanders, possibly Roubaix. I thought one day I could have a good crack at Paris–Nice or Tirreno. GC at the Giro or Tour? No chance. My role there would be to support others. Three weeks wasn't just three times harder than one week. It was for riders with different skillsets, different builds, different teams around them.

And there was one more critical support role to play before the year was out. Mark Cavendish had also been celebrating in Paris, after his victory on the Champs-Élysées took his Tour total that year to five wins and secured him the green points jersey. This was Cav in his first pomp, winning the points jersey at the Vuelta the year before, the Giro two years further on, Milan–San Remo already on his palmarès. When I'd been accepting compliments from photographers at Scheldeprijs, Cav had been winning it for a third time.

I wasn't surprised. Cav hadn't changed from the days of buying knock-off gear from Mancunian wide-boys. He was just earning sufficient money now to get the real thing. He'd lost his temper easily back then and he still lost his temper at the drop of a spanner. And he'd always been fast and he'd always believed in himself, and he'd always had a genius gift for finding the right wheel and the right moment at exactly the right time. Now there was something else he was after: the World Road Race title.

Britain's women had been far more successful than their

male equivalents. Tommy Simpson was the sole British male to have won gold, forty-six years before; when Nicole Cooke won in Varese in Italy in 2008 she was the fourth British woman to take the rainbow jersey. This time, in Copenhagen, it looked like a bunch sprint all day long and so the plan was hatched. Rod Ellingworth was in charge, Cav the figurehead, the rest of us with distinct roles to get him to the front exactly when he wanted. Which is easier said than done when you're racing for almost six hours over 260km, and Australia also have a plan which involves dropping Matt Goss off exactly where he wants to be, and Germany have the same for André Greipel, and of course Fabian Cancellara fancies it, and Peter Sagan, and Eddie Boasson Hagen and a load of others, too.

Once the Tour was done and I'd gone to the Eneco Tour in the Netherlands/Belgium, my whole training programme was geared towards getting to Copenhagen in the best possible shape to help Cav in the best possible way. It was the same for all of us: Steve Cummings, Chris Froome, fresh from coming second in the Vuelta, Ian Stannard, David Millar and Jez Hunt, and Brad was recovered from his collarbone break. We all loved racing for GB, partly because we were mates, partly because it was us British against the rest of the world, but mostly because the preparation and detail from Rod and the backroom staff was so good. We believed in the culture and we believed in Cav, and we all wanted to be there to help him as best we could. Cav was the favourite and we felt ready for it, but we knew we'd have to take the weight of the race.

And that's how it turned out. Australia and Germany looked at us, and let us chase everything down. A year later at the 2012 Olympics, with a smaller team, it would turn out to be too big a task – too many moves to cover, too many threats. This time we had massive engines everywhere. Riders were so keen to crack on that they were putting their hands up to ride before they needed to. Sometimes it can be the hardest thing, sitting there and waiting and soaking up the pressure of being the one to deliver at a certain point. It's almost easier to start riding earlier – get cracking, empty the tank, feel safe in the knowledge you still have team-mates behind you.

As last man for Cav, I didn't have that luxury. Stannard would control it before me, Brad before him. I could sprint, but nothing like the top sprinters. I could do lead-outs from a flat-out pack, but nothing like Mark Renshaw or the top lead-out men. But I was still capable of doing the job and I knew Cav inside out. If you didn't perform for him, he was going to let you know. Sitting there in front of him on the final laps, waiting for our moment, piloting him away from the Aussies and Germans, I had an awful lot of time to think about it – and not very much to get it right when the time came.

And then, coming into the very final corner, 600m from the finish, the Aussies came round us. I moved forward, past Stannard, through a small gap on his right, which he'd left open. Out of the corner I glanced back.

Cav wasn't on my wheel.

'Shit, where is he? Where's he gone? Do I stay where I am or go back? Go back. If he needs to move I'm better doing that for him. What use will I be at 200m to go when the sprint opens up?'

There he was, a couple of riders back, sitting on Gossy's wheel.

'Right, okay. He's alright . . .'

I tried drifting back further, making sure he knew where I was, that I was there if he needed me to go early. But when I got alongside him I could see he was all good. He'd made his choice in the moment, based on what he was seeing playing out. Gossy's wheel was where he wanted to be.

I stayed behind him for 100m or so, and then all these big sprinters massed and began to swamp me, and even had I been needed, that was it.

'Right, I'm out of here. There's 250m to go. There's nothing I can do now . . .'

You don't want to get in the way of sprinters when they're sprinting – not when they're full of caffeine and gels and the rainbow jersey is dangling there for one of them to seize. You don't really slow down and you don't lose touch. It's just they're going so much faster, because this is their moment, and it all comes down to this acceleration and these decisions and this patch of clear or crowded road.

Those last 200m seemed so long. Questions jumping around

in your head. 'Where is he?' 'What's happening?' 'Come on, Cav!'

You're trying to see through all the bodies and shiny bikes, but you can't see the front and you can't focus on the big screens the spectators can see, because you're still travelling at 65km an hour, millimetres from one another. 'Come on, Cav. Finish it off . . . finish it off . . .'

You hear it first. The commentator over the PA system, a single word: 'Cavendish!' You're 95% sure. Then you're through the line and you can see the screens now, and there's an image of your old mate, this kid you've been racing against since you were thirteen. The one who you woke up getting in late on your birthday and who yelled you out in his pants in the kitchen, with both his arms up in the air. And you know he knows and that's all you need.

In a strange way I didn't really feel like I'd contributed. I'd spent 260km waiting in the wheels without ever touching the wind and then he'd taken another option. But I'd been there. Everyone else could ride hard and commit to their job knowing I was still there with Cav if anything went wrong. The other teams made their plans based on ours, hoping we'd use up all our fire power so they could capitalise on that and provide a better lead-out. But Cav, Stannard and me had grown up racing each other, and now we were racing together against the rest of the world. We thrived on that – on the pressure of not wanting to let the others down.

I rode back to the bus on my own. Most of the boys were

well out the back of the peloton, exhausted from their effort, all of us so stoked. When Cav got back to the bus, fresh clean rainbow jersey on his back, we greeted him with huge grins and backslaps and hugs. This is what it was all about. Everyone all in, committing to a single goal, pulling it off. A special feeling on the most special of days.

Cav's a generous man. He had a special IWC watch made for all us with rainbow stripes on the faces, nothing knock-off about them. Not owning a safe, I kept mine in the teapot at home. I reasoned a burglar would look in my pants drawer before they ever thought of the teapot.

I took so much pleasure in seeing my friend enjoying such success. And also, being an elite sportsman, I was delighted for him and to have been part of it, but I wanted a day like this for myself, too. It was the same as when the big wins came to Brad. When people you knew so well were winning things no Briton had won before it expanded the scope of your own ambitions. It made you believe these races were for people like you, from places you knew, rather than just these superstars from hot lands you'd never been to.

It gave you confidence. It wasn't just the French or Italians or Spanish who could win on the road. We could, too. And we were getting better with every year.

Chapter seven

Olympics 2012, London, team pursuit final

So we were a team of planners, at Sky and with Great Britain. We liked fine detail and long-term strategies, and we liked the rewards they seemed to bring. But plans could never be guarantees. We'd seen that with Brad at the Tour in 2011. Just before the biggest Olympics any of us would ever experience, in the summer of 2012, I found that out for myself.

As reigning champions, as world champions, as world record holders, we were hot favourites for team pursuit gold. There were three of us who had won gold in Beijing four years before: Ed Clancy, Steven Burke and me, and there was Pete Kennaugh. We had trained brilliantly. We trusted our bikes and clothing. And then, ten days before, I got sick.

Things wouldn't stay down. Other things flew through without bothering to stick around. Even when I had a couple of easy days to rest up, I still felt weak when I got back on the bike. It was as tough on the head as it was on the body.

We were leaving it late to set off for London. We thought we could afford to, because we had everything we needed at the velodrome in Manchester and in Newport, and there was nothing to be gained by spending too much time around the happy distractions of the athletes' village in Stratford. The hard yards were done. Now it was freshening up, feeling fit and feeling confident. Instead, I was slowing down, feeling sluggish and wondering why the hell this had to be happening now.

It's easy to overthink things in the final few days before an Olympics. You begin analysing every pedal stroke, every lap of the boards you complete. Did that feel better than the last one? Was I pushing the other boys on or holding them back? I missed some sessions and when I dropped in for others I was either having to work much harder to hold the usual pace or not feeling capable of holding that pace at all. We would do a rolling 3000m, so twelve laps of the track, and I felt at 70% of where I wanted to be – of where I had been, through all our preparations. In a race that is measured in thousandths of a second, this is not a good thing.

It's hard not to disappear off into your own private world when this happens. I was still trying to be normal with the boys, which meant upbeat, because they were relying on me to be good. I was the one bringing results from the road, from big time-trials and prologues at elite races. I didn't want to give them any reason to doubt. But inside my own head, that's what was going on.

Over the years, my relationship with Steve Peters had been a relaxed one. While other riders saw him every week, I dropped in every now and then. I seemed to quite naturally do the things he was advising. Talking to him in this difficult period helped me to recognise what I was going through and remind myself how to deal with it. Just like on your bike, you could have average days in your head and bad days, too. Now, when I could hear the chimp he kept talking about rattling at the bars of its cage, I could also hear Steve's calm counterarguments and strategies in my head.

In Beijing I'd felt bulletproof. It had been Brad who had got sick. It was me who had been going well enough in the last few weeks of training to double up in the individual pursuit as well as the team pursuit had I wanted to. Now things felt as if they had been reversed. I was lucky to be part of a strong team. That helped settle me. If all hopes are on you, it's a different story. I wasn't getting carried round. I could still hold my own, but when you're used to being the driving force, that doesn't feel enough.

It helped that we shared an understanding of what each of us brought to the team and how to bring the best out of each other. Pete and I were the part-time roadies again, in and out of the velodrome that spring, both starting the Giro in May to keep our endurance volume and work on our high-end power by being the last two men in the lead-out train for Cav, Sky's latest big-money signing, as he went for the points jersey. That rollercoaster of a Giro ended with Cav crying in my arms in a lonely hotel room off the Stelvio Pass after Joaquim Rodríguez pipped him to the maglia ciclamino, the points classification jersey, by a single point on the penulti-mate stage. Pete also had to pull out in the final week with an injury, which worried him and worried the rest of us in the team pursuit squad. The doctors tried to reassure us. Pete was good at managing himself. We had time.

Back home, we kept it all tight. In Newport and at race meets I roomed with Ed. He was the glue of the team because he was the one constant, the one who led the planning and pushed the backroom staff the hardest on the small critical wins around nutrition or the aero gains on our kit. I led on the track, when it came to getting on to the boards and smashing ourselves to pieces – the easy part, to me.

I would try to chill out Ed if he was worrying too much. You couldn't turn on the TV or radio in those weeks and not accidentally hit something about the Olympics, or London, or how incredible the combination of the two was going to be. There were Union flags hanging off people's houses and in streets and town squares. You'd pick up a packet of cereal or coffee and there'd be an Olympic promotion on the back. You came through an airport and it was all cuddly toys of the mascots Wenlock and Mandeville.

I accepted the talk. In Beijing I had been blinkered. I had shut out any of the experiences of the Olympics. I thought it would mess up our chances if I lifted my head for a moment to look around. In London I wanted to live it. I wanted memories and I knew it could push me on rather than drag me down. I liked doing interviews; I liked the fact that we were favourites. That was a good thing to me. You got used to it when you rode the Tour with Sky and you travelled round France in a bubble where people only talked about cycling and legs and climbs and form.

Ed was less used to it and more likely to be freaked out, but Burkey took Ed's propensity to fret and doubled it. He had lived with me for a few months in the house in Altrincham I shared with Sa and I got to recognise when he was having a little wobble – usually if his last effort on the track before finishing for the day had been a little off, which meant it would stay with him until the next time we rode. 'Mate, it's just one effort, and it wasn't even that bad.'

When it's a speed play and you ride for so little time compared to the road, and every lap is immediately available for review and analysis, there will never be a session or an effort when everything is perfect. The road is relentless, but the track is intense. We might do three hard efforts a day. We'd roll off the boards and be able to see our speed and power tracked on a laptop and displayed in graph form. Of course, you want every one to be flawless. It's not going to happen. Sometimes you'll slow the team up by a tenth of a second or your delivery at the end of your turn at the front won't be quite as good as everyone else's. You have to remember it's happening to each of your team-mates, too. You have to remember it's natural and never the end of the world.

Ed could watch Burkey and recognise his own flaws, and empathise and try to bring him back up. We needed each other, so we looked out for each other. Burkey was a phenomenal athlete. After an off-season he'd turn up with the physique of a partying Ricky Hatton, but within a fortnight his shape would have returned to elite track rider. He had gas to burn. Pete? Pete was always the wildcard. He was looser, but so fast and strong and talented, the exact blend you need in a team pursuit. He lived with us at times as well. I had space. People needed a room. It was one less thing for the worriers to worry about.

The living together bonded us all, too. We had a routine based partly around the practical and partly around pleasures. As a track rider you need fuel. It's not about weight. Which explains the order Sa and I would place at Pizza Express in Hale each week: doughballs to start, Margarita for Sa, Etna for me. The same dance with the same waitress: 'Just to warn you, the Etna is spicy.' 'Thank you, I know.'

Pizza Express for the standard night, wagu steak at the Hale Grill if we had something to celebrate, bowling about with our new puppy Blanche on our laps. Frozen yoghurts from the shop across the road from the train station for pudding, hot chocolate with marshmallows as a nightcap. It's astonishing thinking about this diet as a veteran road rider. I would go months without even inhaling the aroma of chocolate. You were more likely to ride up Mount Etna than order one.

What mattered was that we weren't all the same. We could complement each other, in what we brought to the track and the way we were around it. Pressure brings out the sharp edges in people. There was plenty of that, as world champions and world-record holders, home team and hot favourites if you wanted to go looking for it. We were in each other's pockets all the time, at the track and at races, and at home a lot of the time. But we shared a confidence in the plan and in sticking to it. We tried not to expect perfection and we tried to tick all the big boxes. The rest of it was going with the flow. You can't shape everything around you all the time. Sometimes you have to accept what's coming and make the best of it. The track was so much more controllable than the road. The road was frequently chaos. But we were still just young men on bikes. We weren't robots, even if we looked like them at times.

And, when you dug a little, we were favourites for a reason. The Track Worlds that April were in Melbourne. You got the very definite sense that the Aussies saw this as a dress rehearsal for the Olympics in four months' time. As a result, we deliberately didn't make it a dress rehearsal. While they had all the kit they were planning to use in London, we used our ropey old stuff: helmets that were cracked and had non-deliberate, non-aero holes in them; the tired old skinsuits we had used in training.

When we still beat them in the team pursuit final, and did so with a new world record, you could see what a heinous blow it was for them. Looking back, that's maybe where we won the Olympics: not in London in August, but Melbourne in April. We had them on the canvas and it carried on at the Giro, when the key man in their quartet, Jack Bobridge, was swinging around at the back on one of the big mountain days. I dropped back to the Sky team car to pick up a jacket for Rigo and some of the other boys, and seeing Bobridge struggling to hang on at all felt like it played into the same narrative. Meanwhile, I'd come second in the prologue and then second again in the final time-trial. Even as they tried to pick themselves off the canvas, we had them pinned on the ropes.

That was the immediate evidence. Then there was what Brad Wiggins and the core of Team GB, transplanted to Team Sky, did at the Tour that summer. We watched after our sessions at the velodrome in Newport as Brad went into yellow and stayed there. We watched him get to Paris in yellow and then lead Cav out to win on the Champs-Élysées. Everything touched by British Cycling seemed to be turning golden. Even better, for those of us watching from afar, there had been a rider meeting at our December training camp when we had debated how prize money from races might be divided out amongst us next season. Would we do the usual, where 20% of the money from a race went to the staff who worked on it and the rest to the riders who raced it? Or would we back a new proposal where all the money from all the races that season was lobbed into a single pot and divided at the end?

I voted for the first. More voted for the second, including several of the lads who were piloting Brad to glory in France. Midway through the Tour, just after one of Cav's stage wins, I popped out a Tweet. 'Great job over there in France, boys. Keep earning that money for us . . .' I'm not sure Bernie Eisel saw the funny side. At least it gave the boys a break from the growing Brad vs Froome vs Cav power saga.

Momentum is such a big thing in sport. When a few of you in a team start to struggle, it can seep into all of you. Struggling becomes the norm. When you start going fast and winning, and adding wins to wins, it's like you're all under the same magic spell. When Brad walked out at the opening ceremony of the Olympics at the London Stadium in yellow and the whole place went mad, it felt like we were all there with him. It felt like the same success was coming to all of us.

Maybe that's why we broke our own world record again. When you race in qualifying, it's just the four of you on the track. You're not riding against another team, not yet, so it's usually slower. When there's two teams, starting on opposite sides, there's generally about seven seconds between you. The two sets of four riders create a flow of rotating air. You get pulled along by each other. To break the record all on our own – you could see what it did for the confidence of Ed and Burkey. You could see what it did for the Aussies.

Ed being Ed and Burkey being Burkey, there was still a little doubt, still the occasional, 'Yeah, but . . .'

'Yeah, but maybe the Kiwis didn't go full gas . . .'

'Yeah, but what if the Danes have got something else in the locker?'

'Yeah, but what if the Aussies have got some new kit of their own?'

I was happy to give the sort of answers I'd been giving all year. 'Yeah, but we can't affect their ride or their kit or their tactics, so why bother worrying about it? We've just gone faster than anyone's ever gone before and we were the only team on the track. We're going alright. So let's just keep doing what we're doing and we're definitely going to be in with a shout.'

And we were. Reaching the final didn't feel inevitable, but it wasn't far off. Sa was nervous too, which was a strange dynamic: the athlete who's racing the final having to reassure his partner who's going to be watching him doing it. The only thing I didn't like was the countdown they did before each race. First they played the sound of Big Ben chiming to quieten the crowd. That put the shits up all the riders. Then they'd play footage on the big screens of a celebrity putting a finger to their lips and giving everyone a big shhh. The crowd were well behaved. It would go dead quiet for what felt like a minute. That was peak adrenaline. You knew it was incoming now.

When there were other races going on and we were in the zone warming up, all was fine. You're focused on your ride and exactly what you've got to do. You visualise the perfect race. You close your eyes without actually shutting them and imagine your turns on the front and the changeovers working perfectly. You have your headphones on. Focusing is easy.

Harder is when the warm-up is done. No matter how techy your gear is, getting a skinsuit on over a damp sweaty torso is as easy as typing a book with your toes. Maybe that's why Burkey ripped his, and maybe it kind of helped him. We had spares, of course we did. He now didn't have time to worry about anything else.

The rest of us rolled around the inside of the track on our road bikes. It wasn't doing anything for us physically. It was the comfort of pedalling, the most familiar feeling to us of all. But there were no headphones now to block the outside world, and all these fresh and intrusive sounds keep trying to drag you out of the zone. Suddenly it's not about processes and calm. You realise where you are. The bronze medal race is starting, which means you'll be in an Olympic final in about five minutes. With about 2000m of that preceding race to go, the officials come to get you and take you to four very basic folding plastic chairs. At least when you're rolling round slowly on your bike you're moving. Now there's nothing to do but think.

You sit down and chalk your hands. This is your weakest moment. This is the time the chimp is most likely to jump out of its cage. Instead, I decided to shut it up. Just as I had in Beijing, I looked into the eyes of my team-mates and said what we all wanted to say. 'Right, come on, boys – let's fucking get out there and let's do it.'

Motionless on your bike, four of you in a row, waiting for the electronic beeps that will send you off. Big Ben sounding, everything tightening inside you. I felt locked in now. Like I was a computer programmed months in advance. A big deep breath in at ten seconds to go. Five seconds, breathe in, four seconds, out. Two seconds, move slightly back in the saddle. One second, a fraction more. Gun.

These first five seconds are a max effort, locking your upper body like the arc of a rainbow, 'pulling your trousers on', as Shane would say. All your power is forced down into your legs and away. A good start for me was critical. Those first 15m were maybe more important than any of the rest of the 4000. As we entered the banking I would be travelling slightly further than the guys under me. As the gradient increased they would naturally pull ahead; as we exited the turn I could use the extra height I'd gained to take some free speed and save a few precious watts.

Ed first man, then Burkey, then me, then Pete. Drifting down the track into that one-line formation, still out the saddle coming out of turn two, down the back straight, into the saddle coming into turn three, on to the tri-bars and your aero tuck.

Focus on your breathing, always looking at the same point: the hub of the front wheel of the rider ahead. Looking through their bike gives you a fraction more time to react if something happens. Looking at something dead in front of you, their saddle or rear tyre, and you're too twitchy. You want to be smooth in everything you do.

You're just trying to breathe in those opening laps. To get rid of the lactic you've built up from such an aggressive start. You're pushing a big gear and you're thinking about your turns at the front, when they come. You can hear the crowd, but because you've got a tight aero helmet on you feel like you're in a physical cocoon, as well as one of your own thoughts and your own breathing.

After so many years racing this way you can feel everything, even if you speed up by a tenth of a second a lap. If you want it confirmed, your coach walks the line to tell you – stands just inside the track and takes a pace towards you from the start/finish line if you're a tenth slow, takes a pace away from you if you're a tenth fast.

Each time we passed him he was exactly where I expected him to be. Good. I focused on my change and the change is always the same process: keep the pressure on all the way to the top of the change, and the back down, and just glide to that back wheel. When you nail a change, it's a huge buzz. 'Boom. Sweet. Let's push.' When you don't nail it – when you miss the back and you've got to squeeze to get back on – it's anger. 'Shit. Not ideal. Get back on that wheel. Now breathe. Recover.'

You know you've just burned through some extra watts you wanted for later. Complications in your head, trying to recover fast for your next turn. The better you are, the more likely you are to nail a change. If you're really good, you've got a buffer to correct it if it does go slightly wrong. It's why, six months before this moment, we would hammer effort after effort in training. The coaches wanted us to be able to nail the big moments while on our knees – the changes, the decision-making, individually and as a team.

I feared my buffer had gone after my sickness, but I kept nailing my changes and I never even looked where the Aussies were. Some coaches walk the other team. If the opposition are up, they step away; if they're down, they step towards you. Our coach walked the pace we wanted to ride. We knew that if we nailed it we'd go the quickest we could go and that was all we could do.

And we kept nailing it. Boom, boom, boom, Every time.

I did my second turn, the race almost halfway through. Your mind can wander if you're not careful. It's all about how you're feeling: if you're on the limit, your mind doesn't go anywhere else. All you're thinking is: 'Shit, I'm hurting here. I just need to breathe, breathe.' When you're feeling better, you're more aware of your surroundings. You can hear where you are from the crowd. They're watching the splits coming up on the scoreboard. When they see you're up, you hear this great roar, as long as they're on your side. In London, it felt like the whole country was in there with us.

'Don't chase the pain, it'll come.' That was something Paul Manning said to me back in 2007 and it had forever stuck with me. The pain does always come, but it's also true that the quicker you go, the smoother it gets. The line of the four of you is less choppy. Everyone is in unison. You're spinning that big gear round and the track is almost helping you by throwing you out of every turn. Feeling the lactic burn in your legs the further down the straight you go, then the banking doing its centrifugal trick again. And all the while the crowd are screaming fresh power into your body. It's a magical tailwind. It's those lost watts coming back.

All four of us were on it. No-one was parking up – when your team-mate tightens up, and you can feel the speed go. Sometimes it happens because someone is tired; sometimes because they're trying to be a hero and do an extra half a lap on the front. Don't go chasing the errors. If you're slowing, get off the front. Listen for the shout you'll be getting from the next man back in the line: 'Change! Change!' Not that you could hear anything in that velodrome that evening.

The strangest thing of all? It didn't feel anything special, this ride. Which maybe sounds weird, when we were breaking our own world record again, almost three seconds up on the Aussies and winning Olympic gold in front of our home crowd. I knew we were flying around. I knew we were up on schedule. But our coach was walking independent laps, not the overall time, even if you knew what the aggregation of those individual advantages was giving you. Yet I felt it when I came out of my last turn with three-quarters of a lap to go. I actually bailed. I didn't bother coming back into the line. I swung out and stayed at the top of the track and was almost celebrating before the other three boys had crossed the line.

Even after we had slowed down, found our families in the

crowd and stood there with gold medals being hung round our necks, it took a while to sink in. We had been controlled for so long that it was hard to snap out of the process at last and into the outcome. It really only hit me how big it was the next day when Sa and I walked into a random pub in London and Andy Murray's match was on the big screen, and everyone was jumping around and cheering and completely swept up in it all. I was on the other side of the fence now. I was part of the public, a watcher rather than a doer. Nobody knew who I was or nobody recognised me. And it gave me a sense of how special these Olympics had become to everyone there.

Of course we enjoyed it. When we went out that first night after winning, Sa was adamant I shouldn't take my medal with me. It can work out quite well if you do – free entry to bars and clubs, free drinks when you're in there. I was glad I took her advice. When I woke up the next day, our hotel room door was wide open and my medal was in the middle of the floor. You could see it if you walked past along the corridor.

It was one of those nights so big you don't remember what you did or what time you got back, so Sa was left to fill in the blanks.

'Sa, why were we in a tuk-tuk last night?'

'Because we got in a taxi and you were going to be sick so the taxi guy kicked us out.'

'Ah . . .'

'Do you remember how we got up to our room?'

'I'm guessing we didn't walk?'

'No, the poor guy on night duty had to help me carry you.'

'Ah . . .'

In my defence, I hadn't drunk alcohol since Christmas, and I had just won Olympic gold. I also had ten missed calls on my phone. When you won gold for Britain, you went on *BBC Breakfast* the next morning to talk about it. Unless you were in the team pursuit quartet, in which case you slept in a room with an open door instead.

There's one more memory that puts it all into context for me. A few days later we went to GB House. The big countries take over a building for the duration of the Games and host events there. You can hang out with your friends and family, and other athletes, and watch the action and enjoy a few drinks. The British Olympic Association sent a car to take us there, a BMW wrapped in gold with a big Team GB lion in black on the side. When we arrived there was endless free champagne.

We watched Usain Bolt win his 200m gold. I was blown away by the wonders he was producing. He was an absolute superstar. I wasn't. But I felt part of the same experience as him. I had the same colour medal. Plans could never be guarantees, but when they came off, they could take you to places you barely dreamed possible.

Chapter eight

Commonwealth Games 2014, Glasgow, road race

Professional sport is about glory and it's about big wins, but it's never about looking back at them. It's always about the next target, the next race, the next challenge.

I was good with that. After the Olympics four years before I'd gone large – and by large I mean eight nights on the bounce in Cardiff with my best mate Ian. Our mate Nathan had put in a solid three, back to back, but then said he had to tap out for work. There's always a solution to every problem, in this case him calling in sick, cracking on with Ian and me and – heroically – getting through to the end of the full eight nights with his body and his job still intact. In 2012, though, it didn't need to be so big. I let rip for a day or two, but I wanted to push forward. I wanted to win on the road.

That meant reassessing where I was going to live to train and race. Italy had been a joy, but Sky were setting up a new base in Monaco. Froomey and Richie Porte were there, plus a few other key men in the team. There would be a soigneur for massage, a place to pick up spare parts and sort our nutrition. There was good weather all year round, there were quiet roads in the hills and there were thirty-minute climbs about ten minutes of riding from your front door. Sure, it got hot in summer. That was a good thing, too. If I wanted to be seriously competitive in the Tour I needed to get better in the heat. That meant living and breathing it, not just dipping a toe in on a few training days. Froomey and Richie were fast. They were both probably in the top five climbers in the world. Even better. I could chase them every single day.

There was also my new coach. Tim Kerrison had been around Sky from the start, but, unconventionally for a cycling coach, had a background in rowing and then swimming. People were starting to recognise Dave B outside the insular world of cycling now; he had Premiership managers on his phone and had dinners with NFL coaches. Rod was the doer and the planner, who'd grown up in the sport, knew it inside out. Tim was less high-profile than Dave B or Rod. No-one outside the sport recognised him in the street and he was happy that way, happy to be left to it.

He'd coached Brad to the yellow jersey at the Tour. He was coaching Chris with the same aim and now he was looking after Richie Porte. For a lot of the time, the road for me had been a way of getting in shape for the track. If I was serious about following Brad's trajectory, if I wanted to really see what I could do, Tim would be the coach for me to work with.

With a couple of reservations. Tim was about GC men. My plan for now involved the one-day Classics, plus starting to look at week-long stage races. At Grand Tours I would still be a support rider. The Classics were about one big hit and one big day out. They were all in and they were unpredictable. No corner was the same and every short climb rode differently. There was the less predictable spring weather and tactics that switched around fast. If you made a mistake you didn't have another two weeks of racing to put it right. Tim had never done any of that. Then again, he hadn't coached anyone to a Tour de France title until he did.

He didn't mess about. He pushed you hard and he liked volume. It was a lot of hours in the saddle and it was a lot of hours riding on a low-carb regime. It was a lot of efforts, too. It was a near rethinking of how we trained and, while there was always a plan and always a reason, plenty of riders struggled to cope with that. There was a natural wastage rate with Tim that put some riders off. For every ten who might think they could live with him, only two or three would make it through. You either made it or you broke.

You had to work Tim out as a person to work with him as a rider. Tim is a scientist. He's an introvert and he's quirky. Some coaches can be a father figure or at least an uncle. Others can be like a slightly older mate; you can have a laugh with them and talk about what's going on in your life. Tim was pure athlete-coach. The relationship was professional and it was clinical, apart from the odd occasion in the off-season when you might have a drink together. Then he became more personable. Sa always liked him. He was Tim the person with her, not Tim the cycling coach. They could talk about things he'd never talk about with us riders.

Shane Sutton had been the opposite. Shane saw cycling like an art. He was all about the rider as a person. He had to see you on the bike to understand how you liked to ride and, when he did, he could tell from your position and body language if you were tired and needed to rest or could go again the next day.

Tim was all about the science. He would look at the numbers and work it out from there. He would also push you incredibly hard. That was just fine with me. I loved the hard work. It tapped into the same part of my personality that had tied weights to my bike on training rides as a teenager. I could suffer. I didn't like to whinge. If cycling had a road-specific dating app, Tim and I were both swiping right.

This is how it worked. From the end of August and into September 2012 I got back into some racing, so I could enter the winter in some sort of shape for the road, getting in the base miles and shedding the post-Olympics good times and heaviness. December got intense. On our training camp in Mallorca we would use what we called the rolling road, from Pollensa towards Sa Pobla, and do twenty-minute threshold efforts.

No other team was doing these sorts of sessions back then. Some days it would be the Classics group – me, Stannard, Edvald Boasson Hagen, Flecha, Mathew Hayman, Bernie – setting off twenty seconds apart, chasing each other down, not wanting to get caught from behind, always so competitive. Other days we'd have some sprints or capacity efforts of one to five minutes into a short breather. We called it EPD – explosive power development. The idea? Replicate what we'd need in the Classics: big high watts up the bergs, then be able to continue over the top, recovering and flushing out the lactic while still riding pretty hard.

Then there were what Tim termed 'Classics days', six-hour sessions where you'd start in what we called SAP – sustained aerobic power, the same thing Tadej Pogačar and his team now refer to as zone two. Somewhere between thirty minutes and an hour of that, some zone three stuff, threshold work in the fourth hour and some capacity efforts in the sixth. It was painful and it was different. For some of the older established pros, it was too different. They had their established training regimes and beliefs, and Tim was never about the old assumptions.

Me? The beautiful thing was, through the pain, I could feel it working. At the Tour Down Under in January I felt good. I felt I could ride where I wanted to in the peloton. All the little accelerations were coming more easily. I could think clearly and make the right decisions. Commentators talk about footballers or rugby players who appear to have more time on the ball. It wasn't that I had more time. It was that I knew what needed to be done in that time and I could make it happen.

The Corkscrew stage was always a big fight, a big rush down Gorge Road, hammering down at 80kph six abreast through long, fast corners with gravel up the inside. It was sketchy and tough, but I could float around. I could go where I wanted, when I wanted to. I almost felt like a junior again. That was the freedom Tim's programme was giving me. I could ride off instinct for the first time as a pro rider.

When the road kicked up on Corkscrew, the plan was for me to stay in the lead group and then go towards the top. Instead I attacked at the bottom and ended up going solo over the top. There was a small group behind me, so I eased up and waited for them to rejoin for the descent towards the finish. All of it felt simple. I knew there were some quick guys around me. I also knew I'd been hammering exactly these kind of scenarios in training. I could go long in the sprint and make it to the line. So I took them by surprise and hit them early, 400m to go, laying off and then rushing into the gap I'd left, using their slipstream to steal an extra bit of speed and accelerate away to the line.

I was in the leader's ochre jersey after that. And while I lost it on Willunga a few days later, on an afternoon so hot and dry my jersey turned white with salt and sweat, I came back to take third on GC, and I knew things were happening and things were changing.

It kept going. Fourth at Omloop on those cold, wet Belgian roads, confirmation Tim's training was working for one-day races, too. Fourth in E3 Harelbeke, an even better sign. E3 is like a more compact Flanders. I could feel I still had a way to go, though. At Flanders I finished in the main group, but I finished at the back of it. I tried attacking to go clear, it didn't work and then I was nailed.

From that moment in the year onwards, my focus switched. Now it was all about getting to the Tour in the best shape possible. Brad wasn't going back to defend his jersey; Froomey was moving up. Great though the Olympics had been, a part of me had been gutted not to have been part of Brad's push for the summit. I'd seen enough of Froomey, of Tim and of the team to believe another GC win for Sky was possible, and this time I wanted to contribute. Being part of a winning team was addictive.

It was all hard work from there. Going to altitude camps in Tenerife with Froomey and the outline Tour team, targeting the Dauphiné in June to fine-tune us further. Tim was super-motivated by the big targets. I think he wanted to prove that it wasn't just Brad's magic that had won the Tour; that as a coach he could win it with multiple riders. All this would have a pay-off for me, a few years later.

For now, he pushed me hard and in the process had to learn something about me: nobody pushed me harder than myself. If you told me to ride for four hours, I'd want to do four and a half. If you told me to hold it steady at 350 watts, I'd want to be touching 370.

With a lot of coaches, if you do something that varies from their plan, they don't like it. They can take it personally. Tim looked at me and saw his own work ethic reflected back at him. A lot of the staff sometimes saw him as a pain in the arse. If your standards didn't match his, he'd make it pretty clear. Maybe, looking back, that was one of our great strengths as a team in that first dominant period. The people who mattered all shared the same love of obsessional hard work: Tim, Dave, Rod, Fran, their best riders. If you weren't up to it, you got a hard time and then usually you left.

So I went to the Tour feeling I was on another level to 2011. I had continued to chase Froomey and Richie around, specifically up and down the volcano in Tenerife, pushing them as much as they were pushing me. I rode at the front for them at the Dauphiné and ended up fifteenth on GC without ever targeting places. I was the leanest I'd ever been and I was super-motivated. I didn't just want to be there in the mountains for Froomey. I wanted to be there with him on the last climb.

And then came stage one in Corsica. First the Orica-GreenEDGE team bus got stuck under the finish gantry. We were less than half an hour from the finish. Chaos broke out on the team radio.

'Boys! The Orica bus is stuck under the gantry. They're trying to move it, but maybe they can't . . .'

Two minutes on: 'Right, they've changed the finish. It's now at 2km to go. Got it?'

'Okay, so the 3km rule starts at 5km to go now?'

'Hold on, we're trying to find out.'

A minute later: 'Scratch that. The bus has got through. The finish is back to the usual place . . .'

Then, a couple of kilometres from the old finish line that wasn't the finish line and then was again, I got caught up in a high-speed crash that changed everything.

Tony Martin was the first man down, just in front of me. I hit him, flipped over the bars and did a somersault. Just as my somersaults into the swimming pool on holiday always ended up with me landing on my back rather than my feet, so the rotations did for me again. I knew straightaway that I'd done something serious. Standing up was hard enough and not only because half the peloton seemed to have come down around me. When I tried to lift my leg, it wouldn't move. Of course I got back on my bike. I pedalled one-legged to the finish line, 5km away. Every pedal stroke was agony, but you know the drill – get to the finish in any way you can, get it assessed there. All the time thinking, 'Shit. I missed last year and now this. I'm good, Froomey's good and everyone's motivated.'

I was dreading the results of the scan; praying that nothing was broken, that it was just a big messy bruise. When the doctor told me I had fractured my pelvis I thought I was done for; out of the race, on my way home. But there was good news – or rather bad news that was less bad than the bad news could have been. The fracture was at the top of my pelvis, by my lower back, rather than the circular part you sit on while riding a bike. I asked the doc a question I maybe shouldn't have asked: 'So is it possible to crack on? Am I going to do any more damage to it if I keep riding?' He gave me an answer that was both honest and very welcome. 'Well … yes, it is possible to continue. Obviously crashing on it again is not ideal, but you can ride – if you can put up with the pain …' That's what he said. What I actually heard was, 'Yeah, of course, you can keep going.' The thing about dealing with the pain? I saw that as a challenge. 'I'll show you what I can do …'

It was an interesting experience, trying to get ready to race with a broken pelvis. In the evening I'd be with the physio for an hour or so and then getting the world's most uncomfortable massage. If you fracture something, everything around it goes into shock. Everything around the everything around it also wants to join in with the inflammatory fun. The muscles around my pelvis, my back, my hamstrings, my glutes – nothing wanted to move. The physio wanted them to move. The meeting of two immovable objects slightly made me want to cry.

You lean on what you know in these moments, even when leaning anywhere feels like someone is prodding you with a hot poker. I decided to treat each day like a track race. I'd have a good shot of caffeine. I'd do a proper warm-up. I'd tell myself that I had to focus all my energies on starting well, rather than any challenges further through the day, because this being the Tour there would always be a fight to make the break and a fight to get into it. Get dropped at that point and you're in for a monstrous kind of day. It was like a re-run of 2007, when I'd thought those horrific days were behind me. Robbie Hunter's advice came back at me like PTSD. 'G, you gotta bite the bullet and at least get to this point . . .'

That was the theory. The reality was pretty horrific. I struggled to get on to my bike just to warm up. They had to help me on to it the first few days. When I was on it I couldn't get out of the saddle. You need to get out of the saddle to respond to accelerations from those around you. Because I couldn't, I was constantly yo-yoing off the back of the peloton. Every time we got to a roundabout I would lose the wheel in front. When the road went uphill at any gradient, I went backwards even faster. I was surviving. That was the only aim.

The two days in Corsica were awful. The worst was the team time-trial on stage four, along the Promenade des Anglais in Nice. This was supposed to be one of the big days for me. Just down the road from my new home, pretty much a team pursuit on the road. I was meant to be the man driving the team to a great time, hopefully the stage win.

I threw everything at it. Warm-up with hip-hop playlist. Drinks, gels, oils. TTTs are nervous days at the best of times.

The good riders feel the weight of responsibility, the weaker ones are shitting themselves about letting everyone down. The staff are all on edge: nine riders to look after, all at the same time.

I knew the first 3km was a succession of corners. This was an absolute nightmare for me. I couldn't accelerate. Because the team were worried I wouldn't be able to hold the line, they stuck me ninth man. This would just make it worse. When you're last man, you'll be mid-corner doing 30kph while the first rider exited it five seconds earlier and is already accelerating back up to 60kph. I would have to get off the line as quickly as possible, start well and then visualise every corner before it came. Lay off the wheel in front, and carry more speed around and out of the corner.

The countdown clock in front of us at the start made it feel like a third Olympic final. I got out well, almost ahead of the guy I was supposed to be behind. I drifted on to his wheel and then tried ticking the corners off. One done. Two done. Three to go.

The more corners I got through and was still with the team the better I felt. When we swung on to the long straight boulevards and the Promenade des Anglais the sense of relief was as intense as if we had won it. Once we passed the airport, out on the far west of the course, I knew I could make it all the way. I started taking a few turns on the front, short ones to start. By the time we hit the promenade for a second time, I was doing long turns. The adrenaline was whacking through me. I wasn't a dead weight. I was contributing. I was doing more than anyone had thought I could.

To miss out on the win by just seconds after all that felt like something of a kick in the guts. At the same time I knew nothing could be harder than what I had just survived. I still had to see the physio for an hour each morning and an hour each night. He still wanted to pull my body into places my body didn't want to be pulled into. But it wasn't going to get any more painful from here. I was going to mend, just in a very dysfunctional way.

That's what kept me going, feeling slightly less worse every day. I could ride on the front on road stages. The stage to Ventoux was flat for most of the way there, as usual, and I was able to help control the race, making sure the break that went was the break we wanted to go. Then I rode the front until Ventoux got bigger and bigger, and we were actually climbing up it. Another week on and I was pacing the peloton up one of the big Alpine climbs. I must have been doing something right. Tejay van Garderen rode up to me the next day. 'Ah shit, G mate. You were superb up the Glandon yesterday. All I could think was that you've got a fractured pelvis and you're still making me suffer . . .'

I wonder now, looking back, how I managed to get through. Why I managed. Had it been one of my team-mates, I know what I would have said to them: 'Mate, just go home. Why are you doing this to yourself?' Same as my mum. She never said anything to me during the Tour, because she didn't want to get in my way, but it came out afterwards. 'Ah, Geraint, I just wish you'd just given up and gone home . . .'

Sa had her own take. She was due to fly out with her parents mid-race to watch. I don't think it was just the prospect of a cancelled holiday that meant she wanted me to keep going. She just struggled to watch it happening on the TV. She didn't want to see me out the back all day, struggling.

In this kind of scenario you find your own way through as a couple. You pretend it's not as it is, because you both want to protect each other.

'How you feeling today, Ger?'

'Yeah, alright.'

'Ah, okay. Shall I tell you what we've been up to?'

'That would be great, thanks.'

I'm thirty-nine years old now. I've done almost everything I ever dreamed of doing in my career. I'd like to think I'd never do something like that again. After all, who tries to ride the world's toughest bike race with a broken pelvis? Well, I think I probably would all over again. I'd try to battle through, because I can never bring myself to stop. When I'm there – when I'm at a race, when there's a day's riding to be done – I have to get to the finish and I just have to start the next day. And once I start, there's no chance I'm stopping. I might be outside the time limit and then I'd have no choice but to go home, but if I can still ride I'm not stopping. I would tell a team-mate in the same position to think of other races ahead, to not force himself through the grovelling and battling and pain. But when it's you in that position, it's different. This is the mentality that Rod helped shape in those long-before academy days. The same reason Cav never stopped, either.

And I'm proud that I made it all the way to Paris, that I helped Froomey win his first yellow jersey. I'm secretly proud that I just got on with it and accepted it for what it was, that I got my head down and never moaned. I know how hard it was. I know the pain of it and the suffering. There's maybe an even greater sense of achievement than when I won the Tour, five years later. The grovelling, the battling. I could do it. I wasn't certain everyone else could.

It's the end of the penultimate stage when you can relax as a domestique at the Tour. After stage twenty they let us have a couple of beers on the bus, but Dave and Tim told us to leave it there. While I had great respect for them, I decided to ignore their advice on this occasion. I'd been through too much. A couple of glasses of wine went down at dinner – then, when everyone else went to bed, I headed off to the doctor's room with another bottle of wine.

I'd probably spent more time with the doc and the physio than anyone else in the preceding three weeks. They weren't just sorting me out medically, but looking after my head by chatting about all sorts of nonsense and joining me when we could to watch the British and Irish Lions Test series out in Australia. In their company I had sometimes been able to forget I had a fractured pelvis at the biggest, hardest bike race in the world. Dave and Tim were right. I did have a hangover on the final stage. But it was all worth it.

Something else, too. Maybe that broken pelvis helped me win the 2018 Tour. I'd suffered to a level beyond the point most people would suffer and therefore I knew what I could do. In elite sport it's your mind that gives up before your body. Whatever you think your limits are, you can always do more.

Suffering is an intrinsic part of cycling. The pain is going to come, so just accept it and embrace it. Maybe that's easier to say than live. But the more you believe it, the deeper you can go. If you have ten efforts to do, do the ten efforts. Do eleven. If your weekly training is meant to be thirty hours, do thirty-two. Sure, you can push too hard at times. I certainly have. But it's easier than you think. It doesn't take talent to work hard, or be on time or be committed. You just do it. And you never, ever quit.

So I learned a lot about myself in those three weeks and I learned a lot about what it takes to win. I'd seen Brad transform himself from track rider into Tour champion. I'd known Froomey at Barloworld when he was just a naive kid from Kenya who didn't seem to have ever watched European road riding. I'd seen him as a super-domestique for Brad. Now he was becoming a champion too.

I'd understood before that he had the same attitude to hard work as me. We'd pushed each other to our limits on those altitude camps and loved every breathless moment of it. Now I could see what his greatest weapon of all was: his self-belief. When things were going well, he expected it. When things were harder, there was always something he thought he could do to turn it around. He never gave up. When criticism came in, he had the priceless ability to block it out or use it as fuel. Off the bike he was seldom not in the zone. He'd have three or four weeks of being super-chilled in the off-season. As soon as he started training again, you could see the determination. He could talk about the Tour in November or December as if it were round the corner. I'm pretty sure it was the first thought in his head when he woke up each day. I'd never met a rider as single-minded.

His attitude and his success rubbed off on all of us. It's a wonderful feeling, riding in the dominant team at the Tour. You're allowed to ride as you want, a lot of the time. You get more respect and you get more space. The other teams wait for you to do something. We'd let the break go when we wanted it to go, and we'd decide who we'd let get away and how much time they could have. In the final week of the Tour, riders from other teams would come up to us during the first hour of racing:

'Erm, is it okay if I go? Will you guys chase?'

Depending on who it was and where they were on GC, the answer would be one of the following two options:

A: 'Sorry, mate, you're too close. We don't want to ride hard all day.'

B: 'Yeah, go for it.'

It didn't mean people didn't try. But when they did, we'd make sure they were closed down immediately. It was as much about the psychological as the physical. Keep your foot on their throats. Don't give them any hope.

The same confidence we'd had on the track as Great Britain was coming through as Team Sky on the road. 'Boys, let all those guys go away. There's thirty of them, they're never going to work that well together, especially on the flat.' In any race there will always be guys trying to sit on and not pull. It affects how the break works. Other guys get irritated and start arguing or stop riding.

We knew if we just rode our pace, controlled the break early, we'd save our guys rather than burning through them all and then we'd have more numbers over the top. We would be stronger as a unit. I'd glance across at Ian Stannard sometimes and the same look would pass between us: here's us two, grown up together, racing round suburban parks and pavements, and now we're in the best team at the biggest bike race and we're looking after the yellow jersey. If I say we were loving being the centre of the attention, it makes us sound like a bunch of knobs. But we did love it, because it meant we were doing our jobs as well as possible. We weren't peacocks. This is what the pain and suffering brought you. It was all paying off.

What a time to be there, what a thing to be part of. When you're young and you're just doing it, you inadvertently take it for granted. You don't realise how big it really is, riding at the front of a select group of eight riders on a mountain-top finish, leading the way into cobbled sections, piloting the yellow jersey safely through a treacherous final. You don't think about it too much. You don't reflect. You just want to be better and you want to do more the next time or the next day.

This was me as I recovered from that Tour and my pelvis knitted together again. My seasons would be split into two parts: racing the Classics for wins in the spring, then heading out to Tenerife, losing the weight, improving the climbing skills, getting ready for the week-long stage races and then doing the Tour as Froomey's man. I still had my heroes and I still appreciated the distance between us, but when I went to Flanders now and raced Tom Boonen and Fabian Cancellara, I would race them and I would try to beat them. I knew them personally. I could speak to them.

That was how 2014 would be for me. Third in E3; eighth in Flanders, thirty-seven seconds behind Fabian; seventh at Paris–Roubaix, twenty seconds down on winner Niki Terpstra. I was in yellow at the week-long Paris–Nice – until Fränk Schleck crashed in front of me on the Friday and took me down with him.

The Tour did Tour things to lots of plans. It may have started in Yorkshire in front of an epic crowd, but it didn't seem to want to give much else to British riders. Mark Cavendish had a horror crash in the sprint at the end of the first stage into Harrogate, mangled his shoulder and had to pull out. Froomey was carrying an injury going into the cobbled fifth stage, crashed twice more and went the same way.

Sky immediately tried to initiate Plan P with Richie Porte. We may have lost our leader and reigning champ, but I knew how strong Richie was. I'd seen how well he'd been climbing in Tenerife and the Dauphiné. I believed in him.

'Mate, just stay on my wheel. Let's smash it and see what happens.'

While that day we put time into Contador and a lot of other guys chasing GC, Richie couldn't make it stick. Over the next week or so he gradually slipped out of contention. I went on to finish twenty-second on GC, the only British rider to make it to Paris, which made me wonder afterwards: should I have just gone for it myself in Yorkshire or on the cobbles? I'd felt great on stage two, a tough old day in the Yorkshire Dales. I'd wanted to follow Nibali when he attacked and I had the legs. I decided instead to stick to the plan. I was here for Froomey. I had to trust that my time could come.

I had one more big target that year. I'd won that bronze in the points race on the track at the 2006 Commonwealth Games and then been advised by the medical team to swerve the games in Delhi in 2010. There were so few chances to represent Wales that going to Glasgow for the 2014 Commonwealth Games meant a lot to me.

Straight from Paris to Glasgow on Monday morning, I won a bronze in the time-trial on Thursday. Two days on was the road race, a city centre circuit with lots of corners and lots of climbs. To rachet up the fun a little more, it rained solidly all day.

I felt terrible in the early part of the race. I blamed having the Tour in my legs, but the longer it went on, the stronger I became. I celebrated having the Tour in my legs. I put in a dig with fifty-odd kilometres to go, to test the rest of those around me. Only two others came with me: Scott Thwaites of England and New Zealand's Jack Bauer.

With every short climb I felt better. When I attacked hard on the final lap, the other guys couldn't follow. When I punctured with 6km to go, I thought they were all going to come back to me. You're probably familiar with how long it took the neutral service motorbike to get to me, and how the mechanic's fingers turned to fat sausages as he tried to undo the skewer and change my wheel. Maybe I was unlucky. Why did this have to happen now? Maybe I was lucky. With no team radios, the two chasing riders had no idea that the gold was still dangling there for them, just up the road.

There's no humour to be found in these things at the time. You're just acutely aware that there may be two rivals coming past you at any moment. I wanted to scream at the mechanic, to tell him to just get the wheel in, that he was going to cost me gold. It wouldn't have helped. He was panicking as much as I was.

There was another problem, once he'd sorted that one. A neutral service wheel is completely different to the wheel you've had for the previous four hours. The tyre is a different width and brand. The pressure is too hard for the conditions, so when you're entering wet off-camber corners on city centre roads a lot can happen.

Sa told me afterwards that her dad had gone to get a celebratory bottle of champagne out of the fridge when I was clear, only to get back to the rest of the family, gathered around the TV, with the puncture unfolding in front of their eyes. Seldom has the bearer of bubbly received such a terrible reception. 'Eif! You've jinxed it! Put it back! Put it back in the fridge!'

Maybe it sums up my career, in a way. Never straightforward. Always a drama. Winning gold for Wales was a fantastic feeling. So, too, was being asked to carry the flag at the closing ceremony a few hours later. It might have been raining. I was on my feet at a point when most elite riders liked to be flat on their backs. I didn't care.

When you dream of winning races, you never dream of the aftermath. You never think, 'Ah, I want to win this race so I get this bonus and buy that car.' You just dream of crossing the line first and being on the podium. That's the bit that you dream about. Now I was holding the Welsh flag aloft as I crossed the finish line. I was going to carry it into the stadium as everyone back home watched. One of the sweetest feelings in my entire career so far.

Chapter nine

Tour de France 2015, stage twelve

Maybe what the Commonwealth Games gave me, more than anything else – and a solid outing at the Tour, and going close in the Classics, and riding alongside Froomey and Richie on the training camps – was confidence. I was still about proving other people wrong. By doing so I was proving other things to myself.

Right at the start of 2015 I won the Volta ao Algarve. There are bigger stage races, but there are smaller and easier ones, too. It's a race with a little of everything – a decent time-trial, a proper mountain-top finish (for February) on Malhao – and with proper riders on the roll of honour. You win a race Alberto Contador has won and it means something to you.

At Paris–Nice it was better still. Richie and I were virtual first and second GC on the final road stage back into Nice. These were our training roads. We knew every inch of them. When Richie crashed on the road into La Turbie, I thought the race might be mine.

A couple of kilometres later, coming into a tight hairpin, the other four in my lead group were all going way too hot. They all shot wide and just made the corner. I backed off and I took the inside line. What I didn't realise was that there was a little patch of oil spilled there. I went down and that was it. Richie and I limped home in the next group, and I ended up fifth on GC.

Purely in results terms it was still another step up. It just didn't feel that way. Last year I'd gone close, this year I could have gone all the way. Why did these things keep happening to me? Knocking on the door didn't seem to be working. Maybe I'd have to kick it down.

With the spring Classics next up, I did a final training ride before heading to Belgium. I felt terrible. It was only a three-hour spin with a few efforts. Where had all the good sensations gone? I could feel myself starting to talk myself out of my form. Those efforts had felt way harder than they should have done. Maybe I was coming down with something. Maybe Tim's training wasn't working. I had to have a firm word with myself. Don't be an idiot, G. All that hard work hasn't disappeared. You're not going to feel great every single day. It'll come back.

It did. At E3, the cobbled one-day race that throws a little bit of everything Classics-esque at you, I let the adrenaline and the caffeine and the racing take over. No overthinking, just riding. The crunch point of the race usually came on the famous Oude Kwaremont climb with 35km to go. I was in the lead group as we hit the steeper slopes towards the bottom and the pace felt okay. Actually, the pace felt too easy. So I attacked, without ever really having planned to attack. Only Peter Sagan and Zdeněk Štybar could follow. That was surreal in itself. I'd seen legends like Boonen and Cancellara make similar moves in the past. Now it was me.

We got over the top and stayed away. We rode well with each other, but I had absolute clarity in what I was going to do. I couldn't wait for a sprint. Sagan was Sagan and he was in his prime. I would have to go long. I waited until 4km to go. Sagan, I thought, was likely to be the stronger of the other two. When he finished his turn on the front and swung right, I hit it hard into the slight gap I'd left on Štybar's wheel and accelerated past Sagan on his blind side.

It worked a treat. It turned out Sagan was on his knees. Štybar gave chase, but he couldn't hold on. The 4km distance was perfect for a former team pursuit rider, for someone who loved time-trials. I could combine all my varied skills.

These are the days you don't forget. Riding away in the weak wintry sunshine, my black kit with the bright blue stripe down the back and blue hoop around the arm, white shoes, white-framed shades. No other British rider had ever won E3. No other rider had ever been happier with the prize, which was my own weight in Belgian beer. I did a deal with the organisers and got it delivered to my wedding in Wales later that year. That's how to get your non-cycling mates on board with the cobbled Classics scene.

I was twenty-eight years old now. I was approaching phys- ical maturity as a road rider. I had been a late bloomer as a teenager. I was growing into this in-between role of both support rider and team leader. I was seldom the main man, not yet, but I was no longer a foot soldier. I had a free role sometimes, and I was beginning to wonder what that might feel like at bigger and longer races.

With seniority and the support of the team came a certain amount of pressure. If you're up top, you have to deliver. That's why some riders prefer life in the ranks. There's still responsibility, but the brightest spotlight will always shine on someone else. I enjoyed being up there. Pressure focused my mind in training. It switched me on in races. It made me think about the way I was with those around me.

Brad could be brilliant at times. When he was on it, his ability to prepare and to bring you with him was unparal- leled. When he was struggling, his communication with his team-mates was among the first things to fall away. I could remember big races where he would drop off our wheels without warning, and we would go back and get him and ask if he was okay, and he'd tell us yes and then drop off again. Froomey was the opposite. He was always clear. He always let you know what he wanted. I didn't want to be a copy of either of them. I knew if I took the best bits and fitted them to my own personality, I had a good chance of making it all work.

I had confidence in what I could do on the road and

confidence in what it took to get me there. Weight matters when you want to win on the road. Small amounts of weight tip the racing balance as well as the scales in your bathroom. For the Classics I could keep a little on. When spring was done and summer on its way, I would begin to slim down. Something I had trialled in 2013 and got closer to in 2014 was now beginning to feel more natural, if never comfortable.

Had I been a really active civilian – let's say a good amateur rider who also held down a day job – my weight would probably have been around 75kg. I'm six foot tall. I would have been lean and fit. To do my job in the Grand Tours, I would have to get that down to 68 or 69kg. You still need power in your legs and glutes. Skinny on its own doesn't get you anywhere. So we tried things, and some worked and some didn't, and a lot of them were hard, but by the middle of 2015 we were starting to get close.

It was low-carb stuff in that era. Six-hour training rides in Tenerife when you'd only have an omelette before and a bottle or two of protein drink while you were out, maybe a rice cake if you were struggling. Inevitably, hunger followed you everywhere. You rode past tourists sitting outside cafés, eating pizza and drinking beer, and you were like a penniless kid with your nose pressed up against the toy shop window.

It was pretty extreme, but then so was I. I naturally wanted to push things to the limit. Froomey was the same, which meant we could bounce off each other and drive each other on. When I looked in the mirror now, the last traces of the muscular track rider of Olympic finals had been eliminated. My ears and nose looked like they had grown. They hadn't. Everything else had just shrunk away.

It was an extreme way of living, as a young man, but something that worked for where I wanted to be. I was accustomed now to being put in a particular category by some people within cycling: sport directors, other teams, some journalists. I was the track rider bringing that speed to the road. I was a time-trial specialist. I was a rouleur – I had a good engine, but was too heavy to climb with the best. I was a solid domestique.

What if I were all those things? What if I could be something else again? I remember seeing myself on the front cover of a cycling magazine, underneath the headline: 'Can G podium in a Grand Tour?' It was one of the reasons I was so happy with the way I rode at the Tour de Suisse in June 2015. Suisse, along with the Dauphiné, is one of the two key prep stage races for the Tour. You do a lot of climbing. You have back-to-back mountain days. You have time-trials when you're already tired from multiple days' racing.

The fifth stage finished on Sölden, across the Austrian border. Sölden is one of the hardest climbs I've ever raced up. There's no two ways about it: it's a bastard. It's steep, it's long and it's at altitude. But I held my own there. I didn't lose a heap of time to the pure climbers; I was fifth on the day, forty-seven seconds back on stage winner Thibaut Pinot.

Could I race GC as well as the Classics? Maybe here was the

answer. Suisse can be steep and it can also be super-chaotic in the finals. There are dodgy finishes and one-second gaps and all manner of traps for the unwary. By manoeuvring myself into good positions on these finals I was ending up on the right side of the splits and gaining a couple of seconds on the other GC guys. It was almost as if I had track craft and Classics strength and climbing legs and could put them all together.

I didn't win it. Simon Špilak nicked the overall win by five seconds after the time-trial on the final day. I knew Špilak would be good. He always was at Suisse and Romandie and those sorts of races. But I overhauled Pinot and I held Tom Dumoulin off. Špilak was an unusual character. It was a hot day, that final stage, and he decided to cut the arms off his skinsuit to produce the worst look ever seen on a bike. Being beaten by a rider who dressed like that left me both devastated and happy. Devastated because I thought I should have found those five seconds his bare arms and flappy seams should have cost him. Happy because this was maybe the biggest stage race result of my career so far. Confidence breeds confidence. Confidence leads to big results. Big results lead to confidence.

I'd done my new diet during the race, the low-residue one. I could have white rice and fish, chicken, yoghurt, eggs and cheese. That was about it. I couldn't have any veg, because of the fibre in it, and not much fruit either for the same reason. It was supposed to help us on the big mountain days.

Do it for the preceding two or three days and you should find you were no longer holding any waste in your gut. I could lose up to a kilo and a kilo makes a lot of difference on bastards like Sölden.

I also cut out caffeine before big races, which made my breakfasts an even duller affair. The best I could do was a decaf cappuccino, which felt like a humiliation in front of the Italians in the team. The upside came in races. When you took a caffeine hit in the final hour, you would really feel its kick. We tried other things too – nitrate shots to keep the lactic at bay, different forms of protein. The confidence this gave you mentally was as important as anything it may have been doing physically. We believed in everyone around us: nutritionists, mechanics, coaches, tacticians. They may or may not have been the best in their field. That we thought they were made all the difference.

A simple life, for me, was an easy life and also a strong one. Because I trusted those around me, I could direct all my energies into just riding my bike. I didn't have to research the benefits of beta-alanine, beetroot or any other fad supplement at the time. That had been worked out for us. I didn't have to figure out what my fuelling strategy should be on a long stage, because it had already been worked out. When bad weather was forecast for a race, I trusted that we'd have everything we needed in the right places, from hot tea to the right jackets and gloves. The clothing would be the best on the market. All I had to think about was riding my bike that day: no worrying, no overthinking, just doing what I knew I could do.

All of it came together at the Tour that summer. It was a tough old first week, all elbows-out sprints, cobbles, cross-winds and general first-week-of-Tour peloton nerves. A lot more can go wrong in the first week of the Tour than can go right. I remember seeing Vincenzo Nibali crash on a wet corner, on a day of rain and wind and too many roundabouts. It was one of those things you see in your peripheral vision – a familiar kit, a certain position on the bike, a noise and a reaction to it. 'I've just seen someone who looks very much like Nibali, going down hard . . .' And while you never want to see someone crash, you're in a bike race to win it and the repercussions are impossible to ignore. 'So if that's Nibali, that's not the worst thing in the world for us . . .'

We were keeping Froomey safe. Better than that, we were all riding well. By looking after Froomey, by making sure I was with him as long as possible and often staying with him all the way to the line, I was inadvertently creeping up the GC myself. We were going so well that missing out on a win in the team time-trial on stage nine by a single second really wound me up. A second lost to BMC was never going to decide who made it to Paris in yellow. But it felt like we could have won it and we probably should have done. Typically for our fifth man Nico Roche, he gave it everything. Maybe he gave too much too soon – like we all did – to bury himself for the team. We were used to setting our standards at the top and it leached into everything you did. Being pissed off by a single second seemed quite normal.

In a race of such fine margins, over terrain where you've suffered so badly in the past, your ability to cope with the great challenges and then begin to flourish under them is impossible to miss. I could remember being spat from the back of the group on every climb in 2007, of seeing the proper climbers come past me so easily when I was in that break in 2010. Now I was cruising up second and third category climbs. I wasn't really even thinking about them. First cat climbs – you can't cruise them, but I knew I wasn't on my limit. It was that same confidence in yourself and your preparation. A feeling of almost contentment. Of feeling lighter and stronger, of being conscious that there is less of you, but it's doing more. 'I'm travelling well here. If it kicks off, I can go with them.'

When it came to the real crunch moments, though – the hardest climbs and the last 5km – I was suffering just as much as I used to. I was just suffering at a much quicker pace. You can feel the same level of pain and experience it quite differently. Suffer in the grupetto at the back of the race and you're grovelling. Suffer with the best climbers in the world around you and there's almost a masochistic pleasure to be taken from it. The pain has a purpose. The pain is where you want to be.

The crowds on the big climbs at the Tour are always amazing. What happens when you're in the lead group is like being part of the headlining band at Glastonbury. People have been waiting to see you all day. They've been waiting all year. They've got to the front hours before and they've been drinking heavily for a large proportion of that time. They'll still be pleased to see the other acts, but they'll make more noise for this one and try to get closer. They'll yell and scream and give you all the energy they can.

You can't ignore the strength of that passion, how it makes your heart feel and the extra strength it gives your legs. As soon as you experience it you want it more. You thrive off it and it pushes you on. 'Okay, that was awesome today, being on the last line with 5km to go. Next time I want to be there with 3km to go. I want to be there with 3km to go and then react to a big attack and bring Froomey back to them. I want to go all the way.'

I felt it like never before on stage twelve, a monstrous 195km from Lannemezan to Plateau de Beille. It was 16 July, the middle of the race, the middle of France's hottest month. Plateau de Beille is an uncategorised climb. It's too big – 1780m at the summit, the climb up to it 15.8km at an average gradient of 7.9%. I was riding at the front. All the big dogs were there – Contador, Nibali, Nairo Quintana, Alejandro Valverde. Later that evening I saw a photo of me on the front and all these guys were pulling faces in my wheel. Pain faces. Suffering faces. They were hurting because of the pace I was setting.

On the team radio I could hear the names of the riders

being dropped and I could hear the regularity with which it was happening. When Quintana attacked, I reeled him back in. When he attacked again, I did the same thing.

When you do something like that for the first time, you almost gain 10 watts in morale. I'm actually doing this. 'This is amazing! It's Quintana and he can't get away from me!' It was a practical thing rather than an ego play. At the finish Froomey could sprint away at the summit to gain a few more seconds. It meant he maintained a three-minute lead over Quintana on GC, almost four minutes on Valverde, even more on Contador. Me? I was fifth on GC, sitting comfortably between Valverde and Contador.

I could feel it now. A new certainty about what I wanted to do and where I wanted to be. I loved the Classics. I loved cobbles and I loved the all-or-nothing dramas of the best one-day races. But this was another level. It was the pinnacle: the best riders in the world at the biggest bike race in its most testing moments.

It got better. Midway through the final week Froomey was still well clear of the pack and I was up to fourth. I was so focused on doing my role for the team that I didn't really take the chance to look around. I didn't take in that I was ahead of Contador, that I had a minute and a half on Nibali, that I had serious time on proper riders like Robert Gesink and Bauke Mollema and Warren Barguil. It didn't really matter to me in the moment. My job wasn't to finish as high up the GC as I could; it was to get Froomey to Paris in yellow. It wasn't to conserve my strength or marshal my resources. It was to ride in the wind. It was to do the grunt work. It was to exhaust myself repeatedly for someone else.

So when it did go wrong, I could roll with it. Three days to go, Paris within touching distance. That morning, before the start of stage nineteen, I did an interview with ITV. Walking back to the team bus afterwards, I tried to step over a low rope fence, tripped over it and did a little roly-poly on the grass. It didn't seem like an auspicious way to begin the day. I remember hoping the racing didn't go the same way.

It did. Astana, Tinkoff-Saxo and Movistar knew this was shit or bust for Nibali, Contador and Quintana, and went on the attack on the first climb we came to, the Col du Chaussy. I felt it there and I felt it again on the Col de la Croix de Fer, and this time I got spat out the back. Had I been riding for myself it might have been different. I could have regrouped, got paced back by a team-mate. But that wasn't me. Not yet. When I got dropped, I had to think about the next day's stage up Alpe d'Huez. If I couldn't help Froomey today, I could help him tomorrow. So I sat up and I rolled for the remainder of the day, and if I ended up losing more than twenty-two minutes to slip to fifteenth overall on GC, I was not the story and I was not the victim.

And I got a different level of respect from the big riders, once we'd done our repeated laps of the Champs-Élysées and Froomey had stood on top of the podium in yellow, and waved his flowers and Credit Agricole stuffed toy lion at the crowds. The year before, when I'd been Sky's road captain at the Tour, Mark Cavendish's lead-out man Mark Renshaw hadn't been able to make sense of it. 'Why the hell's G a road captain in the Tour? He's a track cyclist.' No-one was saying that now. They thought I belonged. I knew I did.

Sky had earned the respect of the old school in the peloton too. People were no longer asking what the hell we were doing. They were starting to borrow ideas from us. Where before they had sent only their team leaders and a loyal lieutenant to altitude camps in Tenerife, now they copied our approach and started sending their entire team. You saw more skinsuits on days that weren't time-trials. You saw other riders warming down on stationary trainers after big stages, as well as warming up before them.

We had a strength and depth at Sky that was making other teams reassess the untouchable fundamentals the sport thought it was built around. The size of our budget helped, but we were developing riders who joined, as well as offering them good money. As we kept winning, better riders wanted to be part of it and, because they wanted to win, too, they put the hard yards in and pushed the rest of us harder as they did so. None of us ever got complacent. There was too much competition within the team. I wanted to beat Froomey. So did Richie. Richie and I traded blows, because we both wanted to have our shots as well.

There's something you'll see a lot in elite sport. When something is being done well, it can look easy. It might be

Ronnie O'Sullivan compiling a century break, it might be Mo Salah cutting inside on to his left foot and bending the ball into the far corner. It might be Joe Root scoring all round the wicket or Mondo Duplantis breaking his own pole vault world record again and again. But it's never straightforward. It takes years of finessing and it takes constant hard work.

Critics looked at Sky and complained that we were steam-rollering the Tour by buying in big riders and using them as super-domestiques, setting a tempo on climbs that no-one else could expect to live with. They could only see the end product. They didn't see the turbo sessions before breakfast or those long, low-carb rides when you were so hungry it felt like your own stomach was trying to eat you. They didn't see the effort days in the heat when you would wear a thick undervest to help you acclimatise even more, or the dinners when you would go out with your partner and order steamed fish and spinach as they ate like a normal person in their twenties.

Our budget was a significant help. We could sign great riders. Other teams also had big budgets and were getting nowhere close. No-one was looking at Katusha and accusing them of wasting their millions. We signed good riders and then we worked together. We trained hard and we pushed each other and we gelled, because we brought in good characters as well as strong riders.

It could all feel like the most virtuous of circles in that era. All the management at the top – Dave and Rod, Tim and Fran Millar – were so immersed in the project that they pushed each other and they pushed everyone underneath them. All us riders were the same. If Tim told us to do an effort at 400 watts, that was the absolute minimum. If you were riding at the front of the line on a big day you could put rivals off attacking by your speed, but also by your collective reputation. We all bought in. The standards were so high that you felt bad if you ate an apple that wasn't officially part of your dietary regime. An apple! If it sounds insane, that's pro road racing and it was pro road racing that we were doing. Sometimes, at the very top, insane works.

For me, in the middle of it all, I felt I was both improving by stealth and getting noticed by more people than ever before. I'd been wearing my white-framed Oakleys for a long time. Other riders in the peloton had other sunglasses they were wearing, but few others seemed as distinctive as mine. It seemed to make me easier to spot, when I was in a line of similarly skinny Sky riders in dark jerseys or part of a large mass in a fast-moving peloton.

It was like Justin Tipuric in his blue scrum cap. People who knew the sport could see the work I was doing. People who came to the sport only for the big moments were able to pick me out from riders they might not have known. I could be seen and I could be seen to be working hard.

At the same time, I wasn't the focus. Froomey was in yellow, and Froomey was getting the plaudits, quite rightly so. Maybe if I hadn't blown up on stage nineteen more people would have been talking up my GC chances in the near future. Maybe if I'd tried to stay top ten on GC that afternoon, rather than sitting up to save myself for the next day, I would have popped up on more people's radars. But top ten didn't matter to me. So if you just looked at the results and saw someone in fifteenth, your eyes would log it and then take you quickly on elsewhere. You saw a good rider, but nothing amazing. You didn't think about the reasons for it or the workload I might have got through.

That was fine for me. I didn't need talk from anyone else to know what I could do now. I knew I could ride with the best and I knew I hadn't reached my limits. I knew there was a big chance I could definitely make the big jump to the very top.

I had grown to love the Tour, after that brutal baptism in 2007. Okay, I had always loved the Tour, way before I ever set eyes on it myself. But after so many long hours in its arms – days when you felt it giving you so much, days when it mainly booted you up the arse – I had a connoisseur's appreciation of its charms and challenges now. The Giro was there in my heart, too. Its quirkiness, its traditions, the way it took you to across extremes of that beautiful country. The Grand Tour I had left alone until now was the Vuelta a España. Which meant that when Tim suggested, in the aftermath of our Tour de France post-race party, that I might like to go to support Froomey, I was keen.

I had barely raced in Spain, though, so I was also wary. I'd never been a believer in attempting two Grand Tours in a single season – or rather, I liked the idea, but I wasn't sure you could be at your best in both. I'd also had a big old year already: the Tour Down Under, Dubai Tour, Paris–Nice, San Remo and all the cobbled Classics, Romandie, Suisse and the Tour, plus a Tenerife camp that may as well have been a stage race.

Wary was the right side. It was insanely hot, even for someone who thought he'd got used to the heat. The opening stages felt bad, and I realised I was physically and mentally drained. I could cope with feeling tired. The mental fatigue was worse. I couldn't recharge. I couldn't use my head to fool my legs into thinking they'd be okay.

Early on there was a big mountain day in Andorra. The profile of the stage looked like a comb: either straight up or straight down. Froomey crashed out, which left us with no leader and no real back-up plan. What had been tough, riding hard for a big GC favourite, turned out to be a lot easier than riding hard in pursuit of chasing stages. I didn't have the legs to hunt a stage myself, and I couldn't get motivated by the idea of Sky chasing the team classification – not when it mattered more to Movistar and it hurt so much just hanging on for second.

My suffering felt more extreme, because I was nowhere near the front and no-one really seemed to care. I limped to Madrid, a misery for Sa every time she spoke to me on the phone. The GC top ten looked like a Vuelta top ten from ten years before: four Spaniards, two Colombians. I had to finish. I could never let myself not finish. But it established a relationship between me and the Vuelta which was to endure for the rest of my career: I don't like you and you don't like me. Even the after-party ended in pain. I tried to get the boys into the Roxanne drinking game, where half of you drink on every mention of 'Roxanne' in the Police classic and the other half on 'red light'. I kicked it off as soon as we were on the bus. It continued at dinner. I'm not really sure what happened after that.

The silver lining? Sa and I were getting married in October. Some grooms lay off the beers in the month before they tie the knot, so they can look as good as possible on the big day. They might do a bit of extra exercise, maybe go to the gym. I did a three-week Grand Tour.

Because it was the Vuelta and I was in that much of a hole, I then undid all that good work by moping about eating and drinking shit when I got home. Never naturally a fan of the constituent parts of a salad, Sa had been forced by my own regime to develop an appreciation for quinoa and steamed vegetables. As our wedding day drew closer, the gap between us grew further and she wasn't happy. 'Why are you buying all this crap food now? Can't you just wait a couple of weeks?' She looked great. I was growing with each day.

Things started looking up in the best possible way for a

Welshman: being in the stands at Twickenham as Wales beat England in their home World Cup. We went to the England friends and family do afterwards, courtesy of my old British Cycling colleague Matt Parker, who had moved across to the RFU, which was slightly awkward when you're wearing a red shirt and got through the tension of the match with significant liquid assistance. We went to the next match as Wales beat Fiji in Cardiff, two days before the wedding, and went out on the Friday to Buffalo Bar, where we'd first met and I'd proposed. I managed to pace myself this time. Like Christmas Day, I didn't want to wake up with a raging hangover.

The day itself was shaping up so well. You realise that everyone you care about in the world is there – your closest friends, your family, your favourite team-mates. Everyone was in a great mood. Sa had a pre-match gift for me and the boys: a nice bottle of gin with cut-crystal glasses. That flew down, as did a pint in the pub on the way. Maybe that partly explains what happened when we got to the church and Sa's younger cousins, Mared and Leah, were rehearsing the songs they were going to sing during the service. They were so good that, quite unexpectedly, I found myself beginning to well up.

That was the point when Em, Sa's uncle, came over for a word of advice. 'Don't worry, Ger, you can cry. But it's happy tears. Because last week we were at the funeral of an eighteen-year-old lad. Okay?' Even as I was subconsciously asking a now pointless question – 'Why are you telling me this?' – I could feel myself blubbing up even more. As the tears rolled down my face, a fresh fear hit me: what if I were unable to stop? What if I carried on crying, which certainly felt like a real possibility, and then kept crying throughout the entire service? What if I was crying so hard I couldn't say my vows?

It was still ludicrously early. There was a full hour to go until Sa was due to arrive. I filled that hour by crying. People tried to comfort me. Friends, my mother, my brother. Their kindness just made it worse. It made me want to cry even more. At one point even the vicar told me to snap out of it. Being told off by the vicar on your wedding day is quite the shock. It didn't help.

Sa's reaction, when she walked down the aisle and spotted the state I was in, was entirely fitting. She laughed at me. She was supposed to be the crier. She and her dad had been stressing all week that they were going to spoil things by crying. I'd been bullish. 'Nah, you'll be okay. It'll be fine. Just enjoy the day. Whatever.'

It turned out alright in the end. I got my vows out. The party was great and the one-litre bottles of Kwaremont won at E3 went down well. The venue at St Tewdrics was even better. Sa liked it so much she suggested we bought it and turned it into a business venture. Ten years later she's still running it and it's still going great guns. We honeymooned on a road trip around the west coast of America – LA, Vegas,

Yosemite, San Francisco, Hawaii. It all flew by, all of it too quick. No-one there mentioned the Vuelta, carbs were encouraged and I'd also run out of my year's supply of tears. Everything was good in our world.

Chapter ten

Olympic road race, Rio, 2016

Who was I at the end of 2015? I was a married man. I was a married man with photos of himself on his wedding day with red eyes and a blotchy face. I was heading towards my thirtieth birthday. And I was a stage racer.

I planned to race one more cobbled Classic. Flanders in March was always worth a final hurrah. But when I sat down with Tim and Dave after getting back from my honeymoon to map out how 2016 might look, it was all about the week-long races and the Grand Tours beyond that. We were detailed in our planning. I wrote down a list of positives and negatives. Negatives: I hadn't yet podiumed at Flanders or Roubaix, when maybe my style of riding and love of them meant I should have done. Positives: I'd won the Tour of the Algarve, I'd come close to winning Paris–Nice and I'd finished fifteenth in the Tour while doing nothing to get higher. I wrote down the challenges: get my weight right and hold it there throughout a three-week race; deal with the pressures of leading the team and race; improve my climbing, my general threshold power and handle the spikes that come in a race situation, and perform at altitude and cope with the heat, day after day.

Then we looked at obstacles in the way. At the top of my list, I wrote one word: 'Froomey.'

Maybe that sounds bad from a decade further on. Maybe it sounds like I wanted to take him down, my own team-mate, someone I was always working for, in accidental reprise of the competition between Froomey and Brad a few years before, which had sometimes spread into messy racing days and broken personal relationships.

It wasn't. The two of us got on well. I could be honest with Froomey and I was pretty sure he felt the same way. As I improved I could feel a sharper edge to him, but it was nothing vindictive. It was pure competitiveness. He was there at the top of my list, in part because he was so good. He had an extraordinary engine. He'd won two of the past three Tours de France.

More than any of that, it was because he was number one in the team. He had proved himself, so the team would always be predisposed towards him. It was never personal with Froomey. It was that he stood in the way. I wanted a real opportunity to lead the team. He could ride for himself. I couldn't. If I was called upon I would once again give everything for him. So it wasn't about bringing him down, it was about getting the chance to see what I could do.

I don't think he particularly liked the idea of me going for GC. He was a racer. He wanted me to perform to my best, but because that served him as well as possible, not so that I became a threat to him. He never said that openly to me, although that was the impression I got. I also didn't waste any energy thinking about it. I was normal around him and he was pretty much normal around me. We both wanted the same things. That's conventional in elite sport. That's how you drive each other on.

Froomey could appear quiet and reserved from the outside. He was also a man of incredible ambition and focus. Later in 2016 he would run up Mont Ventoux in his cleats after a crash damaged his bike and the team car was stranded in human traffic further down the climb. It's become an iconic image, an illustration of competitiveness and ferocious determination whatever the odds.

To him it was just racing. He hadn't been brought up in European road racing like most of us, and that set him free. There were no preconceived ideas or beliefs to weigh him down. In his head he was just doing a bike race up a steep hill.

He could be innocent in the most useful way. When Vincenzo Nibali had changed teams in 2013, Froomey had no idea.

'God, G, that Astana guy was strong today . . .'

'Yeah, mate, that was Nibali.'

'Ah right, okay.'

But he became obsessive, as greater success came his way,

and it was Alberto Contador that fixation settled upon. He wanted to know where he was training and how he was training. He wanted to know which domestiques his team had signed. When we got to our training camp on Mount Teide and Contador was there, too, it became even more intense. Froomey wanted to know exactly what Contador was doing. If we saw him and his team out on the bike, neither of them wanted to be overtaken by the other.

Both started playing psychological games. One would ride their turbo before breakfast, knowing the other would find out. All the teams ate in the same dining room at the hotel, so Froomey would skip lunch sometimes or have something in his room, just in the hope Contador would be wondering if he was still out on his bike or skipping meals to be extra lean. We'd get in from a five-hour training ride, nailed, and Froomey would ask his soigneur if Contador was back from his own training.

That part of his character wasn't for me. I've had my rivals down the years and I've watched them closely. I've never obsessed about them. Social media and Strava seemed to make it worse for some people. 'Did you see what they did today?' 'Wow, this guy is flying – what's up with him?' I'd obsess about myself for sure – my weight, my power, my shape. But I couldn't affect anyone else. Why would I worry about them? I had confidence in what I was doing. That was all that mattered.

If you looked at the GC in the Tour around that time

Everything is different in yellow. You have to relish the attention. You start wishing it could always be this way.

Talking pre-race with my coach Tim Kerrison in 2018. Tim is a unique individual, and was a game-changer for me.

Away on training camp in early 2018, Dave B and Tim keeping an eye on things. I don't know why we were all smiling; we knew how much that day and those weeks were going to hurt.

Toasts in the team hotel after winning Stage 11 of the 2018 Tour, to La Rosière. It felt like the greatest day of my riding career. I had no idea what was going to happen on the next day.

The Col de Portet, in the final week of the Tour, where Chris Froome decided to go on the attack.

This might be the best feeling I've ever had on a bike: becoming the first British rider, and first man in yellow, to win atop Alpe d'Huez. This was the point where we all really started to believe.

First beer in a long time, the night before the final stage, with my Tour win guaranteed. Slight irritation that I've had to pause the drinking to pose for a photo. But only slight.

Contrasting suit games at BBC Sports Personality of the Year, 2018. It's a proper trophy to get your hands on. And Harry Kane and Lewis Hamilton felt like a proper podium to top.

The Tour in 2019 didn't end the way I wanted it to. But I was always going to congratulate Egan Bernal, whichever way his win had come.

An image that nicely sums up the Tour in 2022. Pogačar and Vingegaard locked in their own battle, me refusing to go away.

The Giro had always been the one that got away. In 2023, I thought I might finally get there. Primož Roglič had other ideas.

My final Tour de France, in 2025. Celebrating with my team, with my former team-mate and the unstoppable Pogi's current team-mate Pavel Sivakov, and with my lovely boy Macs. Having your son at your races comes highly recommended.

Team G at my final ever Tour. Sa, Macs and me. I did it all for them; their love and support allowed me to achieve everything I did.

you could argue that Nairo Quintana was maybe more of a threat to the yellow jersey than Contador, who had endured a rough time lately. He was starting to hit bad luck on the road: random crashes, mistakes from team-mates, mechanicals when you don't want mechanicals. Quintana could ride the high mountains and he could accelerate towards their summits where the air is thin and your legs are on their limit.

But it was Contador that Froomey judged himself by – maybe for all he had done in the sport, as Froomey gradually found that out, and then for the way he rode. At Sky we did things that made logical and scientific sense. We knew what numbers we'd need to hit to control the peloton and so we trained to be able to do that. Contador, whether at his very best or not, was the great maverick. He attacked when he fancied it. He'd go towards the end of a big stage and he'd go on the first climb. He'd launch in crosswinds and he'd go on a whim. Quintana was a huge threat and Froomey recognised that, but Contador was his obsession.

From November 2015 onwards, Froomey seemed to think about nothing else but the Tour. Other races, other aspects of life a man in his early thirties might be interested in – none of them mattered. When I looked at myself, I could see the same parts of my own character emerging and coalescing. To do well at Grand Tours, I understood now, you had to commit everything you had. You had to go all-in to succeed at the Tour, because it's too hard otherwise.

When I say commit, I mean commit. My thirtieth birthday

fell during our training camp in Tenerife in May 2016. Sa came over to celebrate the big day with me. There wouldn't be any champagne. There might be one small slice of some sugar-free cake. There would certainly be a six-hour ride. If there's one time when you can enjoy a proper cake surely it's four hours into a six-hour ride. Tim was still baffled by Sa's presence. He asked some of the boys: 'What's she doing here? Did you know Sa was coming?' It didn't compute for him. Why would you want to spend time with your wife on your birthday when there was training to do and recovery after that?

Everything had to be about optimising your riding. All the focus was on moving forward: new innovations, cuter science, better ways of doing things. Tim wanted us on a different breakfast, something used by Kenyan runners that was supposed to be high in carbs but easy to digest. I never really took in what it was meant to be called; I just referred to it by how it looked and tasted, which was baby porridge. Was Contador eating baby porridge? I doubted it. Froomey was. And because Froomey was, so was I. We were all on this journey together. Froomey was wanting to maintain and win more, and I was sort of looking to take his crown – for one race, at least.

It worked. I retained my Volta ao Algarve title in February, holding on behind Contador on the big fifth stage to keep my GC lead. In my head that cemented me as a decent stage racer. Now it was time to step up at World Tour level and Paris–Nice.

I had a decent start in the prologue and over the gravel in stage one. In the big mountain test up to the summit of Madone d'Utelle I was second behind Ilnur Zakarin, but finished ahead of Contador to take the overall lead. The next day was the traditional hard stage around Nice and up Col d'Èze. I could feel the nerves banging hard. Would I have the same legs as yesterday? Could I hold off a raging Contador, plus Richie Porte?

Contador went all-in early, attacking up Peille. I knew these roads well, the team around me was great, and we brought him back. When we hit the bottom of Èze, he went again, but once again we responded. My team-mate Sergio Henao buried himself alongside me on the climb and then the descent back to Nice. We kept the gap to eleven seconds and took the race by four seconds – the biggest win of my career so far.

Why was I happy pushing myself so hard? Why did I put baby porridge ahead of a slice of actual cake on my birthday? Because every second counted at the very top. I'm not sure a piece of Victoria sponge would have slowed me by four seconds on the Col d'Èze, but it felt like every mouthful mattered – not just for that one moment, but for the attitude it encapsulated. Commit to everything. Commit so hard even a mouthful is only really a mouth half full.

Flanders went fine. I helped Luke Rowe out in the final; he came in fifth, I was twelfth. Had I won, it wouldn't have changed my focus. It might even have made it easier. There were no guarantees when it came to racing. Maybe that was the lesson of all those cold, windy February and March days in northern Europe. That was fine. Now I was aiming for the GC at stage races, I wanted to know I was giving it my best shot, to not be scared of failing.

Richie Porte had moved on that winter, to BMC, partly for the same reason I had put at the top of my obstacles list. He wanted a tilt at GC, too. His solution was to be number one in a different team. I'd also had some serious opportunities to leave for other teams, including big boys like Garmin and Trek. I stayed because I thought Sky gave me the best chance of improving fastest. What was the point in being leader of another team if I didn't have the legs to win?

Tim was the ideal coach, even with his views on birthday celebrations. He coached riders to victory in four Grand Tours. His expertise would be essential to what I wanted to do. I also had to be the centre of it and I had to be the one driving it along. This was what I had learned, initially from Brad, and then even more so from Froomey. You had confidence in the experts around you, but you had to take ownership of it.

It felt like Tour de Suisse was my chance to prove to the doubters what I could do. Froomey had chosen the Dauphiné as his pre-Tour prep race. That left me Suisse. I wanted to perform – and maybe that's where I went wrong. Dropping my weight from my old Classics build, itself a significant drop from my old track weight, had made such a difference to my performance in stage races that I decided to keep pushing it.

If I had been a low 68kg the previous summer, then what if I could get down to 67kg? Surely then I'd be flying. Surely then I'd make the final step up.

I got down there, even though it was pretty horrendous. I could cope with being hungry all the time. I was sort of used to it now. There was a strange satisfaction in looking at myself in the mirror and seeing sinews sticking out and bones sharper than they had been before. I enjoyed the discipline of the regime. Not eating as much as your body wanted you to eat was an hourly physical manifestation of my total commitment to what I wanted to be. It just didn't work in racing. Rather than that extra kilogram lost making me faster, it made me slower. It cost me power. It cost me energy.

The weather was bad and I felt colder and weaker than I ever had in all the bad weather I'd ridden through before. The first two big mountain stages I was nowhere. I just shivered my way up. I pulled a little something back in the time-trial, coming home ninth to inch up to eighth on GC. But I wasn't doing all this for ninth in a TT against riders I would usually beat in a TT. I wasn't doing it for eighth on GC. I definitely wasn't doing it so I could fall away completely on the final stage, losing eleven minutes to riders nowhere close to Froomey's class on a stage shortened by the weather to a mere 57km. I finished seventeenth on GC, more than twelve minutes down on winner Miguel Ángel López.

I was hugely disappointed, but I was happy to own it. I'd

taken a gamble on the weight and I'd got it wrong. I knew now that 69kg was my starting point for stage racing. If it went longer than a week, the daily privations would bring me down to 68kg by the end anyway; it's almost impossible to physically eat enough at the Tour to match the calories you're expending. So I didn't panic, even as the team seemed stressed. 'G, just stick to the basics. G, stop worrying about shared leadership with Froomey. Just go there and do what you're good at.'

I knew what had gone wrong. I had two weeks before the Tour to correct the imbalance; enough time to freshen up and fuel. I told myself that by the time of the Grand Départ at Mont Saint-Michel I would be fine. Throughout the Tour I would eat properly and I'd have my power back and it wouldn't be an issue.

It wasn't. I felt good in France. It was just that the old power dynamic never looked like it was going to change. Froomey was never flawless. He was human. He would have tougher days. But his confidence never dipped. If he felt a weakness, he was never going to show it to any of his team-mates.

That belief was impressive to witness. He expected a huge amount from himself, but also those around him, so it was Froomey who set the team's tempo and Froomey who owned the narrative. On stage eleven we both followed an attack in crosswinds by Peter Sagan and his team-mate Maciej Bodnar, 12km from the finish, straight out of a roundabout, Froomey third wheel, me fourth. The effort was insane. I couldn't quite believe we were even attempting to nick some time on such a flat finale. There was one thought in my head: 'Oh, we're actually doing this, are we?' There wasn't room for much else. It was too intense. I had to take a turn on the front just to get a breather and hope the others didn't realise what I was doing.

Froomey ended up stealing twelve seconds over the other GC contenders. On stage twelve, when a TV motorbike brought him down, along with Bauke Mollema and Richie, his bike damaged and our team car stuck down the mountain, he set off up the mountain in his cleats. On stage nineteen, from Albertville to Saint-Gervais-les-Bains, he crashed again, sliding out on a long right-hand hairpin. This time he was pushing it a bit too hard on the descent; he had a tendency to push too hard when he didn't need to. Once more the team car was too far back. I gave him my bike so he could crack on. This time I was the one running down the road. When the team car arrived, it drove straight past me to get to Froomey. You become quite direct yourself on the team radio in these sorts of scenarios. 'Guys! You need to stop! I don't have a bike. And we've still got a climb to do . . .'

I finished fifteenth on GC. Exactly the same as the year before. It wasn't what I wanted at the start of the year and from the outside it probably looked like I hadn't stepped up at all. But I took confidence from the context. I'd given my best efforts and my bike to Froomey. I'd had a mechanical on stage fifteen from Bourg-en-Bresse to Culoz, which had cost me a chunk of time, too.

Harder to cope with was the idea I was being overtaken by others who were younger and less experienced. Adam Yates finished fourth on GC at that Tour. Romain Bardet was second. Richie, in his first year away from Sky, was fifth. None of them got within four minutes of Froomey in yellow.

I liked Adam and his brother Simon. Adam had ridden a great race, but I didn't enjoy seeing him performing better than me. Not in a spiteful sense, just in an honest way. I wanted to be in the mix for podium places. I wanted what he had.

You have to be competitive as an elite sportsperson. If you're okay with people your age and your ability beating you, you're never going to make it. You won't even get to the point where you can think about making it.

As a younger rider I'd loved pushing myself against Ian Stannard. That had been quite a friendly one. As I got older, I looked further afield. I looked at Matt Goss in Australia, a track rider getting a lot of wins and hype, and I felt the sharp edges of his success – 'Jeeez, if he's doing it, why can't I?' I'd moved on to riders like Simon Clarke, another Aussie, another rider I could see elements of myself in. None of it negative, all of it motivational. 'Right, if they can do it, why can't I?'

I was aware of some of the chat about me, post-Tour. I was thirty years old now. Yatesy was twenty-three. I had worn the white jersey for the best young rider; he had just won it. I knew some people inside the sport were looking at me and thinking that I was coming into my best years and still not quite delivering. They were wondering how long these best years might last and if perhaps they might not be as best as some of the younger riders coming through.

It was never a thing for me. I might have entered my fourth decade, but I'd still been winning world and Olympic titles on the track four years before. I'd stopped riding the Classics only four months ago. In terms of my GC journey, I was still young and I still had a way to go. There was no sense for me of time running out, only things I wanted to improve upon, only things I could see myself getting better at.

Others could stereotype me if they wanted. I believed.

It's seldom linear, progress. And cycling is seldom consistent in the love it gives you. Sometimes it puts an arm round you on a bad day, takes you off for a six-hour adventure and drops you home again full of weary warmth and good vibes. Other times it just gives you a good kicking. And as you're lying there on the deck, it doesn't walk away. It carries on booting you.

From a distance, the Olympics road race in August 2016 looked good: a super-strong British team representing my past and my present – Stannard, Froomey, Adam Yates, Steve Cummings and me – and a course that was a proper test, starting and finishing on the sea-front at Copacabana, but heading off into the hilly wilds in between. If 2012 had been a route that was hard for the GB team to police for Cav, even with its multiple ascents of Box Hill, this one looked like a proper one-day Classic. The climbs were big climbs, probably enough to take the pure sprinters out of it, but dramatic and punchy enough not to favour the pure climbers too much. A parcours, in short, to make a man raised on Belgian climbs yet at home on the longer stuff very happy indeed.

Froomey obviously fancied it. That was his confidence and ambition, but he'd never done well in a one-day race and I knew that, and Rod Ellingworth, who had stepped across from Sky to coach the team, knew it, too. Of course Rod respected him hugely. He'd seen him transform from an unknown Barloworld wannabe into the best GC racer of his generation, and he thought he had an outside chance if everything went his way. Same for Yatesy. He could definitely perform on this sort of terrain and he was a good wildcard option. Stannard was the dream domestique with Steve Cummings the wise old head, an all-round strong guy.

Me? I came out of the Tour well. As a team we all popped over to race the RideLondon one-day race, which pretty much followed the route of that 2012 Olympics road race. Stannard and I went early and forced a break. I attacked again at the top of Box Hill and went clear. Maybe I should have waited for him; it turns out going solo for 50km through Surrey is a big ask. The peloton caught me 2km from the finish outside Buckingham Palace. It can happen like that after the Tour.

You're either nailed and good for nothing but burgers and a sun-lounger or you have a couple of easier days, and then that whole accidental training load kicks in and your legs feel superb.

We flew to Rio the next day and the plan started coming together. Stannard and Steve would help control the race. We would ride a standard bike for the first half, get across a pretty gnarly cobbled section a couple of times, and then switch to lighter bikes for the climbing. There are no race radios at the Olympics or the Worlds. It's all motorbikes with chalkboards and time gaps scrawled on them. If you got away, you were harder to track. When races get disjointed and no-one's quite sure what the gap is, who's there and who's meant to be reacting and who should be chasing, that's when you can make a decisive move.

There's a question that gets asked on team buses sometimes to pass the time on long journeys from the stage finish to the hotel: would you rather win the Worlds road race or the Olympics? A lot of overseas guys would say the Worlds. Those rainbow bands are iconic and yours for a whole year. I was always about the Olympics. I'd watched them on TV as a kid and I'd won my two gold medals on the track. If you were British, you grew up loving the Olympics, and if you were British in this Lottery era, you loved seeing us climbing the medal table.

Then there was the person I was. You get some riders who are always about individual success. It's just their heads and what motivates them. You get others who love the team role – riders like Luke Rowe. They don't want the individual pressure, but they love the communal success. The balance of the individual and the collective is the tension and the beauty at the heart of cycling. Only one man can win the yellow jersey, but the yellow jersey can never be won by one man.

I was one of those in the middle. I enjoyed helping others, being part of a team, sharing a plan and going for it together. When you're coming through the ranks, even though you're not winning you find success in these other ways. But I enjoyed it as long as I knew there was a point in the near future when I would get that shot as well. Rio felt like that moment. I had raced for Froomey and the team in France. I'd ride for others again if they looked better on the day. If it felt like my day, I'd go for that chance hard. I wouldn't let others elbow me aside. I would seize the day.

I know how to ride one-day races. The trick is to stay calm and to hold back. Of course, you want to go hard early. Everyone does. You've got all that adrenaline and desire inside you. I felt decent in the first half of this race – nothing special, but okay for now. I had a calmness, even when things looked like they might be going wrong. We hit the cobbled secteur and I was glad I wasn't on my lightweight bike, because we hit the cobbles so fast Stannard snapped his frame. Sudden chaos, bikes and bottles everywhere. Stannard was gone, never to make it back.

Froomey and I changed bikes. We got back to the group,

legs feeling the benefit of the lighter frames. Second time up the climbs, attacks going off the front, I was still feeling alright. We had the freedom to race now, and when Nibali and an Italian team-mate launched, I chased after them.

Coming into the final descent out of the forested hills there was only a small group a couple of seconds ahead with everyone pushing it hard – or perhaps too hard. Nibali crashed out on a corner. I passed him as he lay on the dark tarmac. That left just Rafał Majka up the road – a good rider, a great climber, but a man you'd enjoy taking on in a flat finish, a man you could attack by going long with a few kilometres to go, or kick past hard with a big sprint at the death, too.

Louis Meintjes was descending with me, another climber, a group with Greg Van Avermaet and Jakob Fuglsang close behind us, but not taking any seconds back. I felt confident on the descent, although it was an ugly thing. Every corner was different – some bumpy, some greasy, some with washes of gravel, others tightening up unexpectedly.

I went just a fraction too fast into the final one. The road was rough. My back wheel skipped out, bounced into the storm drain at the side of the road and I was down. I got back up. I rode into the finish, but in that moment, my race was over. The race I wanted to win, anyway. I pedalled in with Rui Costa and he started sprinting for tenth place. I let him have it. Who cares about tenth?

Even now, almost a decade on, it's the one race that still

irritates me, that still gets to me. I was confident I could have ridden Majka down. Greg and Jakob did. Even had those two got back to me, I would still have fancied my chances of hitting them long and winning. Instead I rolled across the line with my skinsuit all ripped and half the skin on my shoulder and arse left a few miles back up the road on that shitty, bumpy corner.

Sa was there. Neither of us wanted to speak. We certainly didn't want to think about bike riding. We spent the next day drinking beers and eating chips and watching the beach volleyball, at least until Rod called and asked if I fancied taking one of the spots that had opened up in the time-trial.

I did try pointing out to him that my body was beat up. I mentioned I was already three gin and tonics deep. He still got me to do it. It was grim. I grovelled through and managed ninth, which was decent in the circumstances, but I hadn't gone to the Olympics just to be at the Olympics. I'd gone for glory. I'd gone for the win.

I had to keep the faith. That was in me, too: a belief less obvious than Froomey's, a determination less demonstrative than Brad, but something inside that wouldn't yield, either. Others might think I was stuck in the middle forever. I was looking longer. I was looking for that magic moment.

Chapter eleven

Giro d'Italia 2017, stage nine

It's a tough one to take when you've just crashed out of contention for Olympic gold on the very final corner of the last descent. It must be harder for friends and family that want to message you with some support. What do you say?

'It's only a race, it's not the end of the world.'

'Oh my God, that is an absolute disaster.'

'Eleventh place is still amazing. There were only ten riders better than you!'

'I reckon he deserved to win. Don't you?'

'Poor you, are you okay?'

'Are you okay?'

'Are you okay?'

I felt unlucky, at times. Bumpy roads, back wheels sliding, punctures and bad breaks. I felt lucky, too. Sa and I had been married for less than a year when the crash in Rio happened. She was there at the finish on Copacabana, just as she'd been at the finish in Paris–Nice when that didn't work out either.

She had seen the raw emotion from me every time. And she never once said the wrong thing.

I guess it's easier, if you're the partner and you're not at the scene of the crime. You can speak on the phone for fifteen minutes and offer love and condolences and then hang up and never have to deal with the full effects of what they're going through. Sa? She was there, and she always got it right. She knew sometimes she had to leave me to it. She knew when to let me be angry and annoyed and upset.

It's about giving you space and giving you support at the same time. Sa and I are similar in lots of ways. She's naturally positive. She doesn't like a moaner. She's good at cracking on with things. Her parents Beth and Eif are the same, just like my mum and dad. So she felt the same as me, and reacted the same way, but learned from watching and feeling it too.

The constant desire to cheer the other person up doesn't really work for me. You'll get over things in your own time, I find. I don't need someone telling me every ten minutes that the world hasn't ended. I definitely don't want someone being extra bubbly and extra chatty. I'm not the chattiest of people at the best of times. My bubbliness is below the radar. But Sa could always find the right balance, even as she was experiencing the same disappointments and regrets, just as she could when I'd had a few too many beers and they might be returning to say hello again. Summary: don't rub my back, just leave me to it.

It's great, being in a relationship with someone who's

winning, if your version of great involves a partner whose ribs and hip-bones stick out and who eats less than you do and needs to spend all the time they're not out riding lying around with their legs up. When it's going wrong – and there can only be one winner of a bike race, which means that 180 others might all feel like losers – you absorb all their unhappiness while having to tuck yours away somewhere hidden too. Being with a rider is not like being a footballer, when they're at home every night they're not playing and they train from 10am to midday four times a week and then go home again. I was away all the time, either racing or on training camps. When I was home I was tired and distracted. My focus was on the bike. All my energies were directed at my day job, and the days were seven a week.

When racing days went against me, Sa could gently point me in the right direction without ever forcing it, in a similar manner to my mum and dad in my younger years. She would make it clear she was there if I wanted and when I was ready. She would let me lean on her but also step out of my way. She didn't need to be front and centre.

It helped that we had grown up through it all. When we first got together at the end of 2009 I had been a pro for three years, but it was still the pre-Sky era. As my focus around road riding tightened, we became closer, and she learned with me. It's different if you've been a pro for a decade and then you start going out with someone who has no real idea about the lifestyle. Sa saw the commitment I had to give.

When I was upset after a bad result, when I was tired and trying not to eat too much, when I was hangry – my way of dealing with it was to go quiet. I wouldn't want to talk about what I was going through or how her day had been, and I definitely wouldn't want to go out for a meal or a few drinks. She had a lot to put up with. She never complained.

She changed her life because of me. Missing her graduation from university to be with me in Newport before the 2012 Olympics; getting first-class honours in her degree, and not following up on that because of my day job and where I had to be. Being judged by some people for sacrificing her own ambitions for mine. All of it made us even more of a team.

Humour always helped. Sa could take the mickey out of me, gently, when that was the right thing to do. She could make a joke out of something, if it could take the tension out of a bad moment. She was the safe space where I could recover and rebuild.

So the Olympics hurt, but they didn't break me. We got over them, together. The gin and tonics helped. The caipirinhas on Copacabana were stronger than either of us realised. When we got home and I talked to the team about the targets for the 2017 season, we came up with a tweaked plan: I would go for the Giro d'Italia.

It was one of those ideas that felt like it made sense. Froomey was always going to get priority at the Tour de France, even if I was going better than ever before. The team wanted to make Mikel Landa co-leader with me in Italy, but that was fine. If he was up the road one day, I could sit on and use the others. If I was up the road, others would have to chase. It really could be a two-pronged attack. Sharing with Landa was completely different to sharing with Froomey, because you were never really sharing with Froomey. It was the same sort of sharing that now goes on with my son Macs when we open a chocolate bar. I get one small square and he eats the rest.

In any case, I had a proper soft spot for the Giro. I'd ridden it in prep for the 2008 and 2012 Olympics, which had ended in happier circumstances than the 2016 version. I loved racing in Italy. I had lived in Quarrata with Cav and the boys as we learned the ropes under Rod Ellingworth, and the food and the culture and the pure love of cycling very naturally worked for me. I liked the feel of a different challenge to being Froomey's designated plan B when plan A never failed. I liked the idea of seeing what I could do.

Critically, my legs felt good. Targeting the Giro meant I had to be on the regime sooner than usual. There could be no steady build-up from December to July. I had to be ready for May. That meant training in November with an intent and purpose far beyond normal.

It felt good: strong on the first training camp of the year, not taking a kicking, okay at altitude. Froomey and I went on a camp to Crystal Springs in South Africa. Just the two of us, coach Tim, a swanny, a mechanic and a local chef Froomey knew. I was told it would be baking hot. It rained every day instead. We got some great work done all the same. We mainly managed to prevent the local wildlife infiltrating our apartment and stealing the food. Monkey see, monkey do. When I got home I was lighter and found the more familiar local climbs easier than before. The ceiling of watts I could produce had been raised, and numbers that had taken serious effort before felt easier. I could ride at 350 watts the way I'd ridden at 320 before.

Good form feeds into confidence which feeds back into form. It's the same for all of us, elite road racers or not. If you're feeling good about yourself, you look in the mirror and think that you look okay. That makes you feel even better about yourself. If you've had a big meal the night before and you're hungover, or something went wrong at work and you're down on yourself, you'll look in the mirror and think you look more tired. You'll think your skin doesn't look so good or you've put on weight.

When I stood on the scales now – and I did it every morning – I was the weight I was supposed to be. My legs looked like I wanted them to: skinny and strong at the same time.

I suffered on the bike. So dysfunctional was the strange little world I lived in that I was delighted to find I could now suffer for longer and deeper. The tribulations of the last few years had also given me a perspective that not all riders of my age shared. I understood that I wasn't going to be blasting new peaks of power on every ride. I would have bad days. I would have bad days in Grand Tours, because that's the nature of racing for twenty-one days across three weeks. It's a bloody Grand Tour. It's not supposed to be easy.

Just because you wanted to win or make the podium didn't mean you were going to be floating through every stage. You had to suffer for it. Hence the pleasure to be taken in your pain; with it, you hurt, but without it, you weren't doing enough.

Suffering is a mental process as well as a physical sensation. You see it in every race, and I've done it too, but when you're on a bad day, you lose a bit of faith. You drop to the back in the group or dangle out the back of the peloton. If you're not with your team, and your boys are all at the front and you're at the back, it's twice as hard on your head. You're better with them, in amongst it all, stronger as a unit. At the back on your own you're an outsider, struggling alongside fellow stragglers in your own world of turmoil. You're the kid in the corner of the playground on their own with all your mates in the distance having fun. Between you are the tough kids who want to kick your head in. Don't stay there. Bust a gut to get back to your gang. Make space for each other, take belief from their presence. Don't be the lonely one.

In March I led the team at Tirreno–Adriatico. Seven stages down the west coast of Italy and across the mountainous spine to the east. Perfect as a Giro leg-stretcher.

The team time-trial on the opening stage was explosive. Our new carbon wheels disintegrated as we hit top speed over the multiple potholes there seem to be on Italian roads. Gianni Moscon went down, which left us with a problem: the team's time would be taken on the fifth rider home. When some of your team need new wheels and a few more need picking up and putting back on their bikes, it takes the wind out of your speedy sails.

We limped in a minute and forty seconds down on BMC. That took me out of GC contention, but I had a decent week. I won a stage by attacking up the final climb, getting a gap and soloing the final 8km to the line. That felt good – really good. Even better was the way I was able to race. Sky had a style of racing for GC. It was efficient and successful but very calculated. Out of GC contention I was able to race as if I were at the Classics – more carefree, more on instinct. It spilled over into how I raced at the five-day Tour of the Alps straight afterwards: I took the overall.

All of which meant, going to the Giro, I was feeling like ten men but looking like half a man, in my eyes – the ideal combination for a GC contender. I was confident. I wanted the race to be as hard as possible, because I believed we had trained harder than anyone else, and their hard would be our easy. Deep down I knew that wasn't real. The confidence that came from my benign delusion was.

Sky had never won the Giro. Brad had tried and failed, Richie had a go but couldn't make it, Landa the same. I felt it suited me. The Giro is less controlled than the Tour. There's always tight roads or a tricky descent or bad weather. You've got to have real race-craft and you've got to be technically good.

And I started really well, too. I came home third on stage four to Mount Etna, and was second on GC at the end of the first week. My legs felt great. The internal dynamics of the team were working perfectly.

Ah, the best-laid plans . . . Late in stage nine we were racing into the bottom of the final climb of the day, Blockhaus. A biggie, a nasty one. It's a key point in any bike race, the run-in to the final climb. All the GC teams want their man in the top ten on the road when it tilts upwards.

We were in a good position as a team, on the left behind Sunweb. Then, as we dipped round a long sweeping left-hander, I saw a police motorbike parked on the road. The first rider swerved to miss it. The second, Wilco Kelderman, wasn't as quick to react, and rode straight into him. Instantly there was a chain reaction. Riders going down everywhere, including me.

I hit the deck hard. I felt a lot of things hurt.

I lay there on my right side, barely able to move. My shoulder hurt the most, but what was freaking me out was not being able to lift myself up. Someone came over and helped me sit up. As they did, I felt my shoulder pop back in. It felt extraordinarily nice compared to the second before.

Back on the bike, always back on the bike. A few of the boys waiting for me. Ignoring the pain, brain in racing mode. 'I have to keep fighting. It's early on in the race. Fuck how

I feel at the moment. We can assess that later. Let's get to the finish. Just get to the finish . . .'

Trouble was, by the time we got there I'd lost so much time I'd dropped to seventeenth on GC, more than five minutes down on Nairo Quintana. Then there were the literal storm clouds ahead. Dave had organised a helicopter to spare us a long four-hour bus ride to our next hotel. I didn't fancy it, even in my physical distress. The clouds were too heavy and the chopper too small. Dave persuaded me. Ten minutes into the flight, the pilot changed his mind. The long bus ride became an even longer one.

Sa had been travelling out to support me that same day. Only later did she tell me she'd had a premonition of doom on the plane. When she arrived, she found me trying to shower myself with an arm that wouldn't move beyond 90 degrees. A new landmark for our relationship: sitting in a bathroom modified for wheelchair users, Sa on a chair just to one side, holding the shower head and washing the dirt and sweat from me while I sat there trying to keep the ominous thoughts at bay.

The first stage after that rest day was a time-trial. I knew I could get round, especially after the broken pelvis TT at the Tour four years before. I gave it everything I had left, and somehow managed to finish second, taking some time back on the other GC boys. But a fifty-minute effort is not a five-hour stage. A fifty-minute effort when you're badly injured also takes the last dregs of strength out of you.

It was when the road stages started again that I knew my

lamb was roasted. My knee was the worst. I didn't have the power on the climbs and I couldn't hold a wheel on the flat. Two days after the TT, I got dropped on a small-ish climb and then couldn't get back on the descent, even with five team-mates around me. I felt I was letting them down. All their efforts, and I couldn't make them worthwhile.

That night, I had a long chat with Dave and Tim outside the kitchen truck. They had an idea. I could keep suffering round the Giro, keep using up team-mates, all to maybe get an outside shot at a stage towards the end. The GC was long gone. Or I could go home, recover, and think about going to the Tour to help Froomey. The tried and tested plan they all loved so much.

They were right, really. I knew that. At this stage of my career it wasn't about slogging round for no reason. It was about winning. That Giro felt wide open for me, too. Tom Dumoulin won it, and he's a great rider, but we were really well matched. It would have been a close fight, I'm sure, I just never got the chance to find out. And it doesn't hurt any less, today, for what I would go on to do at the Giro in future years. The Giro would still be the one that got away.

So I went home, and I got fit, fitter than I thought I could in that time, and inadvertently ended up with a decent consolation prize: I would be racing the Tour.

It began with a 14km prologue in Dusseldorf. It rained, for most of the day, but I seemed to flow around the corners nicely. Fast and smooth but never too much.

I always had a tendency to start a bit too hard and end up blowing up, in these sort of short efforts. Rare are the prologues when you feel like you're right on the limit but not quite over it.

This was one of them. Coming into the last few kilometres, the road following the long slow bend of the river to the left, I had this wonderful feeling of free power in my legs. I knew it was a good one. I was able to drive all the way to the line. I just didn't know quite how good until I'd crossed the line.

You go into the hot seat, when you take the lead. There on camera, acutely conscious you're being watched, keen too to take on fuel and not just sit there getting cold and stiff. And as I sat there with my swannie Marko, watching riders coming in and missing my time, I didn't mess about. I hoped they all went slower. It could keep raining. The corners could get trickier.

Froomey was the last man out, as defending champion. Of course I didn't want him to have a bad day. I just didn't want him to have as good a day as me. About 200m out from the finish, I knew he wasn't going to. I was in yellow.

It would have been an amazing feeling anyway, going into the leader's jersey at the Tour. After the heartbreak of the Giro, and all the nearly-not-quites, it was almost unreal. Zipping up the jersey on the podium, being given the stuffed toy lion, going through all the post-stage interviews – all this was for other riders from more exotic places, when I was growing up. It wasn't for kids with Welsh names from suburbs no-one had heard of.

Or maybe it was. I stayed in yellow on the second day, a bunch sprint won by Marcel Kittel. You feel like you stand a little taller, when you're in yellow. You ride through the peloton each morning to start at the front. All the other boys have to make way for you, which is quite symbolic. When you're racing, riders make room for you, slightly.

I loved it. And it didn't feel wrong. It felt like where I belonged. It felt like what I wanted to keep doing.

Froomey took it back, after five days, on Planche de Belle Filles. I guess it was always going to happen, but it didn't make it feel any easier. It's amazing how quickly you get used to putting the yellow jersey on each morning and pinning your race numbers to it. When you're suddenly back in your ordinary kit, it's like walking out of the cinema at the end of an amazing film and finding yourself on a familiar high street in the rain. You knew it wasn't going to last, but it carried you along to another world while it did.

I still enjoyed being second on GC for another four days. It was certainly more enjoyable than what happened next. It was stage nine, again, the cursed stage, and Sa was once again flying out to be with me on the rest day. I've got nothing against Rafał Majka. He's a very good rider. I just wish he hadn't been so keen to descend the Col de la Biche, that he ended up crashing and taking me with him.

It happened so quickly I didn't even have time to swear.

It didn't feel right; it was pretty sore. But I didn't want to believe the team doctor when he told me I'd broken my collarbone. Not because my collarbone didn't feel painful enough to be broken. On that measure we were spot on. It was what it meant.

'Nah, doc, it can't be broken ...'

Thinking about what had happened at the Giro.

'Honestly, it doesn't feel like it's broken.'

Obviously not true, but worth a go.

'G, it's broken. It's definitely broken.'

Our mechanic Gary Blem was standing there patiently with my bike. He asked me if I wanted it. I said yes.

I climbed on. The doc told our second car to stay with me. 'He's got a broken collarbone ...'

I began trying to pedal down the descent. It wasn't great, but I was still moving. I was still technically in the Tour. Then I noticed that my left shoe was loose. I leaned down to tighten it, putting all my weight through my right arm. That's when I realised. Maybe I *had* broken my collarbone.

It was at the bottom of the descent, riding into the valley, that the ambulance was parked up. The second team car came alongside me.

'Right, come on, G. We need to stop now.'

I just needed telling, really. I didn't want to accept it. I wanted to keep going. And then when I was in the ambulance, those thoughts changed. 'This bone better be fucking broken, now ...'

Such a weird feeling, leaving that race. We were in the middle of nowhere, a strange part of France you'd otherwise never go to. An airport where you have all your bags but also your arm in a sling. But it wasn't that. It was the knowledge that the boys would miss you in the team meeting that morning, but as soon as they started racing, you'd be forgotten about. You'd be the same, in their position. You can't look backwards, at the Tour. All the stuff you need to worry about is up the road ahead of you.

I had an operation to put a plate in my shoulder soon after that. I couldn't bring myself to watch much more of the race. Because Sa hadn't planned on me being around so soon, she was on a hen-do, which left me staying at my mum and dad's like I was fourteen years old again. There wasn't even my little brother around to beat on the PlayStation anymore.

At least being in Cardiff meant that I could ignore cycling in a way I couldn't have done in Monaco. We lived in Monaco for the cycling. It wasn't the real world. Cardiff was. I could stroll into a café for a coffee, and it was more normal and a lot easier to forget the Tour was going on without me. I went to a T20 match at Sophia Gardens the day after my op with Sa's father Eif and her brother Rhys. The game was abandoned because of rain, which seemed a little lightweight for a rider used to pedalling through everything.

What did I do? What I always did. Refocus, new goals, get going again. I rehabbed, and I climbed back on my bike, and

I kept believing my luck would change. I rode the Tour of Britain, and it finished in Cardiff. That felt good, other than the weather. I got a good reception.

I had no idea, at that stage, the reception I was going to get in Cardiff eleven months later. How could I have done?

Chapter twelve

Tour de France 2018, stage twelve

Years that had started well and gone a little off course. Years that had promised a lot and delivered but left me wanting more. Years of hope, sprinkled with disappointment and telling myself to keep going no matter what. Keep pushing. Keep trying. Keep doing everything right and putting yourself in the position to reap the benefits.

And then 2018, when you might have stopped the clock at a certain point and said, nah, this one isn't working out for you, mate. And if you had, I'd have missed the most sensational adventure of my riding life. Something that changed everything, forever more.

So, the start. The part that might have fooled you. I was going well at the start of the year at the Tour of the Algarve, and I really fancied winning it for the third time. I was in the yellow jersey on the final stage, then in the opening 20km my team-mate Michał Kwiatkowski jumped in the break with his Polish compatriot Michał Gołaś. You don't chase down a team-mate, so that was that. I was disappointed, but Kwiato won the stage and the overall. I told myself there were bigger fish to fry.

I went to Tirreno, a race I'd always wanted to win, partly for its history, partly for my track record of being unlucky there, slightly more for its incredible trophy. Kwiato won that as well, when I dropped my chain in the last kilometre on the big mountain day and lost time. Tirreno is much bigger than Algarve. My legs felt great, good enough to win it. That one was harder to take.

Then came the strangest Roubaix I ever did. Strange because I was no longer trying to win it. I was GC light, not Classics big. But the Tour had a cobbled stage that year over a decent chunk of the route, and Dave and Tim thought it might be worth doing as a recon and way to get my cobbles muscle memory back up to speed.

The night before, I convinced myself it was a bad idea. The Tour riding a section of Roubaix is not the same as Roubaix. The peloton is a mix of the best, in all its guises: Classics boys, yes, but also GC guys, pure climbers and everything else in between. The Tour also races over cobbles in its own way. GC teams line up to protect their main men. Stage hunters go hunting. In Roubaix, everyone just attacks it and gives it everything they have. You had to be fearless, not half in, thinking of other prizes down the line. You had to fight it to a standstill.

The forecast was bad – rain and wind. I was both keen to

race and harbouring doubts in the back of my mind. 'The Tour isn't until July. Do you really want to risk everything tomorrow?'

The forecast was right. Sure enough, we were only a few secteurs in and some dude crashed in front of me on a massive patch of mud. I tried to avoid him, but it was impossible. I decked it as well, got spat out the back and had to abandon at a feed station. The whole escapade had been pointless.

Next stop: Romandie. I hadn't got the results so far this year, but at least I'd felt good. Romandie? Romandie was a drag. I didn't really feel great at all, and the mountain time-trial at the end was far from enjoyable. Racing being racing, it was still positive in a perverse way. All that being kicked up the backside reminded me how much I wanted to get something special out of the year. It gave me the drive to turn it around and focused my mind. We went to Tenerife for our usual training camp, and while I didn't set the world alight – I never did at training camps – I worked consistently hard. I did extra hours in the morning before breakfast on the turbo or when the boys turned back into the hotel at the end of the ride. I put a jacket on in the heat to make it more unpleasant and more like France in mid-July. I'd under-fuel so I had to hit my numbers while feeling seriously depleted.

I arrived at the Dauphiné in mid-June feeling great. Then, in the time-trial on the very first day, I crashed.

This is where you might stop the clock. This is where you

might look at the evidence and say: Geraint Thomas, talented rider, never quite had his big day in the sun.

It wasn't even wet. I just went too hot into a corner. Entered it at 50kph, lost the front wheel, went down.

I was actually super-lucky, looking back. When I hit the tarmac my arm was stretched right out in front of me. I could easily have done my collarbone again. Instead, I just slid off the road. I jumped on my spare bike and got going again, and only lost twenty seconds to Kwiato, in the end. Yes, it was Kwiato again. No, it was okay. It was my mistake. I was still riding.

I also knew that I must have been flying, to go down and still only lose such a small amount of time. And as the race went on, there was further evidence, everywhere I wanted to look for it. I didn't win a stage, but I didn't need to. I was always where I wanted to be. I felt in control.

Tao Geoghegan Hart did a great job for me in the mountains. Romain Bardet got his team to ride when I punctured on the final descent of the final stage, which pissed me off, and I made it quite clear to him, when we finally got back to the front. There was even a stage up to La Rosière, just as there would be in the Tour, and just like I would a month later, I hit out with a kilometre and a half to go and took time on all my rivals.

You win the Dauphiné, and a troubled year suddenly starts looking a lot better. When the team discussed how we would play the Tour, when it started in Brittany, a new phrase started doing the rounds from management: Chris Froome and I would be joint leaders, but they would 'let the road decide'.

The road could argue all it wanted, but I wasn't in much doubt. When push came to shove, Froomey was their chosen man. I wouldn't say they were scared of him, but he had an aura, by this point. He'd just won the Giro with a remarkable solo ride on the final Friday, which made it three Grand Tours in a row, after the Tour in July 2017 and the Vuelta in September. That had been Alberto Contador's last race. Froomey's obsession had seen him off into retirement.

That unequal balance was confirmed before the team time-trial on stage three. When we went through our plan after breakfast, we were told that if anything happened to Froomey, we were all to wait for him. If anything happened to me, the boys should crack on.

Of course it rattled my cage. I don't like being told one thing and then seeing something different happening. Equally, I couldn't let it get to my head. If I did I would only under-perform on the bike. I could see the issue for the team's sport directors; Froomey was a determined character, with results to back it up. When Sean Yates had been our lead DS, he could stand up to anyone. He was naturally assertive, and he had seen pretty much everything as a rider. He could stand up to Cav, and there's not many people who can do that. Those who were in charge in this period never quite nailed it in the same way.

But I knew, by now, what it took to win a Tour. I'd

watched others do it from the width of a tyre away. I'd given everything I had to help them through the hardest moments. The Tour had been my education and my cruel teacher but my finishing school, too. I understood that you don't win the Tour with one spectacular day in the mountains, although I was to have two of those. I understood it wasn't about blitzing a time-trial, although that would happen too. You had to ride the cobbles, you had to ride in a place in the peloton where you stayed out of danger by fighting to be where everyone wanted to be.

You won it by doing all those things. The Tour de France is the Premiership season of cycling. It's the Ashes Test series. You do it by getting most days right. You conserve your energy and get a draw when you can't get a win. You gradually wear others down rather than being worn down by them.

That's what I did. I stayed out of the crashes in the first week by riding away from where the crashes might be. I didn't try to win the Roubaix stage, because that energy would be needed come the final week. A simple mindset: get through it safely and as easy as possible. Of course, if there's a moment to go and gain some real time, then go. But don't go 100% for a few seconds' gain, when 80% is enough. That 20% could be a minute in the mountains. Another bonus, when I made it through: Sa was coming out for the following day's rest day. We'd broken the stage nine curse, and over cobbles, too.

You can't win the Tour by fluke. That was something else I'd learned. And you can't win it in the first week or on the first big climb, which is why I didn't feel the need to sprint for the stage victory when Dan Martin won on the Mûr-de-Bretagne. You play to your strengths, at the Tour. I'm not the most explosive rider, and to win would have taken an almighty effort and a fair amount of luck. Instead, I picked up some bonus seconds that day at an intermediate sprint, without even sprinting. It was lined across the road, I was behind Luke Rowe, saw nobody was going for it and so jumped out of the peloton to steal three seconds with very little effort. Ideal. The rest of the time, stay in the wheels and save it for another day.

As we made our way eastwards across northern France, as we flew down to Annecy in the Alps for the first rest day, I realised I was riding the Tour the same way I had prepared for it. It might sound boring, but being successful at the Tour, more than anything else, is about being consistent. It's about constantly working hard. You can't just commit a couple of months before and expect it to come good. It's about hard work over a long period of years. It's being committed and driven, about exploring your limits.

What does that prosaic word 'consistency' feel like, in the real world? You'll hear some riders talking about how they've done epic seven-hour rides. When you ask them what else they've done that week, they'll admit they've maybe not done much else – perhaps twenty hours in total. Even if it was a big week, thirty-five hours plus, what about the hours the weeks before and the weeks after? It's not about one big workout or week. It's about thirty-hour weeks, back to back. It's high numbers all the time, not just one or two big days or one or two big stages.

Winning the Classics takes training, but the mentality is different. If winning the Tour is like winning the Premier League, winning a Classic is like winning a big Cup Final. It's about producing your best on one day. You can gamble and it can come off. Anyone can produce an upset, if they get everything right and the opposition have an off-day.

Not at the Tour. It's always big picture. You can't get wrapped up in one single day. Always put that stage, or that moment, or that tactical decision, in the context of the three weeks. For what is to come, for what is best in those challenges and fraught, weary days. It's as much mental as physical. Like a tennis player or golfer, don't sweat the point or the shot you've just messed up. That's done, it's in the past. Just concentrate on the next step. Worrying about the small things takes big things out of you in the end. A simple relaxed race is a strong race.

I felt good, as soon as we hit the climbs of the Alps. On the first day there, when Julian Alaphilippe went away to take the stage. As we began stage eleven, which would finish at the ski resort of La Rosière. Tom Dumoulin attacked on the descent before, with a team-mate up the road ahead of him. Castro was leading us Sky guys, and initially I couldn't work out why we weren't following him. Why would we let such a good rider, such a threat on GC, get away?

We left Dumoulin to it. By the time we hit the bottom of the climb he had a decent advantage. But we were climbing well as a team, Kwiato, Castro and Wout Poels doing good turns to pull us closer.

I just didn't want to ride on the front for Froomey. He wouldn't ride on the front for me. We were joint leaders. So when Kwiato finished his final turn, I attacked.

It was only then, I think, that I realised how good my form was. Looking back, my legs had been giving me little hints over the first ten days. Now there could be no doubt. It was obviously hard, but everyone else seemed to be suffering a lot more than me. I felt like I was cruising. I could get across to Tom quite easily. And Tom was a very good rider, riding well. Riding well enough to finish second on GC, when we got to Paris.

Froomey was not ready for it. Straight away he came on the team radio. 'Don't pull! Don't pull with him! I'm coming!' A little bit of desperation, already, maybe feeling that he wasn't where he wanted to be or knowing where I was.

Watching the race back, you can see he was doing too much, in that moment. Jumping with everyone, trying to get them to ride with him. If that had been me, I would have left it to everyone else. I was his team-mate, the perfect excuse to sit on. Let them take you as close as possible, then jump – one big all-out attack.

What you would find sometimes, with Froomey, was that the tactics the rest of us instinctively understood from having been racing since the age of eleven could pass him by. He had grown up on another continent, doing big miles in the Rift Valley rather than races round local parks and industrial estates. His was the more scenic upbringing and the more astonishing back story; we didn't have pet pythons in Birchgrove or have to worry about hippos crossing the track at Maindy. He went from domestique at Barloworld and Sky to the most successful rider in the world because he was the best, incredibly dedicated to training and capable of riding quicker than anyone else. He hadn't been schooled in race tactics as a youngster, and his engine was so good his wins weren't about being tactically astute.

So when he came on the radio, I didn't feel I needed to reply. Of course I wasn't going to pull with Dumoulin. I didn't have to. I had the reigning champion in my team and behind me, so it was accepted I could sit on Dumoulin's wheel. That's how it worked. I could sit there and it would help me because I could get an easy ride until I was ready to attack again.

And that's exactly how it panned out. I got my free ride. My worry was that we seemed to be going slowly enough that the Froomey group behind us might catch us. We weren't, really. I was just in the sort of shape that made it feel that way.

Suddenly I could hear on the radio that Froomey was coming across. I glanced back down the road and could see him trying to close. That's when I knew it. 'Right, I'm going now . . .'

I attacked at almost exactly the same point as in the

Dauphiné. Mikel Nieve, an old team-mate of mine, was the last man up the road. I didn't think we'd get to him, but I caught him so quickly it almost happened without me noticing. I fizzed past him with 300m to go and took the stage, and all I could think was, shouldn't that have felt quite a bit harder?

An incredible feeling, to win a mountain stage at the Tour de France. An even better feeling, when that win takes you into the yellow jersey, and the next day's stage is up the greatest climb of them all, Alpe d'Huez.

Doing the pre-stage interviews the next day, someone asked me: 'Do you think you can win today?' I had to tell them I hadn't considered it. My task seemed less lofty: stay with the other GC guys, at the very least, keep my advantage. Alpe d'Huez is often won by a break, someone going away for solo glory while the battle for the yellow jersey plays out further down the slopes.

That question did plant a seed. What if I did end up going for the stage? Too much of a distraction, as we rolled out and the racing began. I switched back into my usual mode. Think about the next climb only, think about fuelling for it.

The day began hot and developed hotter. On the Croix de Fer, before we dropped back on to the valley road that would take us to the final climb, I started feeling like I might be running a bit low on fluids. I downed two bottles of water straight away and made a note to myself to keep drinking. When that fluid kicked in, I realised how much I needed it. I felt good to go.

I needed to be. Steven Kruijswijk had a big advantage going through Bourg d'Oisans, at the foot of the Alpe. He wasn't the danger. I was in the group behind, with everyone I had to worry about: Dumoulin, Froomey, Bardet, Nibali. Landa. I assumed Kruijswijk would stay away. I had to concentrate on those around me, and the pace Egan Bernal was setting at the front of the group. It was solid. I could feel it. I needed to hang on.

It was insane, the noise as we climbed. I was buzzing off the atmosphere, maybe too much. There was Cymru Corner and Irish Corner and Dutch Corner up ahead. I was being too much of a fan. I was spending too much time thinking about it and not enough energy riding. 'This is mad. This is great. I'm in yellow on Alpe d'Huez . . .'

The further we rode, the more I settled and the better I felt. Bardet attacked, but in that too-early, never-going-to-stick way. Egan swung off. Suddenly I was on the front, driving us through a corridor of screaming spectators. Now it was almost indescribably thrilling. Now it was beautiful.

Heart pounding, cool thinking. 'Right, okay, I'm pretty sheltered here from all the people anyway, so I'm just going to ride for a little bit, just get through this crowd, keep Bardet within sight and then I'm just going to swing over. I'm definitely not going to start pulling for Froomey.'

That was when Nibali had his crash. A spectator staggering into his path, Nibali going down, me almost going down over Nibali's bike and body on the ground. I even instinctively unclipped my foot from my pedal, but managed to swerve him, and clipped back in and got back up with the others.

Now it was a curious kind of stalemate. I wasn't going to ride on the front. I didn't have to. I was the race leader. If guys were dropped already they'd be dropped again. Everyone I needed to worry about was here in this group. And they were all racing each other, not just me. When someone else attacked, someone else would bring it back.

Maybe not a stalemate, more a curious cycling equilibrium. Chaos and noise and madness all around, the traditional rules of cycling tactics keeping everything in balance in the heart of the storm. Dumoulin was my man. He was a time-trialler rather than a naturally explosive rider, so if Froomey attacked, I knew Dumoulin would chase him down. He did.

When Landa came back and went straight over the top, Froomey reacted straight away, then Tom. I was getting a free ride on the Dumoulin diesel train. When he went at 2km to go, I could respond, and I knew then too that we were going for the stage. It was going to be one of us four: Froome, Dumoulin, Landa or me. I was no longer thinking about how big all this was – this climb, this jersey, this moment. The further we climbed, the more focused I felt. The stronger my legs became.

Coming to the final corner, I think I was the only one to take the racing line and carry my speed around it. Landa went too tight. Froomey and Dumoulin were maybe watching and waiting for each other. I was the one who sprinted out of it.

I just felt so . . . fresh and punchy. Some days, when you have a good sprint – even as an amateur, messing about with your mates, racing each other to the next road sign – some days you feel like, 'Whoah, this is not good.' Your legs are wobbly and the bike's going everywhere beneath you. And then other times it's like the bike is glued under your hands and you can get such a good hold on it. It's like man and machine have become one.

All the power you have is going through the pedals and moving you forward. Maybe it's only 50 watts more you're pushing, but the sensations are so different. I almost felt like Sir Chris Hoy doing a standing start on the track. As Shane used to say to us, in those velodrome mornings so long ago: 'Your arms are part of your frame, boys. It's all rock solid now. It's your legs that are pumping up and down.'

To this day, I think it's probably one my highest peak powers I've ever done in a sprint. And that was after a long day in the saddle, up and down the Col de la Croix de Fer and Col de la Madeleine, off a big mountain stage the day before, after forty-odd minutes climbing up Alpe d'Huez. It's pretty mad, really, and maybe why I celebrated like I did. Like I'd scored the winning try for Wales at Twickenham. Like all the battles and disappointments and dreams of the past twenty years were suddenly pouring out of me in one frozen moment.

You may have heard the interview I did on TV straight afterwards. 'Jeez, man. I just won up Alpe d'Huez . . .' The disbelief and the pleasure all mixed in together. So many facts being thrown at me that I couldn't grasp them all properly – the first time in thirty years someone had won back-to-back mountain stages at the Tour, or was it thirty-five, or forty; the first British rider to win on Alpe d'Huez, the first rider in yellow.

The Brit stat was a cool one, but there wasn't a huge amount of history to it. It wasn't like being the first Frenchman or Italian. The first win in yellow – that's the one that hit me. All this history at the Tour, all these riders I'd read about or watched and never, ever thought I could ever truly match.

It's not got much worse, looking back seven years later. It's almost like the best possible day to have, winning on Alpe d'Huez. It's the cycling equivalent of my wedding day, without needing an exasperated vicar to tell me to pull myself together. High on that Alpine mountain, I felt on top of the world.

Someone sent me an interview, a few months later, that Rod had done that afternoon. He was laughing and excited at the same time. 'It's serious now. G has just won on Alpe d'Huez. This is properly on. He won Rosière . . . okay, well done, good ride. But this is another level. He can win this race, now . . .'

At the time, I never thought what other people might be thinking. It was all about doing the basics and the right things and not getting carried away. It was like a circus, on the mountain. It was only when I got back to my room and closed the door that all the madness was left outside.

I slipped back into normal. I slipped back into boring: 'Right, eat what I need to. Rest. Get my feet up.' Phoning Sa back home, lying on my bed, feet up on the wall and my legs at 90 degrees to help them flush out a little, talking to her about our dog Blanche or what she'd been up to today. Just one unspoken rule between us: don't speak about what's to come in the Tour. Certainly don't talk about possibly keeping the jersey all the way to Paris. Not even to the next rest day. You're just in a hotel room anywhere. Anywhere in the world but here.

So the road was going to decide? Maybe the road should have been given more credit. As the race made its way south-westwards across France, from the Alps to the Pyrenees, the narrative on the outside seemed to be that Froomey's return to the top was an inevitability. He had done it multiple times. Of course it was going to happen again. Except for one thing: the further we rode – the harder the stage, the steeper the climb – the stronger I looked. The road was indeed deciding. It was just reaching the opposite verdict to the one those outsiders had imagined.

It felt natural to me. I knew now how good my form was. Going into the seventeenth stage, from Bagnères-de-Luchon to the top of the Col de Portet, outside Saint-Lary-Soulan, I had a lead of a minute and thirty-nine seconds over Froomey.

Dumoulin was one minute fifty seconds back in third, Primož Roglič two minutes forty-seven back in fourth. I hadn't ever really felt threatened since going into yellow seven days before.

The Portet stage was short, just 65km. The Tour organisers had come up with a different approach for the start, at the bottom of the Peyresourde; we were gridded on our GC position, like a cyclo-cross race or MotoGP start. I think they were hoping for a bit of chaos, that if the GC guys didn't have their domestiques with them at the front then the race would open up from the start. It didn't work. The Peyresourde was still a solid climb but it would all come down to the final ascent up the Portet: 16 km, from the valley floor up to a thin new road built over an old cow track just for the occasion, at a monstrous altitude of 2215m. The highest point of the entire Tour.

That was fine with me. I'd never climbed so well. I felt good at altitude. The higher we went, the wider the gap between me and those chasing seemed to grow.

That was until the team meeting before the stage, when Froomey announced that he wanted to attack. To put it in starker terms, he wanted to attack me. He wanted the yellow jersey back, and this was how he was going to get it.

Being the man he is, he was upfront about it. This is the stage for me. We'll work as a team to the bottom of the final climb, and then we go for it. We put Dumoulin and Roglič under pressure, and then we hit them.

We'd spoken about it briefly the day before, and I had

tried to put my point across. Why attack so early? Force the other boys to go first. The onus is on them. Let them burn themselves, then, if you're good, take advantage.

Chris had appeared to listen without agreeing, but I wasn't just going to let it happen. I spoke to Dave and Nico and put my point across again. Why risk it? To me it was obvious who the best rider was in the team at this Tour. Why would Chris still be allowed to attack?

I thought of all the times I had willingly sacrificed everything I had to help Froomey stay in yellow. That had been my job then. I was fine with it. It felt like it was Froomey's turn now – not because he owed me, or for some unbreakable moral reason, but because of pure, unemotional cycling logic. I was well ahead of him on GC, and I was there not by fluke or accident but because I was in better form and had been for the past two and a half weeks. I was the team's best chance of winning the Tour. That was it.

Froomey had a hold over the team. Management seemed to find it harder to say no to him than to me. So they didn't. We left the team meeting and no-one had told him not to attack.

The strangest scenario in which to find yourself in such a big moment on such a big day. We had a plan until the final climb. Nico's strategy after that? 'You boys don't fuck it up. Everyone on this bus has been working for you guys all race.'

How did that feel? Well, that was the call. I had tried to change it and had no success. I had no choice but to accept the decision. This was not the same as acquiescing to it. As

Steve Peters would say, accept it, move on. Focus on what you can and will do in this situation. I wasn't going to suddenly lose my form. Other riders weren't suddenly going to transform theirs. If I just kept doing what I had been doing, I would be fine.

Something else, tactically. If Froomey attacked, then Dumoulin and Roglič would have to chase him, since they wanted to protect their own positions. I could use them to get back to him. If I needed to, I could jump across from them to Froomey. I had so much faith in my legs by this stage, I think, that I almost felt I could cope with any scenario thrown at me. Everything I had learned and suffered from in my career had carried me to this point. Now was my time. I was ready.

The next day, Froomey went early on the climb. Really early for any long mountain climb, but particularly on the Portet, with how high it went and how steep the finale was. You could take a minute out of someone in the last couple of kilometres, if you were fresh and they were suffering. When he went, he couldn't get away. He didn't have the legs. Dumoulin rode back up to him and Roglič in the sort of controlled, steady-effort way that suited me perfectly, and I sat on and got a lovely tow.

Nairo Quintana and Dan Martin were further up the road. That was fine. Neither was a threat on GC, and while in theory a rider could use them as stepping stones to escape and get away, that rider was more likely to be me. I settled down with Froomey and Dumoulin and Roglič, and our Sky team-mate Wout Poels began riding a nice strong tempo on the front, and all seemed cool.

Suddenly, Froomey came on the team radio.

'Dumoulin's suffering! Let's go! Let's go! He's dropping . . . let's go!'

This was something else. I was fine with Froomey attacking. Whatever. He could do his thing. I could bring him back. But I didn't want him to start burning our team.

Internal dialogue: 'This team is riding for me, mate. I've got the jersey. You can attack, but they're listening to me on the road.'

External dialogue, to the team over our radios: 'Nah, mate. Wout, just keep doing what you're doing. If Dumoulin's getting dropped at this pace, he's getting dropped anyway. There's no need to up the pace even more. There's still 6k to go. So if he's suffering now at this pace, fine.'

Froomey began to launch small attacks and false attacks. Dumoulin got drawn into the same game of cat and mouse, getting dropped and then jumping back on. I didn't care any more. They could play silly buggers all they liked. It just seemed like background noise, now. It wasn't going to affect me. It wasn't going to affect my race. I kept talking to Wout. He kept riding. We were fine.

Almost inevitably, Froome got dropped. He'd nailed himself. Roglič attacked, Tom and I went with him, and we went to the line. My legs felt so good I knew I could go away again and overtake Quintana and Martin for the stage, if I really wanted to. But it was the Tour. It wasn't about another stage win. It was about the overall. It was about being sensible and playing safe and sitting on these boys as long as I had to.

What a feeling, to be in control of yourself and the race at this deep, dramatic point in the Tour. Roglič and Dumoulin were in their own world, worried about each other rather than me. I could use them all the way to the last kilometre, and then jump away in the last couple of hundred metres. It didn't matter that a spectator reached over the barriers and tried to grab me as I passed. My shoulder went through his hand and I barely wobbled.

This was the story of the Tour. I just kept taking seconds. I didn't need a knockout blow. I could channel Floyd Mayweather and just keep jabbing and keep winning points. Don't show any weakness, keep my foot on my opponents' throats.

Quintana won the stage, Dan Martin was at twenty-eight seconds, I was at forty-seven. Roglič and Dumoulin were at fifty-two. Froome was at one minute thirty-five. The only result of his day and his decisions was to drop from second to third on GC.

I've thought about it all from Froomey's perspective, in the years since. I don't feel angry. He had got to the top by being unbelievably committed, by pushing himself incredibly hard, by making sacrifices. He had won the last three Grand Tours. He loved winning, and he was used to it. Maybe this was normal for him. He didn't grow up in cycling. The usual code for how a lot of things are done – maybe that hadn't seeped in as it had for others of us.

Attacking me, wanting to win? We sat next to each other on the bus. I could easily reach out and touch him. You'd think that would be awkward, but it never really was. I'm not really pissed off. I'm a big boy, I've been around elite sport. It's more that line you might get from your mum when you're younger, or a teacher on a school trip when you've been caught messing about at the back of the coach: 'I'm not angry, I'm just disappointed.'

Maybe I'd feel differently if it had cost me the Tour. It didn't. It actually just underlined the gap between us in those three weeks. It shows how desperate he must have been feeling. Even two days later, on the final Friday of the race and the final mountain stage, when he got dropped going over the Aubisque and then brought back by the team, he started riding with Dumoulin to chase Roglič. Those tactics didn't make sense either. Roglič was gaining seconds, but that was it. He was full gas. Froomey could have let Dumoulin chase and both his rivals for the podium exhaust themselves before the time-trial the next day. Losing a few seconds on the Friday would have gained him far more on the Saturday.

But that's what pressure makes you do. It forces your hand. It pushes you into places you don't want to be. And for me, maybe everything he did in those few days made my eventual win all the more satisfying. No-one could say that Tour had been given to me. Froomey had done absolutely everything he could. I didn't win the Tour because I was allowed to, or because anyone stood down. I won it with my team backing someone else, on the key stage. I won it because I was the stronger rider, day after day, challenge after challenge.

And because I stayed calm, amidst all that stress and chaos. Part of me wanted to let the excitement loose, in those final few days before we got to Paris. The kid inside me was jumping around at the unreal thrill of it all. I didn't because I was used to all this. Going to an Olympics as home favourites, winning Paris–Nice, winning E3 and the Dauphiné – I knew emotion could help you, sometimes, when you wanted to tap into it, but it could mess you up too. Process mattered more, although it sounds duller in comparison.

One other critical thing. My entire career had gradually been building up towards this moment. From racing round parks and long rides as a teenager with weights strapped to my top tube, from those drives across Britain with my dad, going to races on old circuits most people never knew existed. From going over to Belgium in a minibus to race against lads with better bikes and smoother calves, to the Track Worlds as a junior. To the GB academy and the Commonwealth Games, to the GB pursuit team, to the Olympics and the start of Team Sky beyond. To races where I fought to compete with the big boys then learned to draw level with them. To the one-day Classics where I learned to be confident in what I could do, to the lessons I learned with Brad and Froomey on my wheel. All of it mattered. All of it had taken me here.

Some people asked a strange question, when I stood on the podium on the Champs-Élysées on that warm Sunday in late July. 'G's won the Tour. How did this happen?'

Deep down inside, I felt they'd got it the wrong way round. If you knew where I'd been, if you understood where I'd come from, you ended up at the opposite conclusion. Why wouldn't this happen?

I think the team always had trust in me. I think they had confidence. Did they actually believe I could win the Tour? I'm undecided. I think Rod did. Tim as well. Tim knew my numbers. He'd witnessed the hard yards.

Dave? He probably thought there was a chance. He knew how good I was, and he knew I had ticked all the boxes. But I think they thought Froomey ticked all the boxes too, and his pen was a little darker. If they'd had to put their money on someone, it would have been Chris.

Fundamentally, Dave is a pragmatist. His job was to get riders from his team to win the big events, and that's what I was doing. Once he got over his, 'Oh, it's Geraint,' he was, 'Okay, it's Geraint.' And he had an emotional connection to it too. We had been working together since 2003. He had been out of Wales for a long time, but he still had those roots. Maybe the emotion was greater for all of them, in the end, because of those connections going so far back. For the shared history, for the collective hopes and dreams.

You know you get that thing with parents sometimes, where they're the last ones to realise that their kids have grown up? Other people can see it more easily. The child is a teenager and now they're an adult. Maybe there was a little bit of that with Dave. He still thought of me as the Geraint who was on his way up. It was a surprise to him that I won the Tour, until suddenly it wasn't. I was fully grown. I was at my peak.

I wonder how I'll look back at it all, when I'm long in the tooth and ready to go back to that wonderful warm place in my memory. When Macs is grown up himself and getting married and we go to the pub the night before for a few pints and a father-to-son chinwag, I'll happily talk about the race all over again. I'll also tell him how glad I am that I enjoyed it properly afterwards, that I didn't immediately park it and look on to the next race and the next season.

Riders always move on. The sport never stops. But the Tour is the endgame, to me. You've completed cycling when you win the Tour. Froomey would win the Tour and think about the Vuelta. That worked for him, and that's just fine. I asked myself a rhetorical question: what did I do all this for? I did it to win. So when I won the greatest prize of all, I wanted to enjoy it.

Dave saw it differently. 'G, don't go too crazy. You can enjoy it when you've stopped.' But I wasn't ready to stop, and in any case, you can't. Try holding a party seven years after you've won the Tour and see how many people turn up. So I celebrated it properly, and I'll never regret it.

Getting a special jersey from Wales rugby, going on the

pitch at the Principality before an autumn international. Doing the same before an Arsenal match at the Emirates and a Patriots game at the Gillette stadium. All the nights out I had with all my close mates, the celebrations with Sa and our families, the people who had given up so much themselves to help me do the thing I wanted to. That is what life is all about. Not racing from one moment to the next, sacrificing everything, never to reflect or enjoy any of it.

There is always something else to chase, wherever you are. The millionaire wants to be a billionaire. The man with a Jag wants a Porsche, and the man with a Porsche wants a Bugatti. The woman who flies first class wants a private jet. When do you stop to enjoy what you have? When do you finally say: I love where I am today, and what's taken me here, and I want to celebrate it all?

Chapter thirteen

Tour de France 2019, stage nineteen

So I enjoyed myself properly, that autumn. Through September and October and November. By December I was done, keen to get back to the old routine of training, eating salad and feeling like an athlete all over again. Feeling tired from training, not from late drunken nights. What I couldn't know, as I took aim at defending my Tour title, was that my build-up would be the complete opposite of the year before.

To summarise: if it could go wrong, it did. At Tirreno I got a stomach bug and couldn't finish. At Suisse, someone crashed in front of me, I went over the top of them and crashed myself. I cut my face where my sunglasses dug into my cheeks, and the doc pulled me out of the stage because he thought I had concussion. It turned out I didn't, but he was doing the right thing, and I had no choice about it, which is also generally the right thing too. I was okay at Romandie, but that was the only time in the entire first half of the season when I raced to the top of a mountain.

It was sort of in keeping with all that had come before. My contract with Team Sky had ended at the end of 2018. Team Sky's contract with Team Sky also turned out to be ending. The day after the Tour finished in July 2018 I found myself in a meeting with Jim Ochowicz, whose BMC team was about to change sponsor and name to CCC. That's a weird vibe for you: sitting in the café opposite the hotel of your team, who are yet to confirm an offer for you, talking to a rival team who really want you, except you're not quite sure if you want them as much. It was all part of the plan hatched by my race agent Andrew McQuaid. He actually wanted me to be seen having a coffee with Jim the morning after the biggest win of my career, the biggest win I could ever take. He wanted to turn the screw on Dave and Sky. Get a bigger, better deal done.

I stuck with Sky in the end, because it had all worked so well. CCC were offering a great deal and they were a great team. But if I went there, I would have to settle into a new regime. New bike, new nutrition. New staff, team-mates and coach. I was finally where I wanted to be in the sport. Now was the time to crack on and keep this winning formula going.

I officially signed it on my phone via Docusign while in the queue at Starbucks with Sa. In football it's all photos on the pitch and manager's hand on your shoulder. Not in cycling. I'd signed my first Sky deal at the Manchester velodrome, using the bench-press machine as a table. Now I was leaning on paper napkins and drinking weak coffee for people who didn't really like coffee. Rock and roll.

It was something of a chastening surprise to be told on our December training camp in Mallorca that the source of our team's funding was over. Fran and Dave pulled me to one side a few hours before they announced it to the team. Dave was confident he could find a new sponsor, at least outwardly. If he didn't, I was on a new three-year contract that would soon be worthless.

James Murdoch was keen to help us find a new sponsor. Dave and Fran flew out to Los Angeles to meet him. I happened to be there with Sa, training for the coming season, so they asked me along. We arrived at James's house before Dave and Fran. We were offered a drink. Water, juice, beer, champagne, whiskey? Me and Sa looked at each other, both thinking, yep, this is probably the place and moment to roll the dice.

'Could we have some champagne, please?'

We could. Dom Perignon, as it turned out. When the time came to leave, James said we should let him know if we ever needed anything. Full of the heady thrills of Dom P, we quickly worked out that we probably needed to stay at his house for a few more days. The highlight? Probably watching the NFL play-offs in his cinema room with adjoining bar, equipped with a secret staircase dating back to Prohibition times. It made up for the Starbucks signing bit. It turned out too that Dave's confidence was well-placed. Ineos came along, the money came in and the transition was seamless.

Something else, that winter. At some point, the Giro d'Italia approached Dave and asked if I would ride the Giro in 2019. Keen to make it worth my while, they offered a fee of around €1.5m, which would be split between me and the team. Standard practice, for riders they really wanted at their race, for riders who might otherwise target the Tour instead. It was great money for just turning up.

I said no because I wanted to go back to the Tour. I wanted to prove to myself, and everyone else, that 2018 hadn't been a fluke. It was never about the money. I was content with what I had. What I was in it for now was the results and the races. The wins, and the glory.

So I wasn't in perfect shape, going to the Tour. The lack of racing, the crash in Suisse. It was a battle to get my weight down in time, and it was a battle to get the sort of backing from the team that I thought their most recent Tour winner might get.

Froomey had his terrible crash, doing a recon of the time-trial at the Dauphiné. His battle would become long-term, and he attacked it with typically impressive focus and bravery. Then Egan Bernal crashed in Catalunya, which ruled him out of the Giro, and ruled him into the Tour. When the team picked him, they announced him as joint leader.

I liked Egan and I rated him highly as a rider. He'd proven himself riding for the team at the Tour in 2018. Equally, he was twenty-one years old. He'd never won a Grand Tour. He'd only ridden one. I also felt I had proved myself multiple times. I felt I was slightly in front of him.

I talked to Dave and Rod and Tim about it. To our lovely DS, the late and much missed Nico Portal. I asked why they thought we were on a par with each other. It was sold to me like this: it's been a busy few months for you. You can share the leadership. He can take some of the pressure and focus off you.

But while it's not a particularly nice thing to admit, I thought I had done enough to prove myself. Egan had ridden one Tour, well. I'd been riding the Tour for a decade. I was fine with the responsibility. I'd been waiting for it. If they had backed me properly, I would have thrived off it all. But as always, the decision is the decision. Accept it and move on. Take the positives. I wasn't going to kick up a fuss about it. I wasn't going to be all diva about it. We were back to where we had been before, that same amorphous phrase: the road will decide. A BBC documentary crew followed us for that race, and they even named the programme after it. And then, as it turned out, it was more of an avalanche that decided it.

Very little in that Tour played out as the Tour was expected to play out. Julian Alaphilippe went into yellow early. That was all good. Most riders in the peloton liked him. The French public adored him. In a long-term drought of home success at the Tour, suddenly they had both Loulou and Thibaut Pinot entertaining them every day, right at the top of the

GC. Riding in very Alaphilippe and Pinot ways – with style and panache, and very obvious suffering.

What none of us anticipated was quite how well Alaphilippe was riding. The short and medium climbs were his thing. On the really long brutal slogs in the high mountains, he was supposed to fall back. Except he didn't. He kept riding out of his skin. Pinot kept pushing him. The French were getting giddier with every day. We were getting more worried.

And I wasn't feeling as good as I had the year before. I could feel the lack of consistency in my training. I had the type of crash that makes you feel unlucky – Michael Woods going down in front of me on a right-hander, taking me out too. The boys worked hard to get me back, and I pushed it harder on a climb to get to the front, but Alaphilippe and Pinot had already gone, and Egan either wasn't ready to ride or had been told not to. I made it clear to him – 'We need to go! We need to ride!' I did a few turns on the front, but he was hesitant.

We ended up losing time to the French pair that we didn't need to, and for the first time I let it get to me. On the team bus after the stage, I said what I thought.

'What the hell are we doing? Are we here to win the Tour or what? We need to have a number one and a number two at least. We need to commit immediately . . .'

I'm not sure they quite knew how to react. They hadn't seen me like this before. It was all very well saying the road could decide, and all would fall into place in the third week.

You still needed clarity to get you to that point. The road could be cruel but it was inanimate. Maybe we could decide. Why wait?

The time-trial in Pau on stage thirteen was what really muddied the waters. I rode a good one. I put time into pretty much everyone – Egan, Pinot, Steven Kruijswijk, Rigoberto Urán. I was the leader in the clubhouse. Then Alaphilippe rode an insane TT. He took the stage from me by fourteen seconds, which meant he now led me on GC by a minute and twenty-six. I was still comfortably clear of Kruijswijk in third, and I was a minute and a half up on Egan in fifth, but I paid more of a price for my efforts the next day on the Tourmalet. With a kilometre or so to the top, I got detached from the group containing Alaphilippe, Pinot, Egan, Kruijswijk and Mikel Landa.

I drifted back at first, lost contact and then had to stay sensible. I knew it got steeper right at the end, so it was about limiting my losses. And I sort of got away with it – only about thirty seconds, in the end – but Pinot attacked at the death to win it, and Alaphilippe rode in just six seconds back. That meant his lead over me was now just over two minutes. It meant my advantage over Egan was now just under a minute.

Those were the two days I lost the Tour, I think, looking back. If Alaphilippe hadn't produced the TT of his life, I would have gone into yellow. That would have ended the arguments. And then, because I had a bit of a bad day on the Tourmalet, the angle in our team changed. No longer would I be looked after. Now it was about cracking the French. 'Right, we need to use both of you – you, G, and you, Egan – to break them. Because they don't look like breaking otherwise.'

So that's what they did. On stage eighteen, the final Thursday of the race, Alaphilippe had one team-mate that was riding with him. We knew we had to make the race harder for him. If we were going to crack him, he would have to be under pressure for a longer part of the day.

The plan was for Egan to attack up the Galibier, in the final 7km or so. Perfect, I thought. He can go, everyone chases to bring him back, I can sit on and then go over the top.

The first part worked well. My legs felt great. But none of the other GC men reacted, when ordinarily they would. It was like they didn't see Egan as a threat. We hadn't made it any harder for them by attacking. We had just made it harder for me.

I was feeling so strong I had to do something. I got on the radio to Nico. 'This is too easy. We're just sat here and letting Quickstep go at their own pace. What's going on? Nico, I feel good. Can I go? Can I go?'

I don't know if it was the altitude we were at, or that the team car was too far back, or he couldn't hear me, but I didn't get much of a response back. I decided to take it into my own hands. With a kilometre or so to go, I went.

Now the reaction came. Pinot went hard and got up to me. Alaphilippe was gapped. Going over the top, we had a small but potentially significant lead over him. But there was a problem: once they had closed the gap to me, no-one continued the chase to Egan. We began to roll rather than race. Alaphilippe made it back to us on the descent; Egan stayed away to the finish and gained thirty seconds on GC.

Why was no-one chasing? Maybe it had something to do with the other men high up the GC. Alaphilippe was over-performing. Pinot was having the Tour of his life, but he was also nursing an increasingly bad knee injury. Kruijswijk was a good rider but he was used to being a super-domestique. Landa was a long way back. Emanuel Buchmann – another good rider but one you wouldn't think of as a contender for the yellow jersey by the time we got to Paris. Rigo was a long way back, so was Alejandro Valverde. There were a lot of riders who might not want to risk that much because they were probably thinking more about a podium than a win.

The end result? More frustration. Alaphilippe's lead was now a minute thirty over Egan and a minute thirty-five over me, but he was still no closer to cracking, and we were running out of days.

On the morning of stage nineteen, 126km from Saint-Jean-de-Maurienne to Tignes, the plan was set. We would attack early, on the Col de l'Iseran. Alaphilippe would have to chase. One of us could sit on. Alaphilippe would be put under so much pressure he would weaken, maybe fatally.

I went first. Straight away Alaphilippe was in trouble. He tried to close, and you could see how much it was costing him. Then Egan went over the top, and quite quickly got a good gap. I could sit on Kruijswijk, because he was getting a good tow from his team-mate Laurens De Plus. Going into the descent, Egan had an advantage of just under a minute. Alaphilippe was going backwards. With the long descent, a stretch along the valley road and then the final climb to Tignes to come, it was all looking good. I could keep getting this tow as long as I wanted. Then, in the last four or five kilometres up to Tignes, I could jump away, feeling fresh. Simon Yates and Warren Barguil were in between. I could use them as stepping stones. Maybe I could get to Egan, or at least put good time into everyone else and close in on him. He'd been riding solo for a long time by then, and we could really see who was the better rider at this Tour. Finally the race, and my year, was going the way I wanted it to go.

Except none of that happened. Five kilometres into the descent, the commissaires' car slowed up in front of us and then brought us to a halt. They never did this, not at the key point of a decisive stage in the world's greatest race. Something serious must have happened.

I couldn't understand what they were talking about, to begin with. They just kept repeating the same thing. 'It's finished. It's done. It's finished.'

All of us were clueless. Then they started talking about a massive landslide on the route ahead. They told us it was blocking the road, and that there was no way past. They told us today's stage was over, but that it wasn't ending now.

It had already ended, at a point where no-one knew it had ended. They were going to take the stage times from the top of the Iseran. The mountain we had just climbed.

Now it was pure confusion. 'What? What are you on about?'

The landslide – I understood that part. The weather had been extreme all the way through the Tour, either incredibly hot or freezing wet. There was little the organisers could have done. But taking the times from a finish line that hadn't been the finish line when you crossed it, let alone when you set off towards it? It felt like deciding the Olympic 1500m final by the position of the runners at 800m, having not told any of them it was going to happen.

And it changed everything. Egan was in yellow now. He had a minute and eleven seconds over me. The next day, the final stage before Paris, was then chopped up too. Mudslides meant that what would have been 130km from Albertville to Val Thorens, including the ascent of the cat two Côte de Longefoy and then the cat one Cormet de Roselend (almost 20km long at an average gradient of 6%) was reduced to a mere 60km, with the only climb the steady one to Val Thorens. Rather than a long, hard day at altitude, the sort of battle of attrition that I loved and that suited me in every way, we had a short little blast. From a Test match to a T20.

In that moment, I knew the yellow jersey was Egan's to keep. A stage that was 10km in the valley and then 20km up to the finish? I couldn't attack the yellow jersey then.

Maybe Froomey could, but I couldn't. It didn't feel the thing to do. What if we had both blown up because we were racing each other, and someone like Kruijswijk took advantage of it? You'd never live it down.

So we rode it, and Alaphilippe got dropped halfway up, and I knew I had second. Vincenzo Nibali rode away for the stage, and a few other boys jumped off the front. My head was gone by now. What was the point of any of it? I was safe in second. I wasn't going to attack my team-mate in yellow.

Egan and me crossed the line together, and I congratulated him. I meant it. He had climbed brilliantly throughout the race. He'd earned it. But it was still a little painful, to be honest. It felt like the most crushing anti-climax. Had we ridden both those stages in full and the outcome had been the same, it would have been easier to accept. Instead it was like the semi-final and the final of the Champions League being abandoned, and our team being awarded the trophy as the leading goal-scorers at that point.

I was genuinely happy for Egan, in many ways. He was the first Colombian to win the Tour. He was a nice guy. I got on with him. It was just the way it ended. The opposite to 2018, and Froomey's attack on the Col de Portet, when I'd been able to prove beyond any doubt that I was the strongest rider. This year Egan proved he was strong without a doubt. I just felt I'd been restricted by tactics and not got everything out. The road had indeed decided, but not in the way any of us had anticipated.

The reason I had made all the sacrifices and commitments to my sport was to get the best result possible. That's why it wasn't the fact I got second that hurt. It was not getting the chance to see if I could have won it. It could most definitely still have ended with the same result. Maybe Egan would have won by a larger margin. It was the unknown that was torturing me.

I had to put a brave face on it. You can't be pissed off on the bus and in the kitchen truck. The boys had been riding for both of us, and we had finished first and second. You couldn't be kicking off with that. There were positives I could take: I was still in the shape to win this great race. Even after everything I'd been through since the Tour in 2018, I had still been in a position to back up winning yellow by winning it again. Brad had found that impossible, Froomey too. I'd proved to the doubters that I was no one-hit wonder.

Something else happened, later that year. Something that changed everything.

I'd always known I wanted to be a dad. Sa and I had got married four years ago. We were ready. But nothing quite prepares you for the reality, does it?

During that Tour Sa had a scan booked. I asked my swanny Marko to let me know when I went through the feed zone if all was good. Being a great swanny, he kept it simple. 'G!

All good with Sa!' Being a good swanny, was he ever going to tell me anything else?

When I first held Macs in my arms, I fell in love with him in that first moment. I couldn't tear my eyes away. Sa and I had always been a team. Now the team was bigger. Now I was doing all this for me, and Sa, and Macs too.

So that was the great silver lining to lockdown, when that began in March 2020, and it was the great consolation in the hard months that followed. As soon as we heard how strict the rules in France were going to be, we escaped back to Cardiff. I rode my bike, and with no racing for months to come, I stepped off the intensity, and I was there for Macs as he grew and I was there with Sa to share the greatest adventure we could experience.

I would have helped whatever my racing schedule. Being at home meant I could help much more. Having no races allowed me to be less selfish than an elite rider usually would be. I washed. I cooked. When you're riding your bike fast for six hours, you don't wash and you don't cook. You just put your kit in the wash and eat the food that's cooked for you.

Nothing quite seemed real, that season. There was no racing for a long time, until suddenly there was a lot of racing crammed into a very short period of time in the late summer and early autumn. I got my head down and worked, and I worked too hard. I didn't have my usual structure of racing and training. Instead I just trained and trained. Tim would give me a rest day, then we'd go again. There was no enforced period to freshen up into and after races. So when the racing finally started, I was empty. I went to a shortened Dauphiné and wasted it, because I had nothing left to give. I was in a box.

I needed someone to hold me back, in the months before. But Tim was like me, always instinctively pushing. At the bottom of a hole, I kept digging. He kept giving me shovels.

We went to a makeshift altitude camp after the Dauphiné, up at a place Ineos boss Jim Ratcliffe owned in Courchevel, close to Col de la Loze, a steep finish climb a Tour stage was due to ascend a few weeks later. We reconned the stage. We had our photographs taken in the new team kit. And then Dave and Tim called me into a meeting, and I knew exactly what they were going to say.

They told me I wasn't going to be picked for the Tour. They told me they wanted me to rest, recover, chip off a bit of weight and then go for the Giro. The Tour was due to start in Nice on 29 August. The Giro was five weeks later.

It was frustrating, because I'd only just run out of time. I had a week off the bike, then had a week of long, slow rides, six or seven hours most days. I clocked a total of forty-three hours in those seven days, but an average of 190 watts. Strange, but sensible.

I went to Tirreno and finished second. I was back on track. I probably needed a week more and I'd have been good for the Tour. But the Giro was okay: a race I loved, a race where I had unfinished business after crashing out three years before. I was the sole leader. I loved the pressure this brought. I thrived on the idea of us being one team working together for one aim. I was ready to give it everything. I felt like my mojo was back.

And that lasted two stages and half the neutralised zone before the third stage. Where do you rank the pain of a crash caused by someone's bidon lodging under my wheel and sending me straight into the hard road? I think the avalanche at the Tour will always be top of my personal horrors. The bidon is next, ahead of Wilco Kelderman hitting a police motorbike on the inside of a blind bend in 2017 and then hitting me, ahead of Rafał Majka crashing in front of me on that descent in the Tour a few months later.

Too many ridiculous things coming together. A neutral zone, where you're just supposed to roll out of the start town and get free of the narrow streets and traffic-calming measures before the race director drops his flag and you actually begin racing. Instead, the commissaires are driving too fast, and everyone's following too fast, so suddenly we're all racing down a steep, narrow cobbled descent. The bidon jumping from its cage on the other side of the road, bouncing straight across through all the wheels and frames and spinning pedals, back-spinning and changing direction and flipping around. Seeing it out of the corner of my eye, then not seeing it, then feeling it hitting my back wheel and jamming in underneath it, and me high-siding and landing directly on my hip.

I knew something wasn't right straight away. I could barely lift my leg, and I struggled to stand up. They actually stopped the race, or rather, since the race hadn't officially begun, they held it at kilometre zero. Our mechanic Diego had to pin my ripped skinsuit back together with safety pins. Sa later sent me the famous image of Liz Hurley in her Versace number at the *Four Weddings* premiere. We looked more similar than you might imagine.

I told myself I was okay. Of course I did. I told myself I had to finish the stage. Maybe I would be okay, even if it didn't help that we were finishing up Mount Etna.

The run into the climb I could tell I wasn't good, struggling to stay in the peloton. I got to the finish as quickly as I could. I had an X-ray there and all seemed okay. But I knew it wasn't right. I pushed the doc to get me another scan in the morning. The team were a bit hesitant. I'm not sure why; maybe they wanted me to push on, as I had at the Tour in 2013. But I didn't want to grovel round again. I'd done that. I'd won and come second in the Tour, I was a different rider now.

We went for a second scan before the start of stage four. I'd fractured my hip.

A ropey 2020, a worse 2021. I was light, when the season started. That's what happens when you've prepared for a grand tour in autumn. But I was probably too light. I probably spent too long on the limit.

My results were okay. Third in Catalunya behind two

team-mates, a win at Romandie and third in the Dauphiné while helping Richie win. But it wasn't plain sailing. I broke a rib at Romandie and then dislocated my shoulder at the Tour. The docs popped it back in, and I felt a million dollars compared to the seconds before, and I rode on. I even gained a couple of places on GC that day, which amused my team-mates no end. Who dislocates their shoulder and moves up on GC?

But I wasn't feeling in great shape. The team was weaker than it had been. Richie Porte was back with the team but not quite at the level to threaten the GC. Richie Carapaz was our leader, so the team wanted me to ride 100% for him and then in the final week look for a stage myself.

I wanted to try for a stage sooner, to take the opportunities as they came. It made for quite an awkward team meeting in the kitchen truck come the first rest day, although in the end it would make no difference. The day I wanted to try for a stage was the Ventoux stage, and I was terrible. I was so bad I was almost dropped with Mark Cavendish at the start. They also wanted us to attack on the descent. Ben O'Connor, who was challenging Carapaz for the podium, wasn't the most confident descender, so they wanted to take advantage. But I wasn't prepared to do it, and I made my feelings clear. It was the first time in my career I'd come head-to-head with the team. It wasn't a nice feeling, but I had to be honest and tell them exactly how I saw it.

Maybe the Tokyo Olympics could turn things around.

Well, maybe they could have done, had my team-mate Tao Geoghegan Hart not crashed right in front of me mid-race and taken me down with him. I landed on the same shoulder I had dislocated before; while it stayed in this time, it was a long way from pleasant. I struggled on and then pulled out, battered and exhausted, as we hit the first of the finishing circuits.

Looking back, this was the moment of rock bottom. I still had the time-trial to ride. I probably shouldn't have raced. But this is the great delusion of being an athlete. You always have hope. It's a great thing, sometimes. Other days it burns you.

I tried talking myself up. 'Look, the Tour was terrible. I got through it, had some good days. There's a great ride in me. It's just hard to find it at the minute in the big hole that I'm in – this dark, damp, dreary hole. But it's in there somewhere. That crash wasn't ideal but at least I didn't go super, super deep that day. So maybe I'll be okay. The injuries aren't too bad. I'm a bit sore and banged up but I should be fine. So get into this TT now and do what you can.'

Twenty-four hours later, Rohan Dennis was passing me in the TT. I don't even know where I finished. I just knew I had never been caught in a TT before. It was blisteringly hot. My shoulder hurt intensely in the TT tuck. My legs were empty and my head was in an even worse state. It was officially grim. I wanted to be anywhere else than there.

All this time, an existential crisis was brewing behind the scenes. Stage fifteen at the Tour had finished up high in Andorra. The next day was a rest day. We did a spin and then got changed on the bus to go back to the team hotel. The other riders left one by one until it was just me and Dave.

Dave wanted to talk contracts. He wanted to talk about a much cheaper contract. The figure was so much lower than my present one it was hard not to reach certain conclusions.

'G, we can only give you this much. Don't worry, we won't hold it against you, we understand if you want to go somewhere else for more. You can go.'

I'm also happy being honest in these moments. 'Oh, okay. Do you even want me to stay?'

'Yeah, no, of course we want you to stay. But we understand if you want to go for more money somewhere else. But yeah, this is all we can sort of offer you.'

It was the same time they were negotiating to tie Tom Pidcock to a long-term contract. He was the coming man. That's where the money was going. They saw him as the future of the team. He was the one who was going to win the Tour back for them.

I parked it all, until after the Olympics. When I spoke to my agent after Tokyo, the figure on offer had plummeted further.

Now this was hard. In a couple of months, I seemed to have gone from one level as a rider to one far below. I made calls to the team. I kept getting the same answers. 'Look, we don't think you can really perform in grand tours anymore. But you could still go for races like Romandie, and the week-long World Tour races.'

It hurt. It really hurt. Other offers were on the table. First in were a Pro-Conti, or second-tier, team wanting a big name to boost their profile and get into bigger races, then a more established Pro-Conti team keen to go for GC in Grand Tours. That got a little more serious, but it was still just money to me rather than anything else. Then, late on, Movistar came in with a really strong offer. The money was good and they were going to let me aim at the biggest races again. They made it clear they believed in me. They made me feel wanted.

I had known Dave forever. I found it hard not to take it personally. If any team boss knew me, if anyone understood what I could give and how I'd always get through these rough periods – it was Dave. All this talk about being older now – of course I was, but I'd spent those years riding track. In road racing terms, I was still middle-aged. There was talk about the sport moving on, about Tadej Pogačar and Remco Evenepoel. Well, the sport was always moving on. There were great new talents coming through.

I felt like I was being stereotyped. The diesel who was running out of fuel. The nice guy who had enjoyed his time in the sun. A throwback to the old days.

It started to drag on. I'd speak to my agent every ten days or so and nothing would have changed. I thought I was worth one thing. They thought I was worth something else. A lesson that maybe I should have learned before: you can get on with people and think of them as friends and be as close as you like, but when it comes to business, it's a separate world. Don't expect business decisions to be made for personal reasons. Don't expect personal relationships to influence business judgements.

I thought about stopping. 'Sod it. It's been a good career, I can do something else.' But I didn't want it to end like that. I wanted to carry on, for two more years.

What should I do? Movistar was flattering. It was also a new environment for me, which could be a good and bad thing. At Ineos I liked all the riders around me. Many of them were mates. I was super close to many of the staff. Marko had been my soigneur for years, and swannies know everything about you. Maybe I was guilty of ignoring what I'd just learned. So I asked myself a simple question: where would I be happiest?

Steve Peters had said something to me once, the sort of thing parents often say to children when they're not happy about something: life is not fair. Accept that and crack on. Either I had to take this offer or not. Being unhappy with it wasn't getting me anywhere.

I agreed and decided to re-sign. For my last contract I always thought we'd have some cool announcement – some sort of video or montage. But it was nothing like that, merely another couple of boxes ticked on a Docusign link on my phone. It was even past the official UCI cut-off period. I trusted the team, but even that was a little worrying.

When I did sign, I made a separate deal with myself. I had chosen to sign. Therefore, I would never complain about it. No-one was forcing me to do it. I couldn't be going out for training rides in March and telling myself I was underpaid and insulted. I'd seen it plenty of times before, and I wasn't going to be that rider.

Of course I talked about it with Sa. It reminded us both of when we had bought a property and turned it into a wedding venue, St Tewdrics. I'd said to Sa, okay, let's go for it, but when we do, don't speak to me about any stress or hassle that comes with it, leave me to crack on with racing my bike. That had worked. So now she said the same thing to me. 'Look, I don't care where you go, as long as you're happy and you don't come home and you're moaning about things.'

So that was it. I signed. I told myself I would enjoy racing my bike for the next two years, and see what else I could get out of the sport. All that, and try to prove everyone wrong.

We had a team meeting in December 2021 about next year's Tour. The management decision was that our two co-leaders were going to be Egan and Adam Yates. Tom Pidcock would be in the squad to have a free rein and try to grab a stage or two. When we were told this, I stood up and made my position clear.

'Right, I just want to say I'm happy to commit to Egan. I know there's been a lot of talk around me and last year in the Tour. Some people might think I'm turning into an old, selfish guy, but that's not right. I'm happy to commit to you and I'll do everything I can. I'd love to go for a stage but, yeah, I'm here for the team.'

About a month later, Egan had his awful crash, out training on his TT bike. The team made the call fast: now the two leaders at the Tour would be Yatesy and Dani Martinez. I realised what this meant. Not only was I not first or second choice. I wasn't third choice. Fourth? With Tom in his free role, maybe not even that.

I didn't say anything. That was the deal. I had made my choice, and I would live with what it brought. All I could do was to train as well as I could, get to the Tour in the best shape possible and then take it from there.

One more thing that gave me a lift as I looked ahead. Roger Hammond had joined the team as a sport director. We had raced against each other earlier in our careers. When we talked about the Tour, he was different to the others.

'G, I know what the team are saying and that, but you can still perform, mate. You can still perform.'

What a feeling to have. Someone did still believe in me. I downplayed it in the moment. 'Ah yeah, I don't know, mate. We'll see. I'm just going to go about my business and do what I do and get there in the best shape.'

But it hit home. I wasn't finished. The future might still be mine, as well as the past.

Chapter fourteen

Giro d'Italia 2023, stage twenty

Did I know what was coming, after the lows of 2020 and 2021? I'd like to say I pictured it all. I didn't doubt myself the way some others seemed to. But from down where I had been, to up where I would go, at the age of thirty-five?

There had been significant changes at Ineos, as we went into 2022. My long-term coach Tim Kerrison had left, replaced by Conor Taylor. Tim had been fantastic; Conor was a breath of fresh air. There was almost no chat from the team about the Tour, and that felt strange, when there had always been chat before. You set up recons of the key stages and you talked about the race and how we might attack it. Now I was being left to my own devices. Unprecedented, but not necessarily disastrous.

Almost unnoticed, I was riding well. My weight was good for this time of year. On our usual high-altitude camp in Tenerife I actually enjoyed myself. There was Luke Rowe, Adam Yates, Pippo Ganna and Dylan van Baarle. We trained hard and relaxed when it was done. I went to the Tour de Suisse with Yatesy as team leader. He went down with Covid and pulled out. I saw the opportunity and took it.

It was hot in Switzerland. Being Switzerland, it was also generally either up or down. It seemed obvious to me that the way to ride was to always do enough and never too much. Go too deep on one day and you'll lose all that time and more on the next.

Maybe it appeared boring. I didn't try to blow the race apart. Instead I put pressure on my rivals every single day. I was comfortable in all I was doing. I knew all the riders around me on GC – their strengths and weaknesses, their preferred tactics, their tells when they were under the pump. Maybe it helped that most of them had been guests on my podcast. You got told things, as you got older. People opened up to you. I was comfortable figuring all these things out while simultaneously riding over 400 watts.

When Colombian climber Sergio Higuita jumped away on a big mountain day, I didn't try to follow him immediately. Instead I used the diesel engine of Jakob Fuglsang, who was in the leader's yellow jersey, to do the majority of the work, and then made my move later. An easy rule to follow: leave the work to others when you can. I was the old man. Nobody expected me to do anything.

I won Suisse. A solid time-trial on the final day after performing well in the mountains the previous days. I lost the stage to Remco by two and a half seconds, and had we not been using a new TT with narrower handlebars, I maybe could have won it. The bike was fine; I just needed more time to get used to it. And the stage didn't really matter, compared to being back on the top step of the podium, especially at Suisse. Suisse was a race where I'd come close so many times, and had maybe started fearing – as with Tirreno and the Giro – that it might be one that got away. Maybe I had set a template for what could follow. Maybe I could keep surprising people. Post-race I was told a crazy stat: only two men had ever won the Dauphiné, Suisse and the Tour: me, and Eddy Merckx. Not bad for a bloke who was supposed to be finished at GC battles.

All of a sudden, messages and plans for the Tour began filtering through. The sort of comments that hadn't been made for a few years – 'Maybe we should look after you at the start', 'Don't lose time early on', 'See how you go, there might be chances here ...'

It was rather satisfying. A confidence I had inside, based on real results, being reflected back at me by people who hadn't shared that confidence before. There was also no pressure at all. These last two years felt like a bonus to me. If I achieved nothing more from my career, I'd still done enough to sleep well in the second part of my life. Macs was getting to the age where he might remember me racing. Sa could bring him to certain days. When the end comes into view, you're able to tap into an enjoyment that was always there but could sometimes get hidden behind more serious motivations.

None of the pundits were talking about me before the Tour. It was all, obviously, about Tadej Pogačar and Jonas Vingegaard, maybe a little about Primož Roglič. That was all good. They deserved it, and it left a lovely space for anyone else who might have a good Tour. No-one was really talking about Ineos, either. The team's period of GC dominance had come to an end, the budgets and line-ups at Pogačar's UAE and Vingegaard's Visma at a level where ours had previously been.

That felt normal to me, rather than a crisis. I'd seen it in the other sports I loved to watch, whether it was the All Blacks winning Rugby World Cups and then being overtaken by the Springboks, or Manchester United being passed by Manchester City and then City's dominance waning. Maybe there was the tiniest bit of selfishness from me too: this was happening as my career was approaching the end, rather than at its peak. Maybe a hint of delusion. I wasn't going to train less intensively or back off in races just because another team and another set of riders now had more cards to play.

It's actually a great feeling, going to the biggest race in your year and knowing you're good and knowing that no-one else knows you are. You don't need to force it. No-one's keeping eyes on you. You can do all the things you've learned are sensible to do and play the long game that all those years of experience have taught you. You let the others make the silly mistakes you once made, tire themselves out starting fights they didn't need to start. You don't talk yourself up and you don't talk yourself down. You don't talk at all, unless you have to. You just ride. Just get on with it.

That's why I think it happened for me, at the Tour. Why I began well and got through a testing first week, and kept doing all the small things well. All the small things except forgetting to take my gilet off at the start of the prologue in Copenhagen. It was a wet day so I'd put it on to ride to the start. An extra-small, nice and snug. And so I completely forgot I had it on, until about thirty seconds into the ride. At which point I didn't want to risk riding no-handed on a TT bike, with the wind and rain, and decided instead to just crack on. Sure, it cost me some aero seconds. It also made some good money for charity, when we auctioned it off after it had travelled the entire Tour route, being passed from fan to fan along the way.

Unnecessary items of clothing apart, in the key stages that would decide the podium, I made the right calls at the key times. Geraint Thomas, undercover GC agent. Whoever expects an old man to be a deadly assassin?

In three weeks at a Grand Tour you're going to have straightforward days and you're going to have dramatic days. You'll have days when you rely on others to get you through and you'll have days when you see a slight weakness in a rival and do everything you can to make it much worse. So I look back now, and I think about stage five, when we went from Lille to Arenberg across the cobbles, and Caleb Ewan crashed into a hay bale coming out of a roundabout and took me and Roglič and a few others out with him. Tom Pidcock stopped and waited for me. He wasn't told to, but he did, and that brought me back to the main group with Jonas and his Visma boys riding hard on the front. It meant a lot to me. People say Tom is very focused on himself. Sometimes he is, and that's not necessarily a bad thing. That day proved to me he's not always like that.

So I went into the first rest day in a rather nice stealth position. Pogačar was in yellow. Vingegaard was second, thirty-nine seconds down. I was in an almost unnoticed third, at one minute and seventeen seconds.

It was around this point that the memes first started appearing. All of them had the same central idea: an unholy dust-up going on, someone else cracking on in the meantime. I have no idea who was coming up with them. They just kept appearing on my social media feeds. The first one: two blokes in a kebab shop, late at night, swinging punches at each other. One had the word 'Pogačar' written over him, the other 'Vingegaard'. In the foreground was a slightly older gentleman quietly eating some chips while absorbed in his phone, not even bothering to glance up. That was me.

It was also an uncanny prediction of what took place on stage thirteen, a monstrous 152km from Albertville to Col du Granon, finishing up that horrible climb, but also featuring the equally horrible combination of the Col du Télégraphe and Galibier on the way. This was the day of Visma's all-out attack on Pog, and I saw it coming.

They were massing in their yellow and black jerseys from the very start. In the old days – or rather, in the Tours I'd grown up in – it would never have got this big this early. We were midway through the second week. There was too much racing ahead. But these two riders were different, and their teams and their tactics reflected that. As soon as I saw Visma looking ominous at the front, I figured out what was coming, and I made sure I was in a decent position going into the Télégraphe.

Sure enough, Visma attacked over the top of the Télégraphe. By the time we started the Galibier a few kilometres later, there were only four of us left: Roglič, Jonas, Pogačar and me. With Pog isolated, just as Visma had planned, they initiated phase two.

Roglič attacked. Pog closed. Jonas went over the top. Pog closed again. At first I jumped on the wheel of whoever was the second Visma guy – whoever was following Pog chasing his team-mate. I could feel the acceleration and the speed, as these one-two attacks kept launching. Pog even put in a few of his own.

Time to play it clever. I knew that if I kept busting a gut to stay with these accelerations then I wouldn't last long. It was already the first time I'd done ten minutes of thirty seconds on, thirty seconds off in a race before, let alone halfway through a stage of the Tour. So I changed it up – rode my pace, and kept coming back to them. As long as they kept shutting down each other's attacks, I'd be able to ride back to them when they momentarily eased.

I'm not saying it was easy. It was brutal. All the time thinking, 'Jeez, boys, we still have 8km of the Galibier to climb here, and then just the small matter of the big matter of the Granon.' None of them seemed to care.

I knew I was part of something special. I knew how mad and thrilling this would be to watch. The kid inside of me in front of the telly would have been jumping around on the sofa with delight. It was also bloody hard. I couldn't get swept up in the surreal drama of it all because all of my energies needed to go into staying with them.

Attacks, truces, attacks that didn't work, chases that did, attacks that almost worked. It was relentless – on the climbs, at the summits, halfway up them, on the descents. Anywhere you could expend some energy, they were doing it. Pog was still a young man having young man thoughts. He thought he could do everything. He could, pretty much. But when you've been chasing everything, all day, and you're at altitude, and your team-mates are way back down the mountain and not able to give you what they have – well, it's going to pay back. It's going to bite your backside sooner or later. Me? I just kept going. Let them light the fireworks, I saved my own. Let them burn their resources, I marshalled mine.

On the Granon, Visma's repeated attacks finally paid off. Jonas launched. Pog couldn't follow, not anymore. I sat on him for a while, and then enjoyed a sensation that had almost never happened, before or since: I thought I could go quicker than Pog, right at that moment.

So I did. I jumped, and got away from him. Jonas took two minutes fifty-one seconds out of Pog. I took well over a minute. Romain Bardet stole a little more on me, but I wasn't too worried about him.

Which led to meme number two. This time it was an image of Mo, bartender in *The Simpsons*, throwing dipsomaniac Barney out of his tavern. Mo was captioned as Pogačar and Vingegaard. I was Barney. In the next image, Mo aka Pog and Jonas was dusting his hands and looking satisfied. There was no Barney. In the third image, Mo/Pog/Jonas is looking out into the street, perplexed. Unbeknown to him, Barney/me has reappeared right behind him.

Other memes would follow. As with all memes, sometimes the most amateurish were the most pleasing of all. There was a still taken from the animated subtitled version of *Thomas the Tank Engine*. Thomas had my white sunglasses superimposed over his train face, just in case you hadn't made the obvious connection. The caption? 'Thomas had never seen such a mess.'

I was so invisible for a man riding so high on GC that on the day I had to wear a certain style of Oakleys, not my usual white-rimmed ones, I seemed to disappear completely. Pog rode up to me to tell me about a conversation he'd had with his partner Urška the night before.

'Is G out of the race now?'

'No. What do you mean?'

'I didn't see him all day today.'

'Ah no, he just had different glasses on.'

'Oh . . .'

I'd never felt so relaxed at a Tour. Of course I still got nervous before these big days. But I wasn't stressed. Steve Peters used to tell us that we could compete as emotional athletes or logical process-driven ones. He'd say that either way could get us to perform at our best, but that only the logical one was sustainable. If you went on emotions every time, you'd burn out far sooner. Staying calm meant I wasn't wasting energy over-thinking and under-sleeping. I had ridden so many big races by now that I didn't panic in the tricky moments. I could go with the flow, confident they would pass and confident in my abilities to cope no matter what. My age may have taken a fraction from my legs. It also gave me an invaluable perspective. I had won the Tour and come second in it. Results still mattered, but my happiness no longer depended on them.

So when the hard days came, as they always will, I survived them. Stage seventeen was another brute, 130km up through the Pyrenees from Saint-Gaudens to Peyragudes. I was still third on GC, two minutes forty-three seconds down on Vingegaard, nineteen seconds on Pogačar, a minute and a half ahead of Nairo Quintana in fourth and a minute forty over David Gaudu in fifth.

The stage wasn't super long. It didn't need to be. We would

be climbing the Col d'Aspin (12km at an average of 6.5%), Hourquette d'Ancizan (8.2km at an average of 5.1%), the Col de Val Louron-Azet (10.7km at 6.8%) and then Peyragudes (8km at 7.8%, with far steeper sections towards the top). It was a day designed for attacking and designed to cause great rifts in the GC.

I was already on my limit when Brandon McNulty went flying up the penultimate climb. Pog and Jonas went with him, and I had a choice: did I try to go with them, knowing there was a good chance I could blow if I did, or did I limit my losses and protect what I had? This had become my Tour in a single decision. I could be gung-ho and go for the win. Equally, I had to be realistic about where I was. I was driving a car with a top speed of 80mph. Pog and Jonas could do 100mph.

So I eased up. With my team-mates Tom and Yatesy way down the mountain and Quintana and Gaudu distanced, I waited for Romain Bardet and Alexey Lutsenko and rode with them down the descent and into the valley. Bardet then messed that up by waiting until I was taking a bottle from the feed zone with a gel and some ice to attack me, which didn't go down well. I rode back up to him and made my opinion of his move clear. He flicked his elbow at me to get me to ride at the front for him. I told him what I thought of his chances, sat on him for the first few kilometres of the final climb and then kicked away again to take another thirty seconds from him. I had lost more time on the two leaders. That mattered less than the time I had put into Quintana, Gaudu and Bardet. A bad day that ends with you three minutes ahead of the rider directly behind you on GC can never be considered all that bad a day.

It's almost taboo in elite sport to be satisfied with third. Well, I would love to have won the Tour again. I was doing everything I could to do as well as possible. I spoke to Luke about it, and I value Luke's opinion extremely highly. We talked about doing something crazy to try to win the whole thing, and we talked about racing to make sure we got on the podium. I was fifty/fifty about it. I loved the idea of going for it. I also realised there was no point in doing anything that was doomed to fail and would throw away a near-certain podium. If you were playing roulette in a high stakes game, would you put all your cash on red or black, or stick it all on a single random number?

We all came to the same decision. We would keep pushing. We would keep trying. If a really good chance came, we would go for it. But we weren't going to try anything totally bonkers. And it felt like exactly the right decision, when we got to Paris and Jonas had three and a half minutes on Pog and Pog had almost five minutes on me, and I had way more than five over Gaudu in fourth. I had now taken first, second and third in the Tour de France. My third was behind the two greatest riders of their generation, one of whom might go on to be the greatest of all time. I had done it by keeping the right attitude and committing to my training and my diet and my team. And I had done it at a time where Macs could join me on the podium on the Champs-Élysées, and we could have that picture ever more of the two of us together in a moment we'd always remember. A moment that gives me just as much warmth inside as seeing myself there in the yellow jersey with the Welsh flag held out behind me.

I had joked when I won the Tour four years before that I had completed cycling. After standing on every step of the podium it really did feel that way now. It also threw me forward into the one big piece of unfinished business I still felt I had left. I'd gone to the Giro twice in good enough shape to win it. Fate had twice intervened in the cruellest of ways. I was ready to give it another go. Rod was in full agreement.

Maybe this hadn't been the end, after all. Maybe we could still go all-in.

Except the 2023 Giro nearly didn't happen at all.

I started feeling unwell at the end of our December training camp. I turned around on the last training day and went back to the hotel, but when I flew home I continued to get worse. I had a fever. I was waking up in the night needing a pee, and seeing bright red blood in the toilet bowl. Pretty scary when it first happened, scarier still when it became every twenty minutes or so.

I spoke to the doctor in the team. He told me it was a urinary tract infection and would clear up. I had some antibiotics and the doc's prediction seemed right, so I cracked on and went to Australia for the Tour Down Under. Once again, I felt ropey in training and had to turn back. More tests, more meds. When I went to New Zealand with Sa and Macs for another training block, the infection came back for a third time.

By the time we got to Los Angeles for another training block, I was having cameras put up body parts where cameras are not designed to go. Being offered the chance to watch the live footage from the camera on a screen as they explored the body part not designed for it did little to ease the discomfort. Only when I returned to Monaco, almost three months later, did they discover the issue was a stone in my prostate, give me some medication to break it up and adjust the saddle on my bike to alleviate the discomfort while the medicine did its work.

It meant my season was slow in starting and my form a long way off where it should have been. I raced Volta a Catalunya, and was so far behind Primož Roglič and Remco Evenepoel that the team started talking about leaving me out of the Giro squad. Remco and Roglič were miles ahead of everyone, but I was nowhere close. I was forty-fifth on GC. That sort of result just tends to persuade management in one direction.

What saved me was my performance at the Tour the previous year and the training camp we did in Sierra Nevada just before. That part of Spain around Granada was a great place to ride, a change-up from previous locations and a freshen-up for the head as well as the body. We also had a group of riders that was more than just a group of riders. We all got on. We enjoyed each other's company. And while a cycling team is often thought of as a machine, when there are bonds between the riders and a sense of shared purpose, that machine can be capable of more power and greater cohesion. We had Ben Swift, Tao, Laurens De Plus, Pavel Sivakov, Thymen Arensman and Salvatore Puccio. Later on we'd be joined by Pippo Ganna, another easy man to like. We did the work but we also relaxed around each other. We worried about the big stuff and let the rest fall into place – not really the way it's done, in the modern cycling world, but something that instinctively worked for all of us.

Swifty and I had known each other for twenty-five years. De Pluski is impossible not to get on with – cheerful, funny, always looking on the bright side. Tao I'm good with; Thymen is quieter, but you need that balance too. Pavel? He was so dedicated that his morning treat was to open the jar of Nutella on the table and just sniff it. Not put it on his toast, or spoon a small amount into his mouth. Literally unscrew the lid, have a sniff, and put the lid back on. It was both dedication and a source of daily amusement to the rest of us.

We had a bond between us already, but by the end of that camp it was stronger still. It was no longer about just doing a job. We could go deeper for each other. I was finding my legs, and the team management saw that. I would go to the Giro as another iteration of the leadership conundrum: the favoured leader, with Tao as back-up. Call it a 65%/35% balance. All good with me; I could feel myself coming good. I knew my role was to deliver, and I thought I could do that. As a leader, I would be myself, at all times: positive with my team-mates, relaxed around the dinner table. When the team leader shows their stress, it affects everyone around them.

We began with a 19.6km time-trial. Remco won it, which surprised no-one, with Roglič at forty-two seconds and me in ninth at fifty-five seconds. That was acceptable. With my lack of racing earlier in the year I knew that first week was all about building into it. Let my form keep coming, don't try anything too outrageous.

I'm not a man for regrets. Had I not missed so much quality training, I would have been closer to Remco in that first TT. Maybe more importantly, given I was to lose that Giro by fourteen seconds to Roglič, I would have been ahead of Primož by more. But I couldn't know that then. I was doing what I thought was right at the time: getting through a tricky hundred-mile out-and-back loop from Naples on stage six, Pippo bringing me back to the main group after an issue with my chain on a cobbled section; producing my best ever five-minute power on the Cappuccino climb on stage seven, working hard with Tao to come in at the same time as Roglič.

I knew my legs were back, then. In the time-trial on stage nine I came second to Remco, by a matter of tenths of a second. Sixteen seconds clear of Roglič. That put me second on GC. I could even have won the stage, had I not ditched the visor on my TT helmet after it became steamed up. I lost it by less than a second; the visor would have saved me at least that. I would have loved to have won a stage of the Giro. I slightly felt it owed me one. But second on GC going into the first rest day, after a week that had been about improving rather than challenging – that was all good.

And then came the big change. We were three years on from the first Covid outbreak, but it still stalked the race. You no longer had to pull out if you contracted it; Roglič admitted he'd gone down with it in the first week. But if it got to you bad and you became unwell, it made the decision for you. You can't race your bike in a three-week race if you're seriously ill. It would cost us both Pippo and Pavel, in that Giro. A crash would take out Tao.

I'd been given all the vaccines. Having lost my spleen back in 2005, the docs were taking no chances with me. Remco may have had his too. But he caught it again, all the same, and by the end of that rest day his team had made the decision to pull him out of the race.

I was sad to see him go. I like Remco. I've always got on with him. I call him the Little Bastard on my podcast as a mark of respect; he's so good at everything it's almost unfair. But there was nothing I could do about his withdrawal, and I was never going to refuse to wear the leader's pink jersey when we started again the next day. I had been promoted from fiftieth to first. But I had also been in fantastic form at two previous Giros and lost my chance through totally random crashes. If bad luck could strike at Grand Tours, I knew all about it.

What was left of our merry band rode brilliantly. I held pink by only a couple of seconds from Roglič and twenty-two from João Almeida, but hold it we did, through stage ten and eleven to twelve and thirteen. When Bruno Armirail took it on the second weekend, we did everything we could to keep it, before realising that we needed to save the team for bigger challenges to come. Armirail was never going to win the malia rosa. Roglič and Almeida could.

Armirail had been part of a thirty-man break we had let go up the road, on the basis that thirty guys never ride well together, so we could control the gap on the flat 100km to the finish after the climb. Problem was, it was a freezing wet day. All thirty guys had worked at the front to keep warm. The gap went from eight minutes at the top of the climb to ten at the bottom. Not catastrophic, except it had then kept growing. Every 10km they gained another minute or so, Puccio and Swifty going deeper and deeper, Pavel starting to ride as well to stop the rot. That had been when I called it. 'Stop, boys. Don't go too deep.' Armirail's group finished twenty-one minutes in front, but it was better for our team and the legs of our riders to lose the jersey for a day or two and let FDJ take the weight off the race rather than destroy ourselves to keep it for now.

So I kept taking it day by day, never looking too far

ahead, never allowing myself to dream. Keep pedalling, keep planning, keep calm. Stay strong for the boys, stay positive around the breakfast and dinner table.

On stage sixteen from Sabbio Chiese to Monte Bondone, on the Tuesday of the third week – maybe that was the day I could have committed more. I finished second on the same time to Almeida and took twenty-five seconds out of Roglič, which put me back in pink, but maybe there was an opening for more. When Almeida attacked I sat behind Roglič and his Visma team-mate Sepp Kuss, not having any team-mates of my own left with me. They either didn't seem keen to chase or couldn't.

Maybe, I thought, Roglič is having a bad day. I jumped across to Almeida, and neither of them could follow, which seemed to confirm it. Except when I reached Almeida, we both started riding as if it were all about the stage win. We played games rather than fully committing. Maybe I could have sat on for thirty seconds to recover and then gone again, go full all the way to the finish. I'm pretty certain I could have taken more time out of Roglič. Would I have taken those fourteen seconds? It's almost easier not to think about it.

But let's do it, because if now isn't the right time, it never will be. Let's say I did take another ten seconds out of Roglič in Monte Bondone. Then he's trying to overhaul a bigger deficit in the time trial. Maybe he goes too hard too early and blows. Maybe he would have gone harder on stage nineteen on the final Friday, and that could have gone either way.

He might have taken some of those seconds back, but would have been more vulnerable the next day.

Swings and roundabouts. It happened and it can't be changed. In the moment I did what I thought was right. Kept pushing a bit to gain time on Roglič, but saved something to go for the stage. I had no idea what would come to pass in the mountain time-trial on the penultimate day. All I can do now is remind myself of that. I made the right decision for that time.

Okay. Stage nineteen, 183km from Longarone to Tre Cime di Lavaredo. A big old mountain day, a final climb taking us to the highest point in the race, more than 2300m above sea level. The air is thin at that sort of altitude. You feel it if you're walking, let alone racing a bike. You feel it walking on the flat, which makes a gradient of 18% the sort of cruel ramp where lots of time can slip away in a very short stretch of road.

It had been my thirty-seventh birthday the day before. No-one in the team had been expecting us to be leading the Giro at this time. I shared my birthday with Ian Stannard, and he was now a DS. Cakes were made. Both went straight to the team cars and the bellies of the staff within them.

We rode the final road stage well, pretty much all the way to the end. I took a few more seconds out of Almeida. I was taking a few more out of Roglič, when I attacked with 300m to go.

But 300m at that altitude and on those gradients is not

300m anywhere else. It may as well be a thousand. I got away from him but then he dug in, and he had the time and the road to pull it back and then come past me. It was only a three-second swing. It shouldn't have changed anything, but maybe it did. My lead at the top of the GC was now twenty-six seconds. Would twenty-nine have been so different? It was more what it might have done to his head. He could have given up and soft-pedalled in. Instead, he was absolutely in the fight. He was the hunter. For the first time since that opening day time-trial, he might be looking the stronger man.

It's different, waiting for a time-trial to start. As race leader I would be going off last. In the Tour in 2018 I'd faced the same scenario on the final Saturday, but my lead had been bigger. I'd filled the morning and early afternoon that day listening to random podcasts in the hotel room. With thinking about the now of my preparation rather than the what ifs ahead.

But that had been a rolling time-trial which I would have had to mess up to lose big time. This was a brute: an 18.6km run between Tarvisio and the top of Monte Lussari with 1050m of climbing squeezed in and a ramp up of almost 19% in the second half. It was bang on the Slovenian border, so would be pure Roglič territory.

I didn't drink enough that morning. When it's that steep and that intense you don't want to be carrying half a litre of fluid in your gut you don't need, but we were too focused on that. When it's stage twenty, after almost three weeks of hard racing, fuel is energy and I should have been fuelled up to the max. If I was carrying a little more weight – well, it was all energy, and it would get used, when it came down to it.

Then there were the tactics. Half an hour before I was due to begin my warm-up, there was still a discussion going on about whether I should wear an ordinary road helmet for the whole thing, a time-trial helmet, or do a switch between the two when the road ramped up. A TT lid saves you a lot of time on the flat. It's also heavy on a climb. It would make sense to wear TT for the first half and then switch to the light road helmet. Everyone would be making a bike change anyway. Would changing my helmet add much more? Ten, twenty seconds?

In the old days of Sky, this sort of big racing decision would have been taken months ago. Tests would have been run to find the optimum solution. The tech boys would have found the answer, and we'd have drilled it to get it right. To be talking about it this late seemed like madness. We hadn't even reconned the climb; it was so narrow and so steep it had been left further down the pecking order.

I think I knew halfway up the climb that I was in trouble. Once the road got steep there were no fans at all; they weren't allowed. Instead of the sort of roaring madness that can drag you on, there was a spooky silence. Just you, the hum of the TV motorbike and the bad thoughts going round your head.

I could have got away with all of that had my legs been

good. If they'd been as strong as they had been for the past two weeks. But, just when I needed them most, they were going. Halfway up the climb, an awful reality began to hit me: I was starting to blow.

Those last two kilometres were horrific. Trying to hold on but knowing I wasn't going the speed I had to. Hearing on the team radio that Roglič was flying. Hearing my precious advantage evaporating and then creeping into the red. Throwing everything I had into it and knowing that my everything was not going to be enough.

Fourteen seconds. *Fourteen seconds.* That's what it came down to, in the end. And I knew, without even looking at the clock. From the expression on my soigneur Marko's face as he pushed me to stop me falling as I crossed the line, from the way Thymen and De Pluski couldn't even look at me as they walked out of the team tent. Hearing the screams and shouts of Roglič and his team-mates in the tent next door.

'Fuck. I've lost this.'

It took forever to get a pee out for doping control. It took forever to get down off the mountain. And everyone I saw, every face trying to be kind or each message of consolation from back home – every one of them choked me up a little more.

The ride itself wasn't calamitous. I'd finished second on the stage. I'd beaten Almeida, and Thibaut Pinot, and Sepp Kuss, and Brandon McNulty. I just hadn't got close enough to Roglič, and the implications of that kept kicking me in the guts. To be in pink from the first rest day, to hold it under the most intense duress in the mountains, to be within touching distance of Rome, after all those years of the Giro breaking my heart – all of it hurt. Seeing Roglič with all the pink touches to his bike at sign-on the next morning; seeing Cav at the start and both of us tearing up. A long way from a small terraced house in Fallowfield, Manchester, so many wins, so many desperate blows too.

Of course I led Cav out in that final circuit in Rome. Of course it happened like it always used to. Cav riding past, shouting out, smiling, joking: 'Ah, lad, when you lead me out, just go on the right, yeah?'

An hour later, going into the last 3km and seeing he only had one guy left with him, and thinking, 'Well, I'm here, so I might as well help a mate out ...'

Getting in position like we'd never been apart. Protecting him, tuning in to him, dropping him off exactly where I knew he'd want to be dropped off. Seeing him accelerating away like he had in the lanes of Cheshire when we'd been young kids, seeing his arms go up. Finding him in the mad melee afterwards and hugging him tight and yelling absolute nonsense into each other's ears.

All the time, this strange back and forth in my head. Standing on the podium with Macs, because I loved taking him into my world, and feeling sorry for him in the same moment, like he should have been standing on the top step instead of Roglič's boy Luka. Getting home the next day and normal life taking over, having to cook Macs some dinner and wipe his bum and find his pyjamas. Realising it was all just a bike race, and then the whole thing engulfing you once again, and knowing it wasn't just a bike race, at all.

I got a one-two-three at the Tour de France. Next year I would have a two-three at the Giro. I was proud and I was sad; I was content and I was dissatisfied. It was like being on the beach on a sunny day, and looking up to see one small cloud covering the sun. A whole sky of the deepest blue, but one tiny cloud blocking the warmth.

Just like Steve Peters always said: life's not always fair. You just have to get on with it. Get comfortable floating around between ecstasy and the catastrophic. 'It's good. I wish it had been better. It's going to bug me for a bit. That's just the way it is.'

Chapter fifteen

Tour de France 2025, stage twenty-one

A nd so we came towards the end.

I rode and I rode, after the conclusion of what was supposed to be my final contract. When those last two years take in a third place at the Tour and an almost-win at the Giro, it makes negotiations rather easier than they might have been before. It went a bit like this.

Management: 'We'd like to give you a new contract.'

Me: 'Okay, how about X?'

Management: 'Yeah, I think we can do that.'

A couple of days later . . .

Management: 'Yeah, that number's all good'

Me: 'Cool. How about two years?'

Management: 'Done. Sign here . . .'

I even got to lead the team at another Grand Tour, and I managed to grab a final podium. As soon as I heard Tadej Pogačar was also going to the 2024 Giro, I knew he would be favourite. I still gave it everything. It's just not that easy taking on a man who wins six stages and the mountain classification as well as the malia rosa.

Was I starting to feel the years? Maybe, just a little. I was more inconsistent than I had been. Slightly less robust. The recovery from the big stages took slightly longer. But I only missed out on second place on GC by thirty-odd seconds, and all that came on one day, stage sixteen, when we were meant to be riding 200km but bad weather saw that chopped in half. A shorter day with one steep 2km climb at the end didn't suit me so much anymore. I needed a little more time to get the old engine going, and Dani Martinez took advantage.

And I knew, in the final week of that Giro, that my GC days were over. On the penultimate stage up Monte Grappa I suffered as much as I ever had since first taking tilts at big stage races. I felt terrible at the start. It rained for most of the day. Then we hit the climb, and Mikkel Bjerg began riding at a pace that hurt me, and Mikkel's a strong rider, but he's definitely not a climber. I came around but knew at the top we'd descend and do all 18km of the climb again.

I was in survival mode when UAE launched Pog. I had to ride my pace, rather than attempt to go with him. I focused on holding on to Ben O'Connor, who was fourth on GC and had a team-mate with him. I had to stay with them. Thinking, 'I'm not getting dropped, not today. I'm not losing the podium . . .'

I suffered and I suffered. It went pretty deep and pretty long, but I made it to the top with the podium still in my grasp. I sat in the team car afterwards, parked up outside some random basketball stadium in the middle of the Italian nowhere. Very last week of Grand Tour. I opened a beer and toasted the feeling of having won third rather than lost first. I thought about five podiums in seven years of Grand Tours, and all the near misses where my form could have won me more. I thought back to all those GC battles, and realised that this part of my life was over. I stood on the podium in Rome the next day with Macs, and we added one more photo to our me-and-him collection.

It all goes so fast, when it goes. The summer of 2025, and my last ever Tour de France, in my final ever season as a bike racer. At my first Tour in 2007 I had been the youngest in the race. Eighteen years later, at my last, I was the oldest. I quite liked that.

I saw a stat, in the first week, that if I made it all the way to Paris I would have cycled 282 Tour de France stages, or 46,485.2km, during my fourteen Tours. Apparently that was more than a lap around the earth's equatorial circumference, which made less sense to me than the way those kilometres had piled up. I had experienced so many things in my career: the velodromes at two Olympic Games, the one-day Classics; week-long stage races, helping better riders at Grand Tours, becoming one of those better riders myself. Time-trials with a broken pelvis, high mountains in the sun and the heat and the rain and snow; cobbles in northern Europe, gum trees in Australasia, sunlit days amid the most glorious Alpine summits.

More than any of that, I felt I'd made the most of it along the way. The most of my talents, the most of the pleasures that can be taken from the high moments and the low points and all the blurry days in between.

I was thirty-nine years old. For an elite road racer in 2025, that was knocking on. I looked back at my Barloworld team-mates from my first Tour in 2007. One of them was now fifty-three years old. Claudio Corti, our team manager, was seventy. I looked at the Team Sky line-up from our debut Tour in 2010. Some of them had retired more than a decade ago. Others had been working as sport directors for years. Brad hadn't ridden a bike in forever.

I looked at my Ineos team-mates. Someone kindly pointed out that Sam Watson was the same age when I did my first Tour as Macs was now. Yet I was ready to move on, even without those ludicrous comparisons. Racing for GC had kept me pushing and searching for fresh speed and better training. Now I was getting around in service of others it was harder to keep going. I didn't want to be the grumpy old guy banging on about how it was better in the old days. I also genuinely was starting to think it *was* better in the old days. Riders were attacking when we stopped for comfort breaks. The unwritten rules of peloton etiquette were starting to feel like they should be written down. And everyone around me was so young. You came into the sport now while only just out of your teens, and you did so with the aim of winning, not gradually learning the ropes. Everyone was training properly now. Entire teams trained at altitude, not just the big dogs. Nutrition was on point; everyone knew about former mysteries like CdA, or coefficient of drag area – basically how aero you were – even far from a TT.

Everyone was at 100%, everyone was racing quicker. At one stage in the second week of the Tour, there were only two riders over the age of thirty in the top fifteen on GC. I was almost forty. I knew more DSs and managers than I did riders. The sport was trying to tell me something, and I was ready to listen.

My whole life had been cycling. I mean that in the fullest sense. The first thing I thought about when I woke up was what training I had and where I was going to go. I looked at food as fuel first and pleasure second. Every month had its own specific purpose, and the collective goal of them all was to be leaner, stronger and faster. I still had the Tour of Britain to come, in September, with the final stage into my home town of Cardiff. That would be a fabulous way to finish – nineteen seasons of racing all over the world, and my final professional race being in Wales, starting at the Geraint Thomas National Velodrome in Newport, taking in the roads I learned on, passing the track at Maindy and finishing in the centre of Cardiff, by the postbox painted gold after my Olympic gold in 2012. How lucky I was to finish on my own terms, in front of friends and family – to be able to reflect on the rider I was, as my journey came full circle. I knew none of it would feel real, this great change in my identity, until I truly was a bike rider no more.

I did everything I could in that final Tour to go out in the style I had entered, in the style I loved to race. I tried to get into the break, on the days when there was a proper break to go, and I made it on the Friday of the first week, when we would be finishing with two ascents of the Mûr-de-Bretagne, just as we had when I won the Tour seven years before.

I knew it was never going to stay away. A massive fight to make the break, then after an hour or so of attacking each other a group got clear, but it was only me and four others. Not enough firepower, too many teams willing to chase behind. We were lambs to the slaughter, chopping off at the front and always knowing we were going to be caught. Soon the other members of the break were racing only to win the day's combativity award. That's still an achievement, but it wasn't where I was. It wasn't what I wanted.

I made it to Paris. I wasn't going to quit it before then. And Sa and Macs were there to greet me, and now I was no longer preoccupied with the cold logic of getting through each stage, the emotions came charging up on me. We had done all this as a team: first me and Sa, then the three of us. All of it with them, all of it for them. I climbed off my bike and sat with a beer while I recorded an episode of my podcast with Tom, and then I went out with the team and turned one beer into several more. It was still Paris, and it was still the end of the Tour. Why would I not? Getting to Paris, no matter what happens along the way, is always a huge achievement. Always a relief, always joyful.

I thought about what it was inside of me that had enabled me to have this career. More than the legs, more than the lungs. It was my attitude, I realised, at some point in that hazy summer night. It was never easy. The progression was seldom linear. I don't think I had anything special. Not like Pog or Froomey or Boonen. I just worked hard, bloody hard. I wanted to be the absolute best I could be. I hurt myself, constantly, and I never took any shortcuts. Bike racing is difficult. You need to accept it, to embrace it, to love it.

I always gave it absolutely everything I had. I stayed positive, whenever I could, and I was consistent in all of that. I tried to live in the moment, make the most of it all, and try to remember that it was just bike racing, whatever happened. And I felt a deep satisfaction in everything I had achieved, too. To be riding the Tour again, eighteen years after my first; to win the biggest prizes, and keep chasing them, and keep coming close. To come back from so many disappointments, and so much doubt from others. To come back from my worst ever season at an age where it finishes most riders, and take three more podiums at a Grand Tour.

And it was always about the simple pleasures and incomparable joys of riding a bike. How a machine made from a few metal tubes and some rubber and grease and compressed air could take you from a quiet suburban street no-one knew to the tops of the highest mountains, from a bumpy concrete track outside a council leisure centre to cobbles and velodromes and Moscow and LA and Sydney, to Paris and Rome and Madrid.

I'd given it everything, but I'd never worked a day in my

life. I won pocket money at races in parks as a kid, so never needed to have a paper round. I took on Belgian kids with smooth legs and beat them and got a tiny contract with a team that folded soon after. I made myself indispensable when the better money came around and fought my way to the top to show that I should stay there. Through all the darker times, I loved every second. It was hard, but that was what I wanted. It was never a chore.

All of this, because of a bike. There was a moment into Carcassonne of my last ever Tour when we averaged 62.8kph for thirty minutes. Speed, glorious speed, rushing through me. Another day, when I looked around and knew exactly which road we were on and where I had to go, because I had been here before. My own personal mental route map of France, etched into my mind and muscle memory, taking me onwards without me ever even consciously thinking about it. Attached to each place, a moment to stay with me forever: Cav winning a bunch sprint here, a young French rider attacking, a Welsh flag by the roadside, a crackle on the team radio telling me to hang in there and give it my all.

This was my landscape. This had been my world. Drop me anywhere in it, and I could always find my way back home.

Everything I dreamt about I exceeded. I got knocked down so many times I lost count, although that's how the cards are dealt sometimes.

But I always got up, and I always gave it everything. And that's the only thing that matters, in the end.

Index

accidents, *see* crashes
Adidas, 116
aerodynamics, 36, 43, 154, 162, 163
Alaphilippe, Julian, 254, 277–82, 284
Albertville, French Alps, 223, 283, 302
alcohol, 1–2, 39, 54, 166–7, 183, 209, 218
All Blacks, 300
Almeida, João, 314–16, 319
Alpe d'Huez, France, 32, 97, 203, 257, 258–61
Alps, 32, 132, 181, 203, 219, 238
  2007 Tour, 21–2
  2011 Tour, 181
  2016 Tour, 224
  2017 Tour, 243
  2018 Tour, 254–61
  2019 Tour, 281–5
  2022 Tour, 302–5
Altrincham, Manchester, 115, 155
American football, 170, 272, 275
Amstel Gold Race, 44–5, 87
ANC-Halfords, 103
Annecy, French Alps, 253
Apple, 106
Appleby, Dale, 85
Ardiden, Luz, 139
Arenberg, France, 122
Arensman, Thymen, 311, 319

Armirail, Bruno, 314
Arms Park, Cardiff, 12, 54
Armstrong, Lance, 24, 89, 111, 118, 125–7
Arsenal FC, 12, 272
Arthur, Sean, 38
Astana, 18, 24, 203, 215
Astarloa, Igor, 92–3
Athens Olympics (2004), 58, 95
Australia, 20
  Commonwealth Games (2006), 79–80, 188
  Olympic Games (2000), 98
  Tour Down Under, 3, 173–4, 208, 310
  Track Cycling World Championships (2012), 80, 157–8
  Track Cycling World Cup (2004–5), 62–5, 80
Austria, 3

Baby Giro, 84–5
Bagnères-de-Luchon, French Pyrenees, 262
Bale, Gareth, 13, 39
Ball, Mike, 38
banana skin hack, 42, 43
Bar G, Quarrata, 91
Barclay, John, 48, 52
Bardet, Romain, 224, 250, 258, 305, 307, 308
Barguil, Warren, 202, 282

Barloworld, 2–5, 13–29, 67, 87, 91–4, 103, 105, 184, 256, 326
  Bergamo course, 92–3, 98
  budget, 19
  Pro-Conti status, 3, 92
Basso, Ivan, 73, 88, 140
Bath Road Road Race, 47
Bauer, Jack, 189
Baumann, Eric, 75
beetroot, 198
Beijing Olympics (2008), 62, 98–102, 151, 153, 235
Belgium, 28, 75
  E3 Harelbeke, 175, 187, 192–3, 211
  Eneco Tour, 145
  Kampioenschap van Vlaanderen, 75, 76
  Kuurne-Brussels-Kuurne, 47–52
  Liège-Bastogne-Liège, 87
  Omloop Het Nieuwsblad, 119, 175
  Scheldeprijs, 135, 144
  Six Days of Ghent, 61
  Tour of Flanders, 111, 130, 132–5, 144, 187, 213, 219
Beloki, Joseba, 126
Bennati, Daniele, 3
Bergamo, Lombardy, 92–3, 98
Berlin, Germany, 35–6

INDEX

Bernal, Egan, 258, 276,
    279–85, 295
beta-alanine, 198
Bettini, Paolo, 3
Bigham, Dan, 83
Bilbao, Spain, 86
Birchgrove, Cardiff, 5–13,
    18, 31–5, 39–44, 48,
    256
birthdays, 1–2, 46, 56,
    65, 79–80, 148, 213,
    217–18, 219, 220
Bjerg, Mikkel, 324
Blockhaus, Abruzzo, 239
BMC, 136, 199, 220, 238,
    274
board games, 52
Boardman, Chris, 11, 91
Boasson Hagen, Edvald,
    106, 118, 136, 137,
    142, 145, 173
Bobridge, Jack, 158
Bodnar, Maciej, 222
Bolt, Usain, 167
Boonen, Tom, 14, 23, 24,
    94, 134, 187, 193
Bordeaux, Gironde, 80
Bourg d'Oisans, French
    Alps, 258
Bourg-en-Bresse, French
    Alps, 224
Box Hill, Surrey, 13, 226
Brailsford, Dave, 64, 66,
    102–3, 106, 109, 170,
    176, 205, 293
  Egypt holiday (2010),
    112–13
  Paris–Roubaix (2018), 248
  Team Ineos establishment
    (2019), 275
  Tour de France (2010),
    118
  Tour de France (2013),
    183, 184
  Tour de France (2018),
    264, 270, 271
  Tour de France (2019),
    277
Brazil, 15, 225–30, 232–4
Brighton, East Sussex, 36
British and Irish Lions, 183
British Broadcasting
    Corporation (BBC),
    130, 167, 277

Sports Personality of the
    Year, 102, 129
British Cycling, 2, 19, 25,
    89, 95, 158
  Quarrata academy, 2, 4,
    20, 80–84, 91, 112–15,
    235
  see also Great Britain
    Cycling Team
British National
    Junior Road Race
    Championships, 46–7
British National Road Race
    Championships, 85–6,
    116–17, 131
Buchmann, Emanuel, 281
Buckley, Peter, 46
Burke, Steven, 151, 155,
    156, 159, 161, 162
Bwlch, Powys, 64, 81

Caerphilly Mountain,
    Wales, 12
caffeine, 22, 147, 178, 192,
    198
Cancellara, Fabian, 14, 24,
    118, 120–21, 123–5,
    133–4, 136, 145, 187,
    193
Cannondale, 14, 32–4, 42,
    43, 92
Canterbury, Kent, 4
Carapaz, Richie, 290
Carcassonne, Languedoc,
    330
Cardiff, Wales, 5–13, 18,
    31–5, 39–44, 48, 245,
    256, 327
Castroviejo, Jonathan, 254,
    255
categorised climbs, 17, 19,
    21, 27, 142, 200, 283
Cavendish, Mark, 2, 21,
    50, 64, 76, 77, 91, 95,
    144, 183, 235, 251,
    320, 330
  G nickname and, 85–6
  Giro d'Italia (2012),
    153–4
  Giro d'Italia (2023), 320
  London Olympics (2012),
    226
  Manchester, life in, 4, 58,
    59, 65–7

Monte Serra test, 83
Scheldeprijs (2011), 144
Sparkassen Giro Bochum
    (2005), 73–4
Tour de France (2007),
    4–5, 14
Tour de France (2010),
    124–5
Tour de France (2011),
    50, 137, 144
Tour de France (2012),
    159
Tour de France (2014),
    187–8
Tour de France (2021),
    50
Tour de France (2024),
    72
Vuelta a España (2010),
    144
World Road Race
    Championships (2011),
    145–9
CCC, 274
chain gangs, 41
Championship of Flanders,
    75
Châteauroux, Indre, 138
Chavanel, Sylvain, 118,
    125–6, 133
China, 62, 98–102, 151,
    153
Cipollini, Mario, 34
Circuito de Getxo, 86–8
Clancy, Ed, 58, 65, 69–71,
    73–4, 77, 95, 96
  Beijing Olympics (2008),
    99, 100, 101, 151
  London Olympics (2012),
    154, 155, 162
Clarke, Simon, 224
Classics, 45, 50, 79, 85, 89,
    110–11, 119, 131–2,
    171, 254
climbing, 3, 11, 32, 41, 44,
    45, 50, 79, 94, 236
  British Road Race
    Championships, 116
  Bwlch, 64, 81
  E3 Harelbeke, 192
  Giro d'Italia, 241, 312,
    314, 316–19
  Monte Serra test, 82–3
  Rhigos, 64, 81

Tour de France, *see* Tour de France climbs
Tour de Suisse, 196–8
Tour of Flanders, 132, 133
Volta ao Algarve, 191
cobbled streets, 79, 92, 111, 187, 188, 208
E3 Harelbeke, 175, 187, 192–3
Giro d'Italia, 288
Kampioenschap van Vlaanderen, 75–6
Kuurne–Brussels–Kuurne, 47, 49–50
Tour de France, 118, 119–21, 248, 252
Tour of Flanders, 132, 133, 213
cocaine, 24
Cofidis, 24
Col d'Aspin, French Pyrenees, 307
Col d'Aubisque, French Pyrenees, 27
Col d'Èze, French Alps, 219
Col de l'Iseran, French Alps, 21, 281
Col de la Biche, French Alps, 243
Col de la Croix de Fer, French Alps, 203, 257, 260
Col de la Madeleine, French Alps, 260
Col de Peyresourde, French Pyrenees, 263
Col de Portet, French Pyrenees, 262–5, 284
Col de Val Louron-Azet, French Pyrenees, 307
Col du Chaussy, French Alps, 203
Col du Galibier, French Alps, 21, 280, 302–4
Col du Glandon, French Alps, 21, 181
Col du Granon, French Alps, 302, 304–5
Col du Télégraphe, French Alps, 21, 302–3
Col du Tourmalet, French Pyrenees, 139–40, 279
collarbone fracture, 244–5

Colombia, 14, 92
Commonwealth Games
2006 Melbourne, 79–80, 188
2010 Delhi, 129–30, 188
2014 Glasgow, 188–90, 191
Commonwealth, 46
Contador, Alberto, 118, 122, 140, 188, 201, 202, 203, 216–18, 251
Cooke, Nicole, 32, 145
Copenhagen, Denmark, 144–9, 301
Cormet de Roselend, French Alps, 283
Corsica, 176, 179
Corti, Claudio, 1–2, 3–4, 17, 91, 93, 326
cortisone, 24
Costa, Rui, 229
Côte de Longefoy, French Alps, 283
Courchevel, French Alps, 287
Covid-19 pandemic, 286, 298, 313
crashes, 32, 45, 61, 72
Critérium du Dauphiné (2018), 249–50
Giro d'Italia (2020), 288–9
Rio Olympics (2016), 229–30, 231
Sydney Worlds (2005), 63–4, 74, 80, 130
Tirreno–Adriatico (2009), 104, 109
Tour de France (2011), 140–41
Tour de France (2013), 177–8, 288
Tour de France (2017), 243–5, 288
Tour de France (2019), 278
Tour de France (2021), 290, 291
Tour de Romandie (2021), 290
Tour de Suisse (2019), 273
Crawforth, Ben, 33–4
Credit Agricole, 203

cricket, 36, 245
Critérium du Dauphiné, 136, 188, 196, 220, 257, 269, 276, 299
2010: 131
2012: 175, 176
2018: 249–50
2020: 287
2021: 289, 299
Cromwell Road, Cardiff, 5
Crystal Springs, South Africa, 235
Culoz, French Alps, 224
Cummings, Nicky, 115
Cummings, Steve, 58, 66, 86, 97, 104, 112, 115, 119, 121, 145
Rio Olympics (2016), 225, 226, 227
Cunego, Damiano, 91, 92, 140
Cycling Weekly, 12, 40
Cyclopaedia, Cardiff, 42, 49

Dauphiné, *see* Critérium du Dauphiné
Davis, Mike, 8, 21, 37, 46
De Plus, Laurens, 282, 311, 319
Delhi Commonwealth Games (2010), 129–30, 188
Denmark, 144–9, 301
Diadora, 93
diet, 9, 19, 38, 40, 44, 45, 61, 82, 84, 107
Barloworld and, 2, 4, 93, 94
Olympic Games and, 99
Team Sky and, 195–8, 205, 206, 218
Dinan, Brittany, 137
doping, 24–6, 88–90
Dortmund, North Rhine-Westphalia, 73
Downing, Russ, 85, 106
Dubai Tour, 208
Dudek, Jerzy, 65
Duffield, David, 12, 19
Dumoulin, Tom, 197, 241, 254, 256, 258, 259, 263, 265–8

Duplantis, Mondo, 205
Dusseldorf, Rhineland, 241

E3 Harelbeke, 175, 187,
    192–3, 211
Ebbw Vale, Blaenau Gwent,
    7
Egypt, 111–13
Eisel, Bernie, 159, 173
Ellingworth, Rod, 20, 80,
    82, 176, 183, 205
    Germany training (2005),
        73
    Manchester houses and,
        58, 59, 61, 66, 75–7
    Quarrata academy, 20,
        80, 82, 235
    Rio Olympics (2016), 226,
        230
    Tour de France (2018),
        261, 270
    Tour de France (2019),
        277
    Tour of Britain (2006), 94
    Track Cycling World Cup
        (2007–8), 102
    World Road Race
        Championships (2011),
        145
Eminem, 22, 143
Eneco Tour, 145
England, 35–6
EPD (explosive power
    development), 173
EPO (erythropoietin), 24
Etruschi, 2
European Junior
    Track Cycling
    Championships, 56
European Track
    Championships, 86
Eurosport, 10, 32, 40, 50
Evans, Cadel, 121, 136, 140
Evans, Ieuan, 12, 39
Evenepoel, Remco, 293,
    298, 310, 312, 313
Ewan, Caleb, 301

Fallowfields, Manchester,
    58–61, 65, 76, 125,
    320
Fiji, 210
Fireman Sam, 5
Fischer, Murilo, 15

Five Valleys Sportive, 46,
    66
Flecha, Juan Antonio, 119,
    120, 122, 124, 133–4,
    173
flip-top mobile phones,
    1, 20
food, see diet
football, 8, 9, 12, 13, 39,
    40, 48, 65, 170, 173–4,
    233, 272, 300
Fordyce, Tom, 328
France
    Critérium du Dauphiné,
        see Critérium du
        Dauphiné
    Paris–Nice, 114–15, 144,
        187, 191–2, 208, 213,
        218–19, 231
    Paris–Roubaix, 55–6, 75,
        85, 92, 144, 187, 213,
        248
    Tour de France, see Tour
        de France
French language, 27, 60
Froome, Chris, 106, 159,
    170, 191, 194–5,
    214–19, 222, 230,
    255–6, 269, 271
    Contador, rivalry with,
        216–19, 251
    Critérium du Dauphiné
        (2016), 220
    Giro d'Italia (2018), 251
    Rio Olympics (2016), 225,
        226
    Tour de France (2013),
        175, 177, 183, 184
    Tour de France (2014),
        188
    Tour de France (2015),
        201, 202, 203, 204,
        206
    Tour de France (2016),
        222, 223, 228
    Tour de France (2017),
        234, 242, 251
    Tour de France (2018),
        251, 255–9, 262–9
    Vuelta a España (2015),
        207, 208
    Vuelta a España (2017),
        251
    World Road Race

Championships (2011),
    145
Fuglsang, Jakob, 229, 230

Ganna, Pippo, 297, 311,
    312, 313
Gap, French Alps, 126, 141
Garmin-Slipstream, 104,
    110, 119, 136, 142,
    220
Gaudu, David, 306, 307,
    308
Geoghegan Hart, Tao, 250,
    290, 311, 313
Geraint Thomas National
    Velodrome, Newport,
    56, 57–8, 152, 154,
    327
Gerdemann, Linus, 142
Germany, 35–6, 73–6, 107
Gerrans, Simon, 115, 135,
    138
Gerrard, Steven, 65
Gesink, Robert, 202
Gianetti, Mauro, 87
Giant, 49
Gibbs, Scott, 12
Giggs, Ryan, 9, 12
Gilbert, Philippe, 14, 134,
    136, 137
Giro d'Italia, 60, 144, 207,
    299
    2004: 91, 92
    2008: 84–5, 105
    2010: 135
    2012: 153–4, 158
    2017: 234–41
    2018: 251
    2019: 276
    2020: 287–9
    2023: 110–11, 309–21
    2024: 323–5
Giro del Trentino, 3
Gladiators, 6, 12
Glasgow Commonwealth
    Games (2014), 188–90,
    191
Gołaś, Michał, 247
Goss, Matt, 145, 147, 224
Gould, Chris, 8, 13, 46, 54
Granada, Andalusia,
    310–11
Great Britain Cycling Team,
    3, 43, 57, 89, 95, 186

Athens Olympics (2004), 58
Beijing Olympics (2008), 62, 98–102, 153, 235
Delhi Commonwealth Games (2010), 129–30, 188
European Track Championships (2006), 86
Glasgow Commonwealth Games (2014), 188–90
Kuurne-Brussels-Kuurne Juniors (2003), 47–52
London Olympics (2012), 103, 146, 151–67, 235
Melbourne Commonwealth Games (2006), 79–80, 188
Paris-Roubaix Juniors (2004), 55–6, 85
Rio Olympics (2016), 225–30, 231–4
Six Days of Ghent U-23 (2004), 61
Sydney Olympics (2000), 98
Tokyo Olympics (2021), 290–91, 292
Track Cycling World Championships (2006), 80
Track Cycling World Cup, see UCI Track Cycling World Cup
World Road Race Championships (2011), 145
green jerseys, 11, 23, 122
Greipel, André, 74–5, 76, 137, 145
growth hormone, 24
grupetto, 16, 19, 21
Guidi, Fabrizio, 2

Hale, Manchester, 156
Hammond, Roger, 85, 86, 94, 296
handicap races, 8, 37–8
Harrogate, North Yorkshire, 188
Hatton, Ricky, 156
Hayles, Rob, 94, 95, 97
Hayman, Mathew, 173

Haynes, Hamish, 86
heat balm, 48
Heath Park, Cardiff, 5, 8, 32
Heaton Mersey, Manchester, 65–71, 85–6
Henao, Sergio, 219
Henderson, Greg, 114
Herne Hill, London, 36
Hesjedal, Ryder, 121, 122
Higuita, Sergio, 298
Hillingdon, London, 33, 137
Hincapie, George, 133, 134
hip-hop music, 22–3, 143, 179
Hourquette d'Ancizan, French Pyrenees, 307
Hoy, Chris, 58, 95, 97, 102, 260
HTC, 110
Hunt, Jeremy, 48, 85, 86, 116, 145
Hunter, Robbie, 2–3, 16, 17, 20, 23, 28, 179
Hurley, Liz, 289
Hushovd, Thor, 120, 121, 124

India, 129–30, 188
individual pursuit, 37, 58, 95–6, 98, 99–100
Ineos, 83
injuries
  collarbone fracture, 244–5
  hip fracture, 288–9
  pelvis fractures, 104, 109, 177–87, 240
  rib fracture, 290
  shoulder dislocation, 290
  spleen rupture, 63–4, 74, 80, 130
Instagram, 51
iShares, 89–90
Isle of Man, 39, 46
Italian language, 60, 67–8, 92, 93, 107
Italy, 1–4, 80–85, 92
  Baby Giro, 84–5
  Giro d'Italia, see Giro d'Italia
  Giro del Trentino, 3
  Milan–San Remo, 114, 115, 144, 208

Quarrata academy, 2, 4, 20, 80–84, 91, 112–15, 235
Tirreno–Adriatico, 104–6, 109, 144, 237, 248, 273, 287, 299

Jay-Z, 143
Jeppesen, Carsten, 130
jerseys, 8, 10, 37
  Giro d'Italia, 92, 154, 313
  Tour de France, see Tour de France jerseys
journaling, 53
Junior Kuurne-Brussels-Kuurne, 47–52
Junior Paris-Roubaix, 55–6, 75, 85
Junior Track World Championships, 67

Kampioenschap van Vlaanderen, 75, 76
Katusha-Alpecin, 205
Kelderman, Wilco, 239, 288
Kennaugh, Pete, 106, 116–17, 151, 153–4, 156, 162
Kenny, Jason, 97
Kenya, 106, 184, 218, 256
Kerrison, Tim, 170–73, 175, 192, 205–6, 220, 297
  Crystal Springs camp (2016), 235
  Tour de France (2013), 183, 184
  Tour de France (2018), 248, 270
  Tour de France (2019), 277
  Vuelta a España (2015), 207
Kirkby, Merseyside, 36
Kittel, Marcel, 243
Klöden, Andreas, 15, 125
Kruijswijk, Steven, 258, 279, 281, 282, 284
Kuipke velodrome, Ghent, 61
Kuss, Sepp, 315, 319
Kuurne-Brussels-Kuurne, 47–52
Kwiatkowski, Michał, 247–8, 250, 255

INDEX

La Rosière, French Alps, 250, 254
Landa, Mikel, 234–5, 238, 258, 259, 279, 281
Landis, Floyd, 24, 89, 90
Lannemezan, French Pyrenees, 201
leg shaving, 31, 35, 36, 49
Leipzig, Saxony, 74–6
Leopold Trek, 142, 220
Liège–Bastogne–Liège, 87
Lille, France, 301
Lineker, Gary, 102
Liquigas, 3, 15
Lisieux, Normandy, 137
Liverpool FC, 65
Liverpool, Merseyside, 94
London, England, 33, 36
   Olympic Games (2012), 103, 146, 151–67, 226, 235
   Tour de France (2007), 4, 13, 24
Longarone, Belluno, 316
López, Miguel Ángel, 221
Los Angeles, California, 57, 275, 310
Lutsenko, Alexey, 307
Lycra, 31

Madone d'Utelle, French Alps, 219
magnesium, 25
Maindy centre, Cardiff, 7, 8–9, 10, 20, 64, 122, 256, 327
Maindy Flyers, 8–9, 13, 21, 31–5, 38, 40
Majka, Rafał, 229, 230, 243, 288
Malhao, Algarve, 191
Mallorca, Spain, 95, 130, 172, 275
Manchester City FC, 300
Manchester United FC, 12, 300
Manchester, England, 4, 11, 38, 56, 58–61, 65–71, 97, 104, 152
   Fallowfields, 58–61, 65, 76, 125, 320
   Heaton Mersey, 65–71, 85–6
   Revolution, 62

Velodrome, 274
Youth Tour, 38
Manning, Paul 'Bern', 96, 100, 101, 164
Marmite, 9, 20, 40
Martin, Dan, 253, 265, 266
Martin, Tony, 118, 177
Martinez, Dani, 295, 324
Mavic Ksyrium, 32
Mayo, Iban, 24
McDonald's, 99
McNulty, Brandon, 307, 319
McQuaid, Andrew, 274
Meintjes, Louis, 229
Melbourne, Victoria, 79–80, 157–8, 188
memes, 302, 305
Merckx, Eddy, 299
Milan, AC, 65
Milan–San Remo, 114, 115, 144, 208
Millar, David, 4, 21, 22, 27, 48, 86, 89, 91, 116, 118, 136, 145
Millar, Fran, 123, 176, 206, 275
Millennium Stadium, Cardiff, 32
minerals, 25
Miracle of Istanbul (2005), 65
mobile phones, 1, 20, 46
Mohammad, Jason, 130
Mollema, Bauke, 202, 223
Monaco, 169–70, 245, 310
Mont Saint-Michel, Normandy, 222
Monte Bondone, Trentino, 315
Monte Grappa, Veneto, 324
Monte Lussari, Italian Alps, 317
Monte Serra test, 82–3
morphine, 63–4
Moscon, Gianni, 238
Mount Etna, Italy, 156, 239, 289
Mount Teide, Tenerife, 135, 216
Movistar, 203, 208, 293–4
Mûr-de-Bretagne, Brittany, 253
Murdoch, James, 103, 275

Murray, Andy, 166
music, 22–3, 106, 143, 179

National Football League (NFL), 170, 272, 275
National Lottery, 58, 98, 227
Netherlands, 28, 40
   Amstel Gold Race, 44–5, 87
   Eneco Tour, 145
   Scheldeprijs, 135, 144
   Tour de France (2010), 118
New England Patriots, 272
New Zealand, 310
Newport, Gwent, 56, 57–8, 152, 154, 327
Nibali, Vincenzo, 188, 199, 201, 203, 215, 229, 258, 284
Nice, Alpes-Maritimes, 179–80
   Paris–Nice, 114–15, 144, 187, 191–2, 208, 213, 218–19, 231
Nieve, Mikel, 257
Nuyens, Nick, 133

O'Connor, Ben, 324
O'Grady, Stuart, 95
O'Sullivan, Ronnie, 205
Oakley, 206, 305
Ochowicz, Jim, 274
Olbas oil, 48–9
Olympic Games
   2000 Sydney, 98
   2004 Athens, 58, 95
   2008 Beijing, 62, 98–102, 153, 235
   2012 London, 103, 146, 151–67, 235
   2016 Rio, 225–30, 231–4
   2021 Tokyo, 290–91, 292
Omloop Het Nieuwsblad, 119, 175
omniums, 8, 37–8
Operación Puerto, 88–90
Orica-GreenEDGE, 176
Oude Kwaremont, Flanders 192

pain, 164, 178, 184, 186, 200

Palmer Park, Reading, 33, 36
Pantani, Marco, 24
Paris, France, 26–7, 143–4, 158, 183, 188, 202–3, 255, 262, 269, 281, 309, 328
Paris–Nice, 114–15, 144, 187, 191–2, 208, 213, 218–19, 231
Paris–Roubaix, 55–6, 75, 85, 92, 119, 144, 187, 213, 248
Parker, Matt, 210
Partridge, Rob, 102–3
Passage du Gois, France, 136
Pau, French Pyrenees, 25, 279
pelvis fractures, 104, 109, 177–87, 240
Pendle, Lancashire, 116
Pendleton, Victoria, 58, 95, 97
Petacchi, Alessandro, 3
Peters, Steve, 101, 102, 153, 265, 294, 306, 321
Peyragudes, French Pyrenees, 306, 307
Phonak, 89–90
Pidcock, Tom, 292, 295–6, 307
Piepoli, Leonardo, 89
Pinerolo, Piedmont, 142
Pinot, Thibaut, 196, 278, 279, 280, 319
Pizza Express, 156
Planche de Belle Filles, Vosges Mountains, 243
Plateau de Beille, French Pyrenees, 201
Platts Fields, Manchester, 38
Pocket Rocket jersey, 37
Poels, Wout, 255, 266
Pogačar, Tadej, 87, 173, 293, 300, 302–8, 323, 324
polka-dot jerseys, 11, 28
Portal, Nico, 277
Porte, Richie, 62, 170, 188, 191, 204, 220, 223, 238, 290

Portet, French Pyrenees, 262–5, 284
Portugal, 191, 213, 218, 247
Postman Pat, 5
potassium, 25
Pozzato, Filippo, 16, 94
Pro Continental teams, 3, 73, 76, 92, 292
prologues, 13, 14, 36, 62–3, 91, 114, 118, 152, 241
Puccio, Salvatore, 311, 314
Pyrenees, 27, 132, 139–40, 201, 262–5, 279–81, 306–8

Qatar, 109–10, 113
Quarrata, Tuscany, 2, 4, 20, 80–84, 91, 112–15, 235
Queally, Jason, 98
Quickstep, 94, 110
Quintana, Nairo, 201, 202, 203, 217, 240, 265, 266, 306, 307, 308

Rabobank, 24–5, 45, 57
RadioShack, 111
Raleigh, 5, 6
Rasmussen, Michael, 24–5
Ratcliffe, Jim, 287
Reading, Berkshire, 33, 36
red polka-dot jerseys, 11, 28
Renshaw, Mark, 146, 204
Revolution, 62
Rhigos, Glamorgan, 64, 81
Riccò, Riccardo, 88–9
Richardson, Simon, 116
RideLondon, 226
Rift Valley, 256
Riis, Bjarne, 24
Rio Olympics (2016), 225–30, 232–4
Roche, Nico, 199, 264, 280
Rodríguez, Joaquim, 154
Roglič, Primož, 263, 265, 266, 267, 300, 302, 303, 310, 312–15
Root, Joe, 205
Rotterdam, Netherlands, 118
Roubaix, Lille, 55–6, 75, 85, 92, 118, 119, 144, 248, 252

Rowe, Luke, 32, 47, 219, 228, 253, 297, 328
Roxanne drinking game, 209
Roy, Jérémy, 140
rugby, 8, 13, 39, 40, 48, 173–4, 183, 210, 271, 300

Sabbio Chiese, Brescia, 315
sacrifices, 53–4
Saeco, 91
Sagan, Peter, 145, 193, 222
Saint-Gaudens, French Pyrenees, 306
Saint-Gervais-les-Bains, French Alps, 223
Saint-Jean-de-Maurienne, French Alps, 281
Saint-Lary-Soulan, French Pyrenees, 262
Salah, Mo, 205
Salzwedel, Heiko, 73
Sánchez, Samuel, 140
Sander, Ross, 65, 68, 71, 81
SAP (sustained aerobic power), 173
Saunier Duval, 86–9, 90, 98
Scheldeprijs, 135, 144
Schleck, Andy, 121, 140
Schleck, Fränk, 14, 120, 124, 140, 187
Schulze, André, 74
Sciandri, Max, 20, 81, 91, 92, 94, 115
Scream (1996 film), 67–71
Scunthorpe, Lincolnshire, 36
shaving, 31, 35, 36, 49
shellfish allergy, 74
Sierra Nevada, Spain, 310–11
Simoni, Gilberto, 91, 92
Simpson, Tommy, 145
Simpsons, The, 7, 10
Sivakov, Pavel, 311, 313
Six Days of Ghent, 61
skinsuits, 100, 109, 116, 136, 157
Sky, 10, 106
see also Team Sky
Slovenia, 317
Sölden, Austria, 196, 198
Soler, Mauricio, 14, 28

Sophia Gardens, Cardiff, 245
South Africa, 2, 92, 235
Spain, 40, 56
Circuito de Getxo, 86–8
Volta a Catalunya, 276, 289, 310
Vuelta a España, 83, 144, 207–9, 251, 271
Sparkasse, 73
Sparkassen Giro Bochum, 73, 87
Specialized, 85
Špilak, Simon, 197
spleen rupture (2005), 63–4, 74, 130
Spring Classics, 50, 192
Springboks, 300
sprinting, 9, 11, 15, 32, 41, 50, 52, 55, 62, 64, 147
St Tewdrics House, Chepstow, 211, 295
Stannard, Ian, 2, 55, 65, 67–8, 77, 81, 91, 106, 173, 186, 224, 316
British Road Race Championships (2010), 116–17
Kuurne-Brussels-Kuurne Juniors (2003), 49–51
Rio Olympics (2016), 225, 227, 228
Tour of Britain (2006), 95
World Road Race Championships (2011), 145, 146, 148
Starbucks, 274, 275
Station des Rousses, Jura, 125
Stelvio Pass, Italian Alps, 154
Stephens, Matt, 47, 85
Storey Arms, Brecon, 44
Street Wolf, 5, 6
Štybar, Zdeněk, 193
Subway, 65
suffering, 21, 84, 183, 184, 186, 200, 237
Sunderland, Scott, 110, 111
sunglasses, 13, 14, 87, 206, 273, 305
Sunweb, 239
supplements, 25, 198

Sutton, Shane, 25, 32, 57, 58, 66, 91, 100, 102, 105, 162, 172, 260
Sweeney, Mark, 57, 58
Swift, Ben, 2, 38, 65, 67–9, 70, 71, 72, 77, 81, 91, 95, 311
Switzerland
Tour de Romandie, 197, 208, 249, 273, 289, 290, 292
Tour de Suisse, 196–8, 208, 220–22, 273, 276, 298–9
Sydney, New South Wales
Olympic Games (2000), 98
Track Cycling World Championships (2004–5), 62–5, 80

T-Mobile, 4, 10, 45, 75
T20 cricket, 245
Tachini, Sergio, 62
Tafi, Andrea, 50
Talent Spotter, 37, 40
Tarvisio, Italian Alps, 317
Taylor, Conor, 297
Team High Road, 104
Team Ineos, 274–6, 291–6, 297
Critérium du Dauphiné (2021), 290
Giro d'Italia (2020), 287–9
Giro d'Italia (2023), 309–21
Giro d'Italia (2024), 323–5
Tirreno–Adriatico (2020), 287
Tour de France (2019), 276–85
Tour de France (2020), 287
Tour de France (2021), 290–92
Tour de France (2022), 295–6, 299–309
Tour de France (2025), 325, 328, 330
Tour de Romandie (2021), 289, 290
Tour de Suisse (2022), 298–9

Tour of Britain (2025), 327
team pursuit, 2, 22, 43
Athens Olympics (2004), 95
Beijing Olympics (2008), 99–102
European Track Championships (2006), 86
London Olympics (2012), 151–67
Track Cycling World Championships (2006), 80
Track Cycling World Championships (2007), 3
Team Sky, 103, 105, 151, 155, 169–73, 186, 204–5, 274–5
budget, 105, 110, 204
Critérium du Dauphiné (2016), 220
Critérium du Dauphiné (2018), 249–50
Giro d'Italia (2017), 234–41
Giro d'Italia (2018), 251
Mallorca camp, 130, 172, 275
Monaco camp, 170
Paris–Nice (2016), 218–19
skinsuits, 116
Tenerife camp, 135, 175, 187, 188, 195, 204, 208, 216, 218, 249
Tirreno–Adriatico (2017), 237
Tirreno–Adriatico (2018), 248
Tour de France (2010), 116–27
Tour de France (2011), 135–43, 151
Tour de France (2012), 158–9
Tour de France (2013), 175–84
Tour de France (2014), 187–8, 204
Tour de France (2015), 199–207

Tour de France (2016), 222–4, 228

Tour de France (2017), 234, 241–5, 251

Tour de France (2018), 248–72, 299

Tour de Suisse (2015), 196–8

Tour de Suisse (2016), 220–22

Tour of Flanders (2011), 130, 132

Tour of Flanders (2015), 213

Tour of Flanders (2016), 219

Tour of Qatar (2010), 109–10, 113

Volta ao Algarve (2015), 191, 213, 218

Volta ao Algarve (2018), 247–8

Vuelta a España (2015), 207–9

Vuelta a España (2017), 251

Team Telekom, 45

Tenerife, Canary Islands, 135, 175, 187, 188, 195, 204, 208, 216, 218, 249, 297

Tennant, Andy, 65, 68–71, 95

tennis, 166

Terpstra, Niki, 187

Thomas the Tank Engine, 305

Thomas, Alun, 5, 13, 31, 32

Thomas, Hilary, 7, 11, 13, 35, 46, 59–60, 181–2

Thomas, Howell, 6, 7, 9–10, 13, 34–5, 38, 49

Thomas, Macs, 235, 271, 285–6, 299, 309, 320–21, 325, 326

Thomas, Sara, 20, 102, 115, 155, 218, 231–4, 299
  birth of Macs (2019), 285–6
  Egypt holiday (2010), 111–12
  London Olympics (2016), 160, 166

Rio Olympics (2016), 230, 231

St Tewdrics House, 295

Tour de France (2010), 117–18

Tour de France (2011), 240, 245

Tour de France (2013), 182

Tour de France (2018), 252

wedding (2015), 208–12

Thwaites, Scott, 189

tights, 42

Tignes, French Alps, 281

time trials, 8, 11, 13, 36, 79, 91, 152, 196
  Commonwealth Games, 188
  Giro d'Italia, 240, 312, 316, 317–18
  kilo, 58, 96, 98
  Olympic Games, 58, 98, 230
  Paris–Nice, 114
  Talent Spotter, 37–8
  Tirreno–Adriatico, 105, 237
  Tour de France, 27, 136, 179–80, 279
  Tour de Suisse, 221, 298–9
  Tour of Qatar, 109–10, 113
  Volta ao Algarve, 191
  Vuelta a España, 83

Tinkoff-Saxo, 203

Tipuric, Justin, 206

Tirreno–Adriatico, 104–6, 109, 144, 237, 273, 287, 299

Tokyo Olympics (2021), 290–91, 292

Tour de France, 3, 10–13, 60, 62–3, 103
  1997: 73
  2006: 24, 89–90
  2007: 3–5, 13–29, 84–5, 87, 105, 141, 207, 325
  2010: 117–27, 135, 141
  2011: 50, 135–45
  2012: 158–9
  2013: 175–84, 288
  2014: 187–8, 204

2015: 199–207
  2016: 222–4, 228
  2017: 234, 241–5, 288
  2018: 110, 184, 248–72, 299
  2019: 276–85
  2020: 110, 287
  2021: 50, 110, 290–92
  2022: 295–6, 299–309
  2024: 72
  2025: 325, 328, 330

Tour de France climbs, 200–201
  2007: 17, 19, 21, 23, 27
  2010: 125–6
  2011: 135, 139–40
  2015: 200–201, 203
  2018: 252–5, 257–61, 262–5
  2019: 278–83
  2022: 302, 304, 307–8

Tour de France jerseys, 11
  green, 11, 23, 28, 122
  polka dot, 11, 28
  white, 123, 129, 136, 139, 141, 143, 225
  yellow, see yellow jersey

Tour de Romandie, 197, 208, 249, 273, 289, 290, 292

Tour de Suisse, 196–8, 208, 220–22, 273, 276, 298–9

Tour Down Under, 3, 173–4, 208, 310

Tour of Britain, 94, 109, 246, 327

Tour of Flanders, 111, 130, 132–5, 144, 187, 213, 219

Tour of Qatar, 109–10, 113

Tour of the Alps, 238

Tournus, Saône-et-Loire, 125

Tower Bridge, London, 4, 24

Tre Cime di Lavaredo, Dolomites, 316

Treforest, Pontypridd, 41

Tudor, Darren, 32

Tupac, 22

tyres, 42, 43, 189–90

INDEX

UAE Team Emirates, 208, 300, 324
UCI Junior Track World Championships, 67
UCI Track Cycling World Championships, 80, 157
UCI Track Cycling World Cup
2004–5: 62–5, 80
2006–7: 95
2007–8: 99, 102
UEFA Champions League (2004–5), 65
Ullrich, Jan, 12, 24, 25, 26, 38, 45, 73, 88
United Arab Emirates, 208, 300, 324
United Kingdom
Glasgow Commonwealth Games (2014), 188–90, 191
National Junior Road Race Championships, 46–7
National Road Race Championships, 85–6, 116
Olympic Games (2012), 103, 146, 151–67
Talent Spotter, 37, 40
Tour de France (2007), 4, 13, 24
Tour de France (2014), 187–8
Tour of Britain, 94, 109
United States, 57, 275
Urán, Rigoberto, 139, 143, 158, 279, 281

Val Thorens, French Alps, 283
Valencia, Spain, 56
Valverde, Alejandro, 201, 202, 281
Van Avermaet, Greg, 229, 230
Van Baarle, Dylan, 297
Van Garderen, Tejay, 181
Van Petegem, Peter, 50
Vansevenant, Wim, 28
Velindre Cancer Centre, Cardiff, 35

Ventoux, Provence, 181, 215, 290
Viagra, 111–12
Vingegaard, Jonas, 300, 302, 303, 305, 307
Vinokourov, Alexander, 18, 24, 45
Visma, 300, 302–8, 315
vitamins, 25
Volpi, Alberto, 92, 93–4
Volta a Catalunya, 276, 289, 310
Volta ao Algarve, 191, 213, 218, 247–8
Vuelta a España, 83, 144, 207–9, 251, 271

Wales, 35–6, 209–10, 271, 309, 330
Wales National Velodrome, Newport, 56, 57–8, 152, 154, 327
Wales Rally GB, 102
Warburton, Sam, 13, 39
Watson, Sam, 326
Wegelius, Charly, 4, 21, 47, 48
weight, 4, 16, 87–8, 94, 112, 156, 187, 195–8, 220–21
weights, 43, 172
Welsh Cycling, 32
Western Mail, 40
Wharton, Debbie, 8
white jersey, 123, 129, 136, 139, 141, 143, 225
Wiesenhof, 73, 98
Wiggins, Bradley, 14, 21, 24, 47, 66, 67, 97, 149, 159, 194, 214, 230, 269
Athens Olympics (2004), 58
Beijing Olympics (2008), 100, 101, 153
Garmin-Slipstream, 104
Giro d'Italia (2010), 135, 238
London Olympics (2012), 159
Team High Road, 104
Tour de France (2007), 4, 18, 20, 21, 24

Tour de France (2010), 118–19, 121–4, 126, 135
Tour de France (2011), 135–6, 138–9, 143, 151
Tour de France (2012), 158, 170
Tour de France (2013), 175, 184
Track Cycling World Cup (2006–7), 95–6
Williams, Shane, 102
winter riding, 42–3, 49
Woods, Michael, 278
World Championships, 3
World Cup, *see* UCI Track Cycling World Cup
World Junior Track Championships, 57
World Road Race Championships, 93, 144–9
World Track Championships, 95

Xbox, 52

Yates, Adam, 224, 225, 226, 295, 297, 307
Yates, Sean, 114, 115, 251
Yates, Simon, 47, 282
yellow jersey, 11, 89, 93, 114, 186–7, 228
2010 Tour, 118, 125–6
2011 Tour, 136, 143
2012 Tour, 158, 170
2013 Tour, 183
2015 Tour, 199, 202, 203, 206
2016 Tour, 224
2017 Tour, 243
2018 Tour, 258, 261
2019 Tour, 277, 279, 281, 283–5
Yorkshire, England, 187–8
Youth Tour, 11
Yvonne McGregor, 98

Zabel, Erik, 45
Zakarin, Ilnur, 219
Zandio, Xabi, 135
Žigart, Urška, 305

Acknowledgements

Sa and Macsi.

Mum, Dad, Alun, Michelle, Emrys and Sophia.

Beth and Eif, Rhys, Carys, Al and Jac.

Em, Pauline, Mared, Sion, Leah and the gang.

Tex, Dewi and Emma, Daf and Tom.

Menna and Graham.

Rich, El, Eila and Emi.

Phil, Teri, Gruff and Ffion.

Glyn, Menna, Rob and Louise, Claire and Callum.

Christine, Adrian and the whole Ebbw gang.

To the sky OG's Dave B, Tim, Fran, Rod. Nico – always remembered.

My UK-based mates who I don't see too often but when we catch up it's like I've never been away – Ian, Cath, Molly and Jack, Ed, George, Becky, Jac and Tomi, D, Han, Brody and Oscar, Alun, Rob, Soph, Jude and Jessie, Luke, Cath, Ollie and Alfie, Matt and Dani, Gouldy, Mike Davis, Ross HR.

For being such amazing friends to Sa – I know how much

you all mean to her: Ffion, Sian and Cadi. Morgs and Idris, Emma and the whole Plasmawr gang.

To my team-mates who are life-long friends – Swifty, Lizi, Arthur and Harry.

Stannard and Helen.

Bernie and Tanjia.

Cav and Peta.

Brad, Burkey, Bern, Pete.

Connor, Pippo, Tao, Pav and Puccio, Thyman and Claire.

Richie and Gemma, Edvald, Daryl, Hayman, Robbie H.

The Monaco crew – Penny and Matt, Eddie and Niamh, Pluski and Charlotte, Wout and Alice, Caleb and Ryann, Sam and Tara.

To Marko, who's been my swanny and, more importantly, my friend. Also, possibly, my Tour curse – the only one he missed was 2018.

Everyone else who's helped me on my journey on the bike – Darren, Shane, Murph, Aitor, Adrian, Conor, Matt Parker, David, Dani and Claudio, Diego, Ivan, Gary, Kelly, Alan and Dan G.

At Quercus – Richard Milner, Jon Butler, Megan Schaffer, Beth Wright, Siobhan Peters, Jill Cole and Tania Wilde.

Jay de Andrade, David Luxton and Archie O'Reilly.

And to my ghost-writer Tom Fordyce.

RAISING READERS
Books Build Bright Futures

Dear Reader,

We'd love your attention for one more page to tell you about the crisis in children's reading, and what we can all do.

Studies have shown that reading for fun is the **single biggest predictor of a child's future life chances** – more than family circumstance, parents' educational background or income. It improves academic results, mental health, wealth, communication skills, ambition and happiness.[1]

The number of children reading for fun is in rapid decline. Young people have a lot of competition for their time. In 2024, 1 in 10 children and young people in the UK aged 5 to 18 did not own a single book at home.[2]

Hachette works extensively with schools, libraries and literacy charities, but here are some ways we can all raise more readers:

- Reading to children for just 10 minutes a day makes a difference
- Don't give up if children aren't regular readers – there will be books for them!
- Visit bookshops and libraries to get recommendations
- Encourage them to listen to audiobooks
- Support school libraries
- Give books as gifts

There's a lot more information about how to encourage children to read on our website: **www.RaisingReaders.co.uk**

Thank you for reading.

---

[1] National Literacy Trust, Book Ownership in 2024, November 2024
https://nlt.cdn.ngo/media/documents/Book_ownership_in_2024

[2] OECD. 2021. 21st-century readers: developing literacy skills in a digital world. Paris, France: OECD Publishing.
https://www.oecd.org/en/publications/21st-century-readers_a83d84cb-en.html